Elections American Style

A. JAMES REICHLEY
Editor

Elections American Style

THE BROOKINGS INSTITUTION
Washington, D.C.

Library of Congress Cataloging-in-Publication data

Elections American style / A. James Reichley, editor.
    p.   cm.
    Includes bibliographies and index.
    ISBN 0-8157-7382-X   ISBN 0-8157-7381-1 (pbk.)
    1. Elections—United States. 2. Voting—United States.
    3. Political parties—United States. I. Reichley, James.
    JK 1976.E447 1987
    324.973—dc19

9 8 7 6 5 4 3

THE BROOKINGS INSTITUTION is an independent organization devoted to nonpartisan research, education, and publication in economics, government, foreign policy, and the social sciences generally. Its principal purposes are to aid in the development of sound public policies and to promote public understanding of issues of national importance.

The Institution was founded on December 8, 1927, to merge the activities of the Institute for Government Research, founded in 1916, the Institute of Economics, founded in 1922, and the Robert Brookings Graduate School of Economics and Government, founded in 1924.

The Board of Trustees is responsible for the general administration of the Institution, while the immediate direction of the policies, program, and staff is vested in the President, assisted by an advisory committee of the officers and staff. The by-laws of the Institution state: "It is the function of the Trustees to make possible the conduct of scientific research, and publication, under the most favorable conditions, and to safeguard the independence of the research staff in the pursuit of their studies and in the publication of the results of such studies. It is not a part of their function to determine, control, or influence the conduct of particular investigations or the conclusions reached."

The President bears final responsibility for the decision to publish a manuscript as a Brookings book. In reaching his judgment on the competence, accuracy, and objectivity of each study, the President is advised by the director of the appropriate research program and weighs the views of a panel of expert outside readers who report to him in confidence on the quality of the work. Publication of a work signifies that it is deemed a competent treatment worthy of public consideration but does not imply endorsement of conclusions or recommendations.

The Institution maintains its position of neutrality on issues of public policy in order to safeguard the intellectual freedom of the staff. Hence interpretations or conclusions in Brookings publications should be understood to be solely those of the authors and should not be attributed to the Institution, to its trustees, officers, or other staff members, or to the organizations that support its research.

Foreword

ROBERT BROOKINGS believed that a free society requires government that is both efficient and responsive to the public will. Following our founder's mandate, the Brookings Institution has always sought not only to find ways to make government work better but also to improve the system of popular elections through which the preferences of individual voters are translated into public policy. In the past, Brookings has sponsored studies of the presidential nominating process, the electoral college, and the role of parties, among other aspects of the electoral system. With this book, we undertake for the first time a comprehensive examination in one volume of the American system of elections, from the presidential level through congressional elections to voter turnout and vote fraud in city wards and rural counties.

Since the late 1960s, the electoral system has been extensively and repeatedly reformed and re-reformed. The presidential nominating process has been fundamentally altered. Laws regulating campaign financing have been substantially changed. Registering to vote has been made easier in many states. And yet the result is a situation that almost no one finds satisfactory. Campaigns go on for too long and cost too much. Voter turnout has steadily declined. Candidates increasingly tailor their appeals to fit the strictures of thirty-second television commercials. Proposals for further changes in election laws and procedures abound.

One lesson that emerges from the experience of the last twenty years is that reforms that are not carefully conceived and realistically designed are likely to do more harm than good. This does not mean that no changes should be made in the current electoral system. But it does indicate that before reforms are proposed or enacted, problems should be scrupulously analyzed to determine whether change is really needed, and necessary alterations should be based on practical knowledge and the best available scholarly research.

The aim of this book, edited by Brookings senior fellow A. James Reichley, is to increase understanding of the electoral system, identify genuine problems, and offer practical solutions where they are required. Experts on various parts of the electoral process were called on to make fresh examinations of their specialties. Papers were presented and discussed at a Brookings conference on the electoral process, attended by scholars, journalists, and political activists (listed at the end of the book). The resulting book, as Reichley writes in the opening chapter, presents "a shared and informed exploration of crucial aspects of the American electoral system."

The editor wishes to thank the many people who helped produce the conference and the book. Paul E. Peterson, former director of governmental studies at Brookings, participated in all phases of planning and execution of the project. Nancy D. Davidson directed the editing of the manuscript, and individual chapters were edited by James R. Schneider, Barbara de Boinville, and Jeanette Morrison. Diana Regenthal prepared the index. Timothy C. Bladek verified the accuracy of factual statements and citations in the chapters, assisted by Judith Newman-Holt and David R. Sandman.

Senate Republican Leader Bob Dole spoke on "Rebuilding the Parties" at the Brookings Council dinner that climaxed the conference. Walter Dean Burnham, Michael J. Malbin, Samuel Kernell, and Steven S. Smith critiqued papers at the conference. Milton C. Cummings, Donald E. Stokes, Charles O. Jones, Thomas E. Mann, and Burnham read the entire manuscript and made many valuable suggestions. Diane Hodges and Renuka D. Deonarain coordinated the conference, and Ms. Deonarain oversaw preparation of the manuscript. Mark B. Arnold, G. Bliss Austin, Jon Buffington, Carleigh McLeish, Vida R. Megahed, Eloise C. Stinger, and Emily E. Stinger assisted at the conference.

This study was financed in part by generous grants from the Dillon Fund and the Ford Foundation, for which we express our gratitude.

The views expressed here are those of the authors and should not be ascribed to the foundations whose assistance is acknowledged above, or to the trustees, officers, or other staff members of the Brookings Institution or to the other organizations with which the authors are affiliated.

BRUCE K. MACLAURY
President

August 1987
Washington, D.C.

Contents

Figures

CHAPTER ONE

The Electoral System

A. JAMES REICHLEY

ELECTIONS are fundamental to any political system based on principles of democracy and republican government. Under democracy, elections in which all eligible voters may participate are the ultimate source of governmental authority. In a large, complex society like the United States, elections provide the chief means through which most voters influence the formation of government policy and exercise the rights and responsibilities of citizenship.

There is currently a widespread sense, shown by public opinion surveys and complaints by informed observers, that the American electoral system is in trouble. Some believe that this trouble is minor and can be dealt with through moderate reforms; others think it goes deep and requires extensive political surgery, perhaps accompanied by sweeping changes in the larger social order. Complaints include the huge cost and long duration of campaigns, the power of the media to shape public perceptions of candidates, and the undue influence exerted by "special interests" over both nominations and general elections. The low level of voter turnout in recent elections is ascribed variously to restrictive electoral regulations, enlargement of the eligible electorate, and profound alienation within American society. Some observers, reacting in part to the outcomes of particular elections, charge that the current system tends to exclude from consideration potential leaders better qualified than those usually offered as candidates to the voters.

Some of these troubles probably have sources in larger social and political trends. Many historians perceive in American national politics short-term cycles of two or three presidential terms, at the end of which the party holding the presidency tends to become vulnerable. But there

1

seems also to be a longer cycle of sixty to seventy years during which a set of political ideas—usually embodied by a party—rises, achieves fulfillment, and sinks into decline. Each stage in this longer cycle is characterized by developments in the electoral system.

So far the United States has passed through two complete long cycles, not counting the nation-building period of the first three presidential terms (itself the completion of a cycle that began with the Great Awakening of the 1730s), and appears to be in the final phase of a third. The first long cycle, shaped by ideas of agrarian democracy, was initiated by the election of Thomas Jefferson as president in 1800, reached its apex under Andrew Jackson and Martin Van Buren in the 1830s, and then sank under the unsolved problem of slavery and the advance of industrial capitalism. The second cycle, dominated by the Republican party's program of free-enterprise nationalism, began with the election of Abraham Lincoln in 1860, achieved its peak under William McKinley and Theodore Roosevelt around the turn of the century, and fell through failure of its guiding philosophy to cope with problems of economic equity and efficiency and the international challenge of totalitarianism. The third, built around theories of welfare state internationalism developed by the New Deal Democrats, began with the election of Franklin Roosevelt in 1932, peaked under John Kennedy and Lyndon Johnson in the 1960s, and has been in gradual decline ever since.[1]

Although history does not exactly repeat, and changed circumstances may drastically alter the patterns of earlier cycles, the period of transition through which we are now passing may be the prelude to a new age of creative growth and achievement, with normal dominance by one or the other of the two major parties or perhaps some new party as yet unborn. The Republicans at this point have the better chance of embodying the spirit of the new age, simply because as the minority party in the last cycle they are less tied to the solutions of the recent past. But there is nothing

1. Some commentators place the duration of a long cycle at about thirty years, finding major realignments in 1828 and 1896 as well as in 1800, 1860, and 1932. This leads to the puzzle of why a new majority party did not emerge in the 1960s. But what really was scheduled to happen in the 1960s was for the long cycle to peak—which is exactly what did happen. As James Sundquist has pointed out, McKinley's victory in 1896 "reinforced" rather than weakened the alignment coming out of the 1860s. The same is true of Jackson's victory in 1828 with regard to the Jeffersonian alignment of 1800. James L. Sundquist, *Dynamics of the Party System: Alignment and Realignment of Political Parties in the United States,* rev. ed. (Brookings, 1983), p. 169. The other classic on realignment is Walter Dean Burnham, *Critical Elections and the Mainsprings of American Politics* (Norton, 1970).

foreordained about this. If the Republicans fail to produce effective responses to current problems, the Democrats again will have their chance or possibly some entirely new political formation (like the Republicans in the 1860s) will move in to fill the gap.

Many of the difficulties currently being encountered by the electoral system are entirely characteristic of the final phase of a long cycle. The 1850s and the 1920s were periods of weak national parties, emerging third-party movements, voter alienation, and charges of rampant manipulation of the system by political special interests. To some extent, it may be that such troubles will have to be endured until the larger political order achieves some new definitive direction. But here, too, determinism need not apply. Development of sensible reforms in the electoral system, where needed, may actually help launch and shape the new age.

In designing such reforms, it is important, as shown by the baneful effects flowing from attempts at reform of the presidential nominating process and campaigning financing in the 1970s, to begin with careful analysis of what the problem really is and then to find cures that will attack the true sources of trouble.

The chapters of this book, growing out of a Brookings conference on the electoral process, study each of the major current criticisms of the electoral system, seek to determine their validity, and where necessary prescribe remedies. Each writer was assigned a particular aspect of the system and was asked to find whether it is in fact displaying serious flaws and if so how these might be corrected. The resulting book does not express a collective judgment, though the commentators refined and revised their initial presentations in the light of discussion and debate at the conference. There were differences, some sharp and deep, among the contributors, who were drawn from a wide range on the political and ideological spectrum. Some of these differences persist in the chapters as finally written. Taken together, however, these analyses present a shared and informed exploration of crucial aspects of the American electoral system.

Complaints about the system cluster around four main concerns:

—The presidential selection process—whether because of changes made by the Democrats in their rules for choosing national convention delegates since 1968, or the influence of special interests on nominations, or the ability of the media to shape perceptions of candidates, or some other causes—is malfunctioning, unduly limiting the choice of candidates for the nation's highest office.

—Voter participation is in steady decline, now placing the United States at or near the bottom among developed democracies in electoral turnout.

—The system is being corrupted, or at least distorted, by the huge amounts of money needed to run for office at the national, state, and congressional district levels.

—The weakness of the political parties drives candidates to rely for both financial support and campaign workers on special interest groups, thereby undercutting the capacity of the federal government to function on behalf of a larger "national interest."

Each of these problems is serious, or potentially serious. Any one of them, if left untended, could tear a gaping hole in the fabric of American democracy. But it is worth noting that they are problems of a system not living up to its own highest standards, rather than of the more fundamental corruption found in systems that are repressive at the source. Very few Americans would replace free elections with any kind of authoritarian or dynastic means of choosing governmental leaders. Some, particularly among intellectual elites, would like to abolish representation by state in the electoral system or to extend the reach of public authority, and therefore of the democratic polity, into areas now reserved for private decisionmaking. Most Americans, however, still prefer to give some weight to the principle of federalism in apportioning representation and to keep a large share of life, personal and economic, outside of government control.

It is also worth noting that the American electoral system did not flow along smoothly, without hitch or flaw, before the problems that developed in the late 1960s and 1970s. The electoral system has encountered difficulties, some very serious, throughout its history. Vote fraud has been a frequent presence in American elections. Seven times the system's underlying structure has been altered through constitutional amendment.[2] On three occasions the presidential candidate with the highest number of popular votes was not elected president. Twice the outcome of the presidential election was so hotly disputed that it appeared that a duly elected president might not be available by inauguration day. On one

2. The amendments are the Twelfth, discussed below; the Fifteenth, forbidding that the right to vote be abridged "on account of race, color, or previous condition of servitude"; the Seventeenth, requiring popular election of the Senate; the Nineteenth, giving women the right to vote; the Twenty-second, limiting the president to two terms of office; the Twenty-fourth, prohibiting the poll tax in federal elections; and the Twenty-sixth, lowering the voting age to eighteen.

tragic occasion, some participants on the losing side in the presidential election were so dissatisfied with the result that they set out to remove their states from the federal Union.

Before considering the electoral system's more critical current problems, it will be worthwhile to examine the constitutional and political structures on which the system is built, and to review some of these earlier instances when it seemed close to ruin.

Rules of the Game

The American electoral system is governed by rules that are basically majoritarian, with important modifications. At the federal level, the Constitution as originally enacted called for three election systems, each applying to one of the major governing units. The U.S. House of Representatives was to be apportioned by population, with Indians excluded and each slave counted as three-fifths of a person; members were to be chosen by the voting public as defined by the states in their requirements for "electors of the most numerous branch of the State Legislature." U.S. Senate seats were apportioned two to a state, with members to be elected by the somewhat more elitist mechanism of the state legislatures.

The president, heading the executive branch, and the vice-president were to be chosen through a complicated scheme based on what has come to be known as the "electoral college" (though the term does not appear in the Constitution). Members of the electoral college were to be elected in each state in a manner determined by its legislature, with federal public officeholders specifically excluded—thereby, it was hoped, placing the process at least one remove from ordinary politics. The number of electors would equal the state's total representation in the Senate and House (small states, therefore, being disproportionately represented, though much less so than in the Senate).

Electors would meet to vote, not as a collective body in the federal capital, but in their respective states, which it was thought would dampen electioneering. Each would vote for two persons for president, at least one of whom could not be an inhabitant of the elector's state. Ballots would be transmitted "sealed" to the president of the federal Senate, who would count them "in the presence of the Senate and House of Representatives." If one candidate had a majority of the total electors, he was elected president, with the runner-up vice-president. In case of a tie between two candidates, each of whom had a majority of electors (which was possible since each elector was to vote for two persons), the House would elect one of the two president, each state delegation voting as a unit and casting one vote. If no candidate had a majority in the electoral college, the House, again with each state casting one vote, would select the president from the five with the highest number of electoral votes.

The Founders do not seem to have expected that the president would always, or even usually, be chosen through majority support from the electors. This would be the case when a popular individual like George Washington was the clear national favorite. But when support was scattered among a number of candidates, the electors would in effect serve a winnowing function, leaving the final choice to the House (the more popular body, but operating in this one instance through a federal structure rather than by district).

All these public leaders were to be elected for fixed terms—two years for members of the House, six for members of the Senate, and four for the president and vice-president—giving them a measure of protection against transitory shifts in public opinion, but keeping them ultimately responsible to the people. The fourth major governing unit, the federal judiciary, was rooted in politics, through appointment by the president and confirmation by the Senate, but was made virtually autonomous by unlimited terms "during good behavior" and was not intended to be politically responsive.

Among the election systems called for by the Constitution, that for the House has changed the least, altered mainly by expansion of the electorate to include all citizens over the age of eighteen. The means of election for the Senate was sharply altered by the Seventeenth Amendment, moving voting authority from the state legislatures to the electorate as a whole. But it is the means for electing the president, the crux and apex of national leadership because of the chief executive's singular visibility and control over the administrative departments and agencies, that today probably differs most from the Founders' expectations.

As James Sundquist points out in his chapter on the political parties, the Founders expected that the presidential electors would be public-spirited notables, not deeply involved in the rough-and-tumble of ordinary politics, who would cast their ballots much as the respected elders of a gentleman's club might participate in the choice of the club's presiding officer. Consistent with this view, the office of vice-president was designed primarily to provide a high public post for the individual judged by his peers to be the second most qualified for the highest office. The vice-president's availability to succeed a president unable to complete his term was for the Founders a secondary purpose.[3]

Nothing in the Constitution requires that the states choose their electors at large or cast their electoral votes as a bloc, and in fact for the first several presidential elections some of the states did neither. In 1789 and 1792, about half the states chose electors through direct popular election, while in the other half they were elected by the legislature. Among those holding direct elections, about half elected at large and half by congressional districts.[4]

A Constitutional Crisis

For the first two presidential elections, the system worked about as intended. Election of Washington as president and John Adams of Massachusetts as vice-president neatly symbolized the alliance between the planter class of the South and the merchant class and Puritan divines of New England that effectively dominated the new republic. The crucial middle states were not in the early rounds represented in the elected executive establishment. But the fact that the third-place finisher in both 1789 and 1792 was a New Yorker (John Jay in the first election and George Clinton in the second), and the practical power of Alexander Hamilton of New York as secretary of the treasury, seemed to point toward regional accommodation.

When Washington stepped down in 1796, however, the system began to operate differently than the Founders had planned. The two principal rivals for the presidency, Adams and Thomas Jefferson, instead of running purely on their personal merits, presented themselves as candidates of the two great factions known as Federalists and Republicans, that had begun, to the dismay of almost everybody, to form during Washington's second term. Adams was linked electorally with Thomas Pinckney of South Carolina, for whom Federalist electors were urged to cast their second ballots with the understanding that Pinckney would become vice-president. Republican politicians were unable to agree on a running mate for Jefferson,

3. Arthur M. Schlesinger, Jr., *The Cycles of American History* (Houghton Mifflin, 1986), pp. 338–40; and Alexander Hamilton, *The Federalist*, no. 68 (Modern Library, 1937), pp. 444–45.

4. *Congressional Quarterly Guide to U.S. Elections*, 2d ed. (Washington, D.C.: Congressional Quarterly, 1985), p. 254.

so Republican electors in different states gave their second votes to a variety of candidates. Adams carried all of New England, and Jefferson most of the South. The middle states split, New York, New Jersey, and Delaware going for Adams, and most of Pennsylvania for Jefferson. Adams eked out a narrow majority in the electoral college. But enough of the spirit of the Founders' intention survived so that twelve of Adams's seventy-one electors cast their ballots for candidates other than Pinckney. As a result, Jefferson finished second and became vice-president—following the Founders' design, but with the consequence that the president and vice-president represented hostile factions within the national government.

In 1800 the original system essentially collapsed, producing the young government's first constitutional crisis. The Federalists supported Adams for reelection, with General Charles Cotesworth Pinckney of South Carolina (Thomas's older brother) as his running mate. Republican members of Congress caucused in Marache's boardinghouse in Philadelphia and picked Aaron Burr of New York to form a slate with Jefferson—thereby forging a bond between the political establishments of New York and Virginia that would endure for almost two centuries, profoundly affecting the shape of American politics. In the election New York switched sides, and both Republican candidates received majorities. This time, however, party unity held, so Jefferson and Burr were given identical votes.

Under the Constitution, the decision went to the House, in which eight state delegations were under Republican control, six were Federalist, and two were divided—thus neither party commanded a majority. Federalist House members supported Burr, hoping to keep out the hated Jefferson, split the Republican party, and perhaps share the fruits of victory if Burr should pick up the votes of a few Republican House members. Burr played a cautious game, declining to deal with the Federalists but avoiding the one act that would break the deadlock: his announcement that if elected president he would not serve. For thirty-five ballots both sides held firm. Then, as many began to doubt the very survival of the republic, the single member of the House from Delaware, a Federalist, declared he would vote for Jefferson, giving the Virginian the necessary majority.[5]

Aiming to avoid a similar impasse in the future, the Republican majority in the new Congress pushed through the Twelfth Amendment, requiring that the electors vote separately for president and vice-president. Signifying the trend from a primarily personal politics to a politics based on

5. John C. Miller, *The Federalist Era* (Harper, 1960), pp. 268–73.

well-defined factions, the pool from which the House could select the president if no candidate won a majority in the electoral college was reduced from the highest five to the highest three.

During Jefferson's two terms, Republican leaders in Congress, now often called Democrat-Republicans to acknowledge the party's equalitarian ethos, increasingly functioned as the high command of a national party. In 1804 the party's congressional caucus chose George Clinton, boss of the powerful New York machine, to replace the mercurial Burr as Jefferson's running mate. In the next three presidential elections, the congressional caucus, in which all Democrat-Republican members of Congress were entitled to one vote, selected slates for president and vice-president. For each of these, the caucus appointed a committee of its members to manage a victorious national canvass. It seemed that national parties might form around the leadership of legislative factions, as was occurring at the time in Britain and has since happened in most democratic countries employing the parliamentary system.

Emergence of National Parties

As matters turned out, however, legislative parties were not to become the focus of national politics in the United States. By 1824 the caucus had itself become a political issue, giving fuel to those who aimed to break the domination of the southern planter elite that had flourished under the administrations of Jefferson, Madison, and Monroe. The political power of the states, commanding campaign resources that evaded centralized control, was crucial in supplanting the caucus. But the ability of the president to exercise independent political clout far beyond that available to parliamentary premiers or prime ministers, at least before the rise of the welfare state, would probably in any case have been enough to assure a different structure for American politics.

Perhaps if the Federalist party had survived as a significant force in Congress, its legislative leaders might have been able to present themselves as the natural alternative to the political status quo. But in 1824 Federalists held only 12 percent of the seats in the House and 8 percent in the Senate. John Quincy Adams, son of the last Federalist president, was a Democrat-Republican, serving as secretary of state in the cabinet of President Monroe. Politicians desiring change needed some other fulcrum on which to hoist the political nation.

When the Democrat-Republican caucus convened in Washington in February 1824, only 66 of the party's 231 members of Congress attended. The caucus proceeded to award its presidential nomination to William H. Crawford of Georgia, secretary of the treasury in the Monroe administration and logical standard-bearer for the incumbent elite. The other major candidates, John Quincy Adams of Massachusetts, Andrew Jackson of Tennessee, and Henry Clay of Kentucky, were in no way deterred, and in fact used the caucus's designation as a symbol of oligarchic rule with which to bludgeon Crawford (much as insurgent candidates long after made party organization endorsement a liability for their slated opponents in many state and municipal elections).

Adams, Jackson, and Clay turned to their respective state legislatures to pass resolutions launching their candidacies. The resulting free-for-all produced a division in the electoral college of ninety-nine for Jackson, eighty-four for Adams, forty-one for Crawford, and thirty-seven for Clay. No candidate possessing a majority, the election once more went to the House. John C. Calhoun of South Carolina, originally a candidate for president, had switched to the competition for vice-president and was elected by a large majority in the electoral college.

Under the original provision of the Constitution allowing the House to choose among the top five presidential contenders, Clay, the political virtuoso of the day, might have been able as Speaker of the House to swing the prize to himself. But under the Twelfth Amendment, limiting the choice to the top three, he was removed from the pool. Clay backed Adams, who thereby was able to win a one-vote majority among the twenty-four state delegations in the House.

Jackson and his supporters were outraged, pointing out that he had not only been first in the electoral college but also led in the popular vote (though the significance of the popular vote was somewhat undercut by the fact that six of the twenty-four states still did not choose electors by direct election). When Adams appointed Clay secretary of state, the Jacksonians claimed to have evidence of a sordid political deal—a charge that clung to both Adams and Clay during the rest of their public careers.[6]

It is an interesting question why this accusation was so damaging.

6. Robert V. Remini, *Andrew Jackson and the Course of American Freedom, 1822–1832* (Harper and Row, 1981), pp. 74–99; and James F. Hopkins, "Election of 1824," in Arthur M. Schlesinger, Jr., and Fred L. Israel, eds., *History of American Presidential Elections 1789–1968* (Chelsea House, 1971), vol. 1, pp. 349–81.

Under a multiparty system of the kind now found in many democracies, Adams and Clay could be said to have formed a coalition government. All four candidates identified themselves loosely as Democrat-Republicans, so no betrayal of party was involved. Between them, Adams and Clay had considerably more votes than Jackson, though less than a majority. But there clearly was a widespread feeling that Clay and Adams had employed a political maneuver to evade the will of the voting public, which already was seen as the real source of legitimacy for national leadership.

Shrewd politicians, notably Martin Van Buren of New York, took from the 1824 election the lesson that while the congressional caucus was no longer an acceptable means for proposing national leaders, the various state legislatures would not suffice as launch pads for presidential candidacies. In 1828, Jackson again ran on the basis of a resolution by the Tennessee legislature. But Van Buren and others put together a national party organization to manage the campaign. Jackson heeded the published recommendation of the *United States Telegraph,* a Washington newspaper, to accept Calhoun as his running mate. Adams was nominated for reelection by a convention of state political leaders in Pennsylvania. Both Jackson and Adams gathered endorsements from other state legislatures and public assemblies.

After Jackson's landslide victory, Van Buren and other Democratic strategists used federal patronage to build an efficient national party machine—a rarity, as it has turned out, in American political history. In 1831 the short-lived Anti-Masonic party, a curious amalgam of evangelical piety and populist class resentment, held the first national party convention in American history, in Baltimore, nominating candidates for president and vice-president. Clay and Van Buren took note. Within a year the recently formed National Republican party held a national convention to nominate Clay for president, and the Democrats met to endorse Jackson for reelection. Jackson's new running mate was Van Buren, replacing Calhoun, who had quarreled with Jackson over South Carolina's attempt to nullify the so-called Tariff of Abominations. The team of Jackson and Van Buren brought to the peak of fulfillment the program of agrarian democracy launched thirty years before by Jefferson.

For the next seventy-two years, from 1836 through 1908, as James Ceaser relates in his chapter on the presidential nominating process, the national party convention operated as the effective selector of finalists in the competition for president. Since convention delegates were for the most part picked by state party organizations, the choice of presidential nominees was made mainly by professional politicians, with some coaching from their financial backers.

The emergence of strong national parties in the 1830s reinforced the trend toward making presidential electors little more than tokens, elected at large in each state on slates picked by party leaders and pledged to support the party's national ticket. Before long, the idea of an elector exercising independent judgment, as the Founders had intended, began to seem contrary to the spirit of the Constitution. By 1832 all states except Maryland and South Carolina chose electors at large and through direct popular election. In Maryland electors were chosen by popular vote in congressional districts, and in South Carolina the choice was still made by the state legislature. In 1836 Maryland went to at-large elections. South Carolina, which for many years remained Calhoun's personal satrapy, chose its electors through the legislature until after the Civil War, when it too switched to at-large popular elections.

Since that time the system of choosing electors statewide by popular election has been almost universal.[7] Individual electors, whose very names are unknown to most voters, retain the constitutional right to cast their ballots for whom they please, and a few, the so-called faithless electors, have in fact deserted the ticket they were chosen to support. But a strong moral assumption has developed that electors are ethically bound to vote for their party's national candidates. And state party leaders have of course taken care to pick persons of proven reliability as candidates for elector. In the entire history of the electoral college, fewer than twenty electors have been "faithless"—the most recent in 1976, when a Republican elector from the state of Washington voted, possibly with an eye to the future, for Ronald Reagan rather than Gerald Ford.

Traumatic Elections

In only five elections since the party system formed in the 1830s has the national political order approached or reached constitutional crisis: 1860,

7. In 1967 Maine passed a law, still in effect, allocating two of its four electors to the presidential candidate carrying the state, and giving one of the other two to the candidate carrying one of the two congressional districts and the second to the candidate carrying the other. It is therefore possible for Maine to split its electoral votes three to one candidate and one to another. In practice, the same candidate has carried both congressional districts in all succeeding presidential elections and therefore received all four electoral votes.

1876, 1888, 1912, and 1968. The first of these traumas was, of course, by far the worst, leading to actual disruption of the federal Union and four years of bloody civil conflict.

In 1860, four major presidential candidates competed in the general election: Stephen Douglas, representing the regular Democrats; John Breckenridge, representing a southern offshoot of the Democrats determined to preserve slavery; Abraham Lincoln, representing the recently organized Republicans, dedicated at a minimum to checking the spread of slavery; and John Bell, representing the Constitutional Union party, composed mainly of southerners who wished to avert the breakup of the Union. Lincoln, with just under 40 percent of the popular vote (not counting South Carolina, which still chose electors through the legislature), carried eighteen northern states, giving him a twenty-eight-vote majority in the electoral college. By the time of Lincoln's inauguration in March 1861, seven southern states had seceded. Civil war followed.

Could some other electoral system have prevented this political catastrophe? Under direct popular election without a runoff, Lincoln, with a third again as many votes as Douglas, his closest rival (who finished last in the electoral vote), would still have won. Reaction among those supporting Lincoln's opponents would no doubt have been even more bitter, since his victory would not then have enjoyed the legitimacy conferred by an absolute majority in the electoral college. This difference probably would not have mattered much in the South, where rejection of the election's result could hardly have been more decisive. But it might have made it more difficult for Lincoln to maintain effective leadership in the North.

Under a system of direct popular election with a runoff, if no candidate receives a majority—or more than 40 percent, as called for in some direct election proposals—Lincoln would have faced Douglas in the second round. Most supporters of both Breckenridge and Bell would probably have switched to Douglas, giving him victory and perhaps providing him with the political means to hold the Union together for at least a few more years. Under a parliamentary system, with either "first-by-the-post" (plurality) elections in single-member districts (the method of election usually employed for the House of Representatives), or some form of proportional representation, the Republicans would probably have emerged as the largest single party in the national legislature, but with less than an absolute majority. The two kinds of Democrats and the Constitutional Unionists quite possibly would have formed an anti-Republican majority coalition, again averting disunion. Some other electoral system, then, might have kept the Republicans out of national power in 1861, and the union might have hobbled along for a time without settling the slavery issue.

What these speculations do not take into account, however, is the aura of historic inevitability conveyed by the Republicans in 1860. Like the American revolutionaries in 1776 and the Russian Bolsheviks in 1917, the Republicans seemed to represent an unstoppable social force whose hour had come. They appeared to be agents not only for the great moral and political principles underlying the Declaration of Independence and the Constitution, but also for the economic dynamism of market capitalism then beginning to transform the globe. It is hard for me to believe that any conceivable electoral system based on democratic rules could long have kept them out.

During the first decade after the Civil War, the Republicans used the prestige associated with preserving the Union and their control of most readmitted southern states through support from former slaves to maintain national dominance. But by the election of 1876, national economic troubles and political scandal had made the Republicans vulnerable. White-supremacy Democrats had regained power in most of the South. Samuel J. Tilden of New York, the Democratic candidate for president, ran 3 percentage points ahead of Rutherford B. Hayes of Ohio, his Republican opponent, in the popular vote. On election night Tilden appeared to have won a clear majority in the electoral college as well. Early on the morning after the election, however, two strategists from the Republican National Committee and the editor of the *New York Times*, then a Republican paper, put their heads together and discovered that if Hayes won all the electoral votes of three southern states, Florida, South Carolina, and Louisiana, still controlled by Republican administrations, he would have a one-vote majority in the electoral college. Both parties launched all-out efforts, involving widespread vote fraud (at which the Republicans excelled) and voter intimidation (the specialty of the Democrats), to secure the electoral votes of these states.

Two sets of returns from each of the contested states were delivered to Congress, which at the time had no rule on how electoral votes were to be counted. A few days before the count was to begin, Congress established a special commission, composed of five senators, five representatives, and five Supreme Court justices, to decide all disputes. The congressional members of the commission were divided evenly between the parties, but as there were only two Democrats on the Supreme Court, three of the justices had to be Republicans (a political independent who had been expected to hold the swing vote resigned at the last minute to accept election to the U.S. Senate from Illinois), giving the Republicans a one-vote overall majority.

All disputes brought before the commission were settled along strict party lines. The Democratic majority in the House threatened a filibuster to prevent completion of the count, but this maneuver failed when southern Democrats, promised by Republican leaders that Democratic administrations would be allowed to resume control of all southern states, declined to support it. Hayes's election in effect was purchased at the price of Republican acquiescence in disfranchisement of blacks by white Democrats in much of the South.[8]

Democrats at the time customarily referred to Hayes's victory as "stolen." The consensus among modern historians is that an honest count would probably have given Hayes the electoral votes of South Carolina and Louisiana, but that Tilden was entitled to the four votes of Florida, giving him a seven-vote majority in the electoral college. It is worth noting, however, that Tilden's majorities in many southern states were achieved with the help of ruthless intimidation of black voters, who undoubtedly preferred Hayes. An honest count of those voting, therefore, probably would have elected Tilden; but a free vote by all eligible voters might well have swung victory back to Hayes.

In view of the common claim today that voters would be outraged if the runner-up in the popular vote were to win victory in the electoral college, it is interesting that Tilden's acknowledged lead in the popular vote was not a major factor in the 1876 controversy, despite intensity of feeling that at times seemed to be leading to civil war. The important question was who was entitled to the electoral votes of the three contested southern states. That Hayes would be elected if he won all these votes was accepted by both sides, though everybody agreed he had come in second in the popular vote.[9]

8. I have here summarized a highly complex and still to some degree controversial chain of events. Besides the disputed electoral votes from the three southern states, one Republican elector from Oregon was challenged on the ground that he was a federal government employee at the time of his election and therefore ineligible. If this challenge had been sustained, Tilden would have been elected, regardless of the outcome for the three southern states. But this electoral vote too was awarded by the commission to Hayes. C. Vann Woodward, *Reunion and Reaction: The Compromise of 1877 and the End of Reconstruction* (Doubleday, 1951), remains the best account of the entire dispute.

9. The Democratic *New York Sun,* supporting Tilden, and the independent and relatively impartial *New York Herald* barely mentioned the popular vote issue during the months of controversy that followed the 1876 election.

In 1888 the winner in the popular vote again lost in the electoral college. Grover Cleveland, the incumbent Democratic president, ran almost a full percentage point ahead of Benjamin Harrison, his Republican challenger, in the popular vote. But Harrison, by winning narrow majorities in New York and Indiana, was able to assemble a majority of sixty-five in the electoral college. The Democrats cried foul, but their protest focused on alleged vote fraud in the two pivotal states rather than on Cleveland's popular lead. Again the disparity between the outcomes in the popular vote and the electoral college was not itself a significant source of controversy. (Four years later, Cleveland won a rematch against Harrison.)[10]

In 1912 the general election contest for president among three major candidates—William Howard Taft, Republican; Woodrow Wilson, Democrat; and Theodore Roosevelt, Progressive—raised the possibility that for the first time since 1824 no candidate would achieve a majority in the electoral college. In the end, Wilson was supported by the great majority of Democrats, while Taft and Roosevelt divided the normal Republican vote almost evenly. Wilson, with only 42 percent of the popular vote, carried all but eight states and 435 out of a possible 531 electoral votes.

Roosevelt's failure to make much dent in the electoral college in 1912—he carried six states for eighty-eight votes—showed that even a highly popular third-party candidate could not capture the balance of power if he crippled one of the major party candidates while taking few votes from the other. In 1968 George Wallace, running for president on the ticket of the segregationist American Independent party, almost overcame this problem. Whether or not by deliberate strategy, Wallace won a substantial bloc of electoral votes in one region, the South, while leaving Republican Richard Nixon and Democrat Hubert Humphrey competitive in most of the rest of the nation. Though Wallace attracted a much smaller share of

10. James A. Kehl, *Boss Rule in the Gilded Age: Matt Quay of Pennsylvania* (University of Pittsburgh Press, 1981), pp. 109–12; Eugene H. Roseboom, *A History of Presidential Elections* (Macmillan, 1957), pp. 282–83; and Robert F. Wesser, "Election of 1888," in Schlesinger and Israel, eds., *Elections*, vol. 2, pp. 1615–52. The *New York Sun*, which supported Cleveland, conceded in an editorial on November 14, 1888, one week after the election: "The framers of our Constitution never expected or intended that the majority of the Presidential Electors would invariably reflect the wishes of the majority of the voters. . . . The composition of the Senate and the method of electing the Executive were regarded by the smaller states as guarantees against their own eventual effacement through the numerical preponderance of voters in the larger communities. . . . Such being the circumstances under which our method of electing Presidents was incorporated in the Constitution, we can see that even if the larger states were now able to change it, they could not do so without a gross breach of faith toward their weaker companions."

the popular vote than Roosevelt had done in 1912, and only about half as many electoral votes, he came much closer to putting himself in the position of kingmaker or throwing the election into the House.

This possibility was not much discussed during most of the campaign because Nixon was thought to be safely ahead. But when the count came in on election night, the division between Nixon and Humphrey in the popular vote was found to be very close. For several hours after midnight, Nixon hung just short of a majority in the electoral college. Television anchormen lectured their audiences on the constitutional and political horrors likely to result from an electoral college deadlock. Finally, as dawn broke along the East Coast, Illinois put Nixon over the top, and the prospect of a constitutional crisis was packed away for another day.[11]

Should the Electoral College Be Replaced?

Currently, the specter of electoral college deadlock can hardly be said to haunt the American public, partly because three of the last four presidential elections have been won by landslides (1972, 1980, and 1984). The exception, in 1976, was close, but there was no significant third-party candidate, so a clear winner in the electoral college was virtually certain.[12]

Many political scientists, constitutional scholars, presidential campaign technicians, and media seers, however, view the electoral college as a disaster waiting to happen. A shift of about 9,000 votes in Ohio and Hawaii in 1976, they point out, would have given Gerald Ford victory in the electoral college, although he would still have trailed Jimmy Carter by more than a million and a half in the popular vote. Yet in a nation certainly not lacking in enthusiastic causists, no highly visible effort is now under way to amend the Constitution to replace the electoral college. Why is this so?

When the Brookings Governmental Studies program designed this study of the electoral system, we deliberately did not assign a separate chapter on the electoral college. Arguments for and against the electoral

11. In the last week of the campaign, polls showed the race in the popular vote getting closer, and one poll in the final weekend even showed Humphrey ahead in the popular vote. The prevailing assumption remained, however, that Nixon would win a comfortable majority in the electoral college.

12. Eugene McCarthy won about 750,000 popular votes and may have cost Jimmy Carter a few states, but he did not come close to winning any electoral votes.

college, we decided, have been rehashed so often that they are familiar to most readers. But since the electoral college forms the constitutional base of the presidential election system, these arguments need at least to be summarized and some kind of judgment offered.[13]

The fundamental objection to the electoral college is that it is undemocratic. Not only does it represent voters unequally (since smaller states are weighted disproportionately); it also interposes an elite body of practically anonymous electors between the voters and the actual election of the president. Critics of the electoral college further charge that the states' practice of casting their electoral votes on a winner-take-all basis, rather than in proportion to the division of the popular vote within the state, is anachronistic, springing from a time when states were far more meaningful to the lives of most Americans than they are today.

The combination of disproportionate weighting of states with winner-take-all, moreover, poses a constant threat that the loser in the popular vote may be elected president. That this outcome was accepted by the voters with relative equanimity in 1888, and even in 1876 under politically trying circumstances, has no bearing on today. The contemporary public would withhold moral legitimacy from a president who had finished second in the popular vote.[14]

On the other side, the defense most often advanced for keeping the electoral college is simply that it is there. Many politicians and commentators who freely concede that if we were creating a presidential selection

13. For a balanced and concise discussion of the arguments for and against the electoral college, see William R. Keech, "Background Paper," in *Winner Take All: Report of the Twentieth Century Fund Task Force on Reform of the Presidential Election Process* (Holmes and Meier, 1978), pp. 27–69. See also Wallace S. Sayre and Judith H. Parris, *Voting for President: The Electoral College and the American Political System* (Brookings, 1970); Neal R. Peirce and Lawrence D. Longley, *The People's President: The Electoral College in American History and the Direct Vote Alternative,* rev. ed. (Yale University Press, 1981); and Judith V. Best, *The Case against Direct Election of the President: A Defense of the Electoral College* (Cornell University Press, 1975).

14. Some political analysts and Republican partisans contend that in 1960 Richard Nixon probably ran slightly ahead of John Kennedy in the popular vote. The official count credits Kennedy with all the popular votes cast in Alabama for a Democratic slate of electors composed of five pledged to Kennedy and six to Senator Harry Byrd of Virginia. If Kennedy had been credited with only five-elevenths of the popular vote cast for the Alabama Democratic slate, as seems reasonable, Nixon would have led nationally by about 115,000 votes—even without getting into the question of alleged fraud in the returns from Illinois. But the result was sufficiently muddied that Kennedy was perceived by the public to have won a narrow popular vote victory. And perception, in this argument, is the thing that counts.

system today we would not produce anything remotely resembling the electoral college contend that it has in fact functioned reasonably well and enjoys the large asset of being familiar in both its strengths and weaknesses (the "devil-we-know" argument).

Furthermore, all the generally discussed alternatives to the electoral college have serious flaws of their own. Direct election of the president by the voters would increase the likelihood of a minority president—perhaps with as little as 30 percent of the vote, as occurs in some party primaries for governor in states where nomination by the dominant party almost assures election. Direct election with a runoff would lead to political turmoil and encourage the development of independent candidacies and small parties that could demand concessions for their support in the second round. Keeping the electoral college with modifications, such as choosing electors by congressional district rather than statewide, would not be worth the effort, and the modifications would not necessarily be improvements. (Under the district system, in 1960 Nixon would have won a narrow majority, though he was perceived as having finished second in the popular vote.) Switching to a parliamentary system of any kind is chimerical and would not suit a nation as large and diverse as the United States.

Some positive arguments have been advanced in favor of the electoral college. The procedure of winner-take-all by states makes it difficult for third-party candidates to win electoral votes, thereby strongly reinforcing the two-party system, which experience has shown works best for a complex country like the United States and probably for any democratic polity. The very fact that winner-take-all often converts a narrow victory in the popular vote into a decisive margin in the electoral college (as in 1948, 1960, 1968, and 1976) gives a much-needed boost to the winning candidate's public legitimacy. Disproportionate representation of the smaller states in the electoral college protects small-state interests, as the Founders intended. On the other hand, winner-take-all causes presidential candidates to devote most of their attention to populous urban states, heavy with electoral votes and also with economic and social problems. Presidents, therefore, are likely to build their political bases in big urban states, balancing the strength of rural and small-state interests in Congress.

Some commentators have concluded that on balance the electoral college is preferable to its available alternatives, but nevertheless they insist that one or two major reforms are needed to cure its more glaring defects. The most frequently proposed of these is a constitutional requirement that electors vote for the candidates on whose ticket they are elected; another is that electors be eliminated altogether and each state's electoral votes awarded automatically to the ticket carrying the state.[15]

The difficulty with these proposals, besides addressing a problem that so far has never produced a harmful consequence, is that they would remove a worthwhile quality of flexibility from the system. In 1968 several candidates for elector pledged to Nixon or Humphrey indicated privately that if the candidate of the other major party had a plurality but not a majority in the electoral college, they would break their pledge and switch their vote if necessary to prevent Wallace from playing kingmaker or the election being thrown into the House. How these individuals would have behaved in the event is of course conjectural. But if the electors had been constitutionally bound to vote for the candidate to whom they were pledged, or if they had been mere notations in a computer, the election would have gone automatically to the House—the real quagmire of constitutional quicksand, as I will discuss below.

Another proposal is that the possibility of the leader in the popular vote losing in the electoral college should be eliminated by giving the popular vote winner some kind of electoral vote bonus. For instance, a task force of eminent political scientists, historians, journalists, and political activists established by the Twentieth Century Fund in 1978 to examine the electoral system concluded that the electoral college should be kept, but that the candidate with the highest number of popular votes should be given a bonus of 102 electoral votes (two for each state and the District of Columbia), thereby virtually assuring his or her election. This solution, it was argued, would preserve most of the good features of the electoral college system while removing its most dangerous flaw.[16]

The trouble with this and other proposals involving electoral vote bonuses is that they would deeply undermine the system's philosophic foundation in federalism, without achieving pure democracy, and would further complicate an already complex system. Moreover, the problem at which these remedies are aimed quite possibly does not exist. The supposition that voters would be morally repelled by the election of a president who was runner-up in the popular vote may well misread the public's

15. See, for instance, Schlesinger, *Cycles of American History*, p. 319.

16. *Winner Take All*, p. 5. The task force also recommended replacing the actual electors with electoral votes automatically assigned.

willingness to accept a verdict won fairly under long-established rules that give great weight to majoritarian principles but also allow expression of other interests and values. Majorities in the U.S. Senate are often elected by minorities in the voting electorate without noticeable public outcry. Even the House of Representatives, as Thomas Mann shows in his chapter in this book, almost never closely reflects the division of party preferences among the voters (although it does reflect the preferred majority).

The electoral college, like the Senate, is rooted in the Founders' intention of forming a federal republic, not a pure majoritarian democracy. Can it be that the voters' apparent lack of interest in changing the electoral college indicates that most of the public have not moved so far from the Founders' intention as many commentators now assume? The states, it is true, do not now express community interests and values to the extent they did in the eighteenth and nineteenth centuries. But the states probably possess more social vitality, as shown by periodic waves of activism in state government, than intellectual elites imagine; and in any event they may serve as surrogates within the federal system for other bases of community: economic, vocational, ideological, and ethnic.

The one feature of the current system that genuinely risks disaster is the provision for election of the president, if no candidate wins a majority in the electoral college, by the House of Representatives with each state delegation casting one vote. Under this contingency, the president could be elected by representatives of so small a minority in the national electorate that democratic values would indeed be offended.[17] And, since support by an absolute majority of state delegations is required for election, the presence of even a few delegations evenly divided between the parties and therefore unable to vote could paralyze the selection process for an indefinite period. This problem could be cured by a simple constitutional amendment stipulating that the House in this capacity should act through a majority of its entire membership, as on most other matters. Why has not such an amendment been proposed and enacted? Because most politicians, perhaps sagely, fear to touch any part of the present system. If reform began, they are convinced, it could not stop short of some kind of direct popular election of the president, with attendant pitfalls.

17. Theoretically, delegations representing the twenty-six least-populated states, including only 18 percent of the national population, could elect the president. A winning coalition of lightly populated southern and western states would be by no means beyond the realm of political possibility.

Achievable Reforms

Major change in the constitutional structures on which the electoral system is based is unlikely, at least in the immediate future. But beneath the constitutional level, significant reforms in some statutory and procedural areas are both desirable and possible.

The presidential selection process, in part because of changes that were made in the 1970s, is again a prime object for public and scholarly concern. Campaigns for party nominations go on for too long and cost too much money. Groups not representative of the party, let alone of the general public, exert too much influence in state preferential primaries and local caucuses. The national party convention, except perhaps in 1976 when Gerald Ford and Ronald Reagan went down to the wire for the Republican nomination, has not played a decisive role in picking presidential nominees since 1952.

James Ceaser argues, in chapter 2, that restoration of real authority to the convention would improve the quality of the process and is potentially achievable, though more likely because of an accident than by design. Ceaser holds the reforms of the 1970s responsible for many of the system's current troubles and fears that a fresh wave of comprehensive revision at the national level would make matters even worse. He prescribes a moratorium on national reform, accompanied by action by the states to give more control over presidential nominations to elected public officials and other practical politicians.

Partly because of the increased importance of the primaries, but even more because of the vast influence of television, the news media have had a steadily growing effect on presidential campaigns. This is true of newspapers as well as television, Albert Hunt shows (chapter 3), because television still takes most of its cues on news coverage from print journalism.

Hunt argues that the media, with some notable exceptions, try to use their power responsibly, but he finds that they often employ their resources poorly to improve public understanding of what is happening and what is at stake. Like Ceaser, Hunt recommends improvements to remedy specific abuses rather than comprehensive restructuring.

Beneath perplexity with particular aspects of the presidential selection process lies a more fundamental concern: is the present system giving the United States the quality of political leadership it needs to deal with complex national and international challenges? Stephen Hess takes a fresh look at Lord Bryce's famous question, Why are great men not chosen president? Hess queries whether Bryce's judgment is still accurate, and if so whether anything can be done about it (chapter 4). He finds that Bryce probably asked more of politics than politics, under any system, can be expected to give. But he does worry that, even within the limits of the politically possible, our system is not drawing on the full pool of potential national leaders. Hess does not believe that structural reform will do much to alleviate this situation and suggests we may just have to live with it.

Sharp decline in voter turnout, the second major cause for concern with the electoral system, is troublesome, not only because it allows some elections to be won almost by default, but also because it may signify deeper disaffection within the social order. Some analysts attribute falling turnout primarily to voter registration requirements, which are more restrictive in the United States than in any other major democracy. Walter Dean Burnham shows that making registration easier would, all other things being equal, increase turnout by about 10 percent, but that this would still leave the United States far behind most other democracies in voter participation (chapter 5). Burnham finds that decline in turnout since 1960, while present at all social levels, has been heavily skewed toward the lower ends of the social and economic scales. He argues that many voters find current "personalistic" politics irrelevant to their concerns and probably cannot be brought back to the polls until elections offer more meaningful choices.

While overall voter turnout has been going down, political participation by blacks as a percentage of the total has risen substantially since enactment of the Voting Rights Act of 1965. Nevertheless, some aspects of the political and governmental systems are still stacked against full participation by blacks and other racial minorities. Eddie Williams and Milton Morris find that some structural barriers, such as use of at-large elections to block minority representation, still impede black progress (chapter 6). But probably the biggest obstacle now is the persistence of racial attitudes among many whites that make it difficult for blacks to be elected to office except from black majority districts.

The rising cost of election campaigns, item three on the agenda of major concerns, exposes the system to potential corruption, or at least distortion, by the power of money. Not many elected public officials take actual bribes or sell their votes in return for campaign contributions. But money certainly buys access. "The financially articulate," according to

Senator Paul Simon of Illinois, "have an inordinate access to policy-makers."[18] Republican Senate Leader Bob Dole told participants in the Brookings conference on the electoral process: "I think PACs [political action committees] play a legitimate role in expressing the political preferences of particular constituency groups. But if members of Congress become largely dependent on PACs to finance their campaigns, the public interest is bound to suffer."

The growing role in campaign financing of PACs, themselves the indirect product of post-Watergate restrictions in the 1970s, has been singled out as a target for reform. Larry Sabato demonstrates, however, that PACs are no more than the tip of the iceberg in the campaign financing problem (chapter 7). Limiting spending by PACs while making no other changes, Sabato argues, would protect entrenched incumbents and cause special interest money to find other channels. The best way to restrict the influence of PACs, Sabato prescribes, is to provide candidates with alternative sources of support, whether through some measure of public financing of congressional campaigns, or raising limits on giving by individuals, or, most promising of all, strengthening the parties. A reform that would go a long way toward bringing the problem under control would be to require television stations to make blocks of prime time available for use by the parties during campaigns. The parties would then allocate time as they saw fit among individual candidates. This would both take some of the financial pressure off candidates and improve the capacity of parties to act as buffers between candidates and special interests.

Another long-established source of political corruption, vote fraud, has not recently received much attention from political scientists. Robert Goldberg shows, on the basis of interviews and study of recent court cases and congressional hearings, that vote fraud, though much reduced nationally, continues to thrive in some areas and remains an abuse to be guarded against (chapter 8).

The weakness of the parties, the fourth major concern, spills over into the other three problems. Stronger parties, many commentators claim, would improve the presidential selection process, increase voter turnout, and reduce the power of PACs. Even more important, James Sundquist argues, strong national parties are needed to offset the centrifugal forces in government generated by the separation of powers at the federal level and the dispersion of authority between the federal government and the states

18. *Congressional Record,* daily edition (June 4, 1987), p. S7621.

(chapter 9). The weakness of national parties, Sundquist holds, results from political attitudes and structures that go back to the Founders. He takes encouragement from the recent development of more cohesive parties in Congress and believes that party realignment should help revitalize party organizations.

Everett Carll Ladd contends, in contrast, that decentralized, loosely disciplined parties reflect enduring economic and social realities rather than alterable political attitudes or structures (chapter 10). Such parties, Ladd maintains, are well suited to the genius of American life and compare favorably in their utility with the more rigid and tightly structured parties common in most other democracies.

Whether one accepts a Sundquistian or a Laddian model of the party system, strong state and local parties are called for. Kay Lawson shows that laws governing party procedures in many states undermine the cohesion and effectiveness of state and local parties (chapter 11). She offers both a "wish list" of desired reforms and ones she thinks are achievable under current political conditions.

Thomas Mann examines a special aspect of the contemporary party system: a House of Representatives that some believe has been made impregnable to change in party control (chapter 12). The Democrats have held unbroken control of the House since 1955, while party control of the presidency has shifted four times and of the Senate twice. Mann concludes that, although the advantages of incumbency and gerrymandering have had some effect, the basic reason the House has remained Democratic for so long is that the Democrats have continued to be the larger of the two major parties in the electorate. He offers, however, a scenario through which the Republicans could gain control of the House.

Underlying Beliefs

At the end of the Brookings conference on the electoral process, from which this book is descended, I made concluding remarks, as a chairman must. I acknowledged that no single set of conclusions or point of view had emerged during our two days of discussion. Perhaps surprisingly, several papers emphasized the basic soundness of the existing system and warned against the danger of attempts at sweeping change—a point made in our final colloquy by Everett Ladd. At the same time, many papers

called for specific reforms to make the system more equitable or effective—a point made by Kay Lawson.

Skepticism toward constant or undisciplined change, Ladd said,
showed increasing intellectual maturity within the community of political
and social analysts and scholars. I agreed with this. And yet we were not
satisfied. Conservatives (or neoconservatives) like Ladd and Ceaser were
really no more satisfied than liberals (or equalitarians) like Sundquist,
Lawson, and Burnham. The conservatives regretted the deterioration of
commitment to shared values, and the liberals complained of structural
constraints that prevent the emergence of moral purpose. Perhaps, I suggested, both kinds of dissatisfaction may rise from a common American
instinct: the itch to have things better.

Whether conservatives or liberals in our structural preferences, we are
as Americans all in a deeper sense progressives—products of a tradition
that was founded on the belief that human beings are not mere bundles of
molecules and atoms driven by blind forces of nature or history, but moral
creatures, endowed with the capacity and responsibility to do what we can
in each generation to make the world a better place. Despite the wisdom of
Stephen Hess's counsel that we must be prepared to live with some forms
of imperfection, we will never finally give up on the possibility of
progress—nor will Steve Hess himself.

Rereading the conference papers as I edited them for inclusion in this
volume, I was again struck by the commonality of underlying beliefs,
though these emanate, because of differing analyses and experience, in
widely varied, sometimes antagonistic, specific applications. Two shared
convictions stand out: the American electoral system is basically sound;
we can do better.

What common themes do you expect to find? Tom Mann asked, as the
conference broke up and we started downstairs to hear Senator Dole's
speech at our postconference dinner. I suggested then, and feel more
confident now, that these two starting points are theme enough.

PART ONE

Presidential Selection

CHAPTER TWO

Improving the Nominating Process

JAMES W. CEASER

A continual change of good measures is inconsistent with every rule of prudence and every prospect of success. —James Madison

THE SUCCESS of an institution depends nearly as much on its stability as on its quality. A political institution is a structure that channels political activity, setting the limits of permissible behavior and patterning action in predictable ways. An institution that is constantly being reformed in response to normal political activity is failing in its essential task, regardless of its quality at any given moment. Institutions can always be improved, but the more stable they become the more useful they are.

If quality and stability are the two principal standards for assessing institutional health, the best situation is clearly found when a good institution is firmly in place. Other situations cannot be so easily judged. Where a deficient institution exists, instability, although harmful in its own right, might be welcomed if a better replacement is a genuine possibility. By the same reasoning, the worst situation is found when an institution is both deficient and unstable and when there is little prospect for improvement.

Judged by these standards, the nominating process today does not fare very well. Over the past two decades it has been the least stable of all the major national institutions. It has also been the most deficient. Flawed in conception, it has been harmful in operation and, if continued in the form of the past decade—a form that has almost ensured instability—it could threaten the well-being of the entire political system.

29

Dire as this assessment may sound, there is some basis for hope.
Among those having influence over the development of the nominating
process, there has been in the past few years a growing appreciation of the
dangers of instability and a partial recognition of the system's defects. A
few hesitant steps have already been taken to modify the dominant
character of the system, and room has been opened for more such steps
to be taken. Accordingly, the argument of this chapter—paradoxical, but
not, I trust, overly refined—is that the present arrangement should be
maintained, in part because it offers the best way to secure its own
modification.

Instability of the Nominating System

The nominating process over the past two decades has suffered from
constant instability. Other institutions, such as Congress, have experienced what proponents of change like to call *reform,* meaning a major
improvement of some enduring significance. The nominating process,
however, has not only been reformed, but re-reformed and re-reformed
again to the point where even advocates of change shrink sheepishly from
using the term.

Since 1968 no two successive nominating contests have taken place
under the same general rules. This will hold true for 1988 as well, with the
introduction of the much discussed "Mega-Super Tuesday" in early
March. While it is correct to speak of the existence of a single system
during this period, the changes from one contest to the next have been
substantial enough for many analysts to argue that candidates have often
won or lost in large part *because* of the rules. Since the outcome of any
nominating contest can always be said in a sense to depend on the rules,
this kind of explanation is of interest only where the rules are either of
recent origin or under serious question. One or both of these conditions has
applied now for nearly twenty years, with the result that the nominating
process has come to be widely regarded not as a constant, but as a variable
that can be manipulated for short-term advantage.

This attitude has been especially prevalent in the Democratic party, for
the Democrats, unlike the Republicans, developed a mechanism for devising detailed national party rules for delegate selection. Before the 1970s
the rules for delegate selection were made by each state or state party.
After 1970 the Democrats not only built their new mechanism for rule-

making, but virtually established a precedent that it would be used after each election. A Washington-based group of delegate selection experts sprang into existence and launched careers by staffing party rules commissions, attending delegate selection conferences, and serving as advisers in candidate campaign organizations. Like ancient Egyptian priests, these experts became masters of an occult science with a jargon (*windows, frontloading, thresholds*) that few others could fathom.

Although this new rulemaking instrumentality never possessed the full control of the nominating process that its advocates claimed, it certainly had enough power to attract the participation of many groups. Among those who at one time or another had a hand in rulemaking were pure reformers, concerned with achieving a perfect replication among the delegates of the voters' candidate preferences; rights activists, concerned with increasing the number of delegates from certain minority groups; and, more recently, friends of political parties, concerned with the well-being of the party as an ongoing institution. Also numbered among the rulemakers were representatives of some of the candidate organizations, who sought to ensure that the rules adopted served the aims of their candidate. The rules of the game became part of the game.

Initially, campaign managers strongly denied such involvement. But as the practice of fixing rules became more obvious, the denials became less heated. By the time of a Harvard University Institute of Politics debriefing on the 1984 election, there was a nice marriage between the journalist's quest for the "real" story and the modern campaign manager's pride in shaping the system to benefit his client:

> Mr. Bode [NBC News network correspondent]: John Reilly, you were on that commission. What was the most important goal that the Mondale campaign had, shortening the season, bunching it up so that the quick-kill strategy was viable, thresholds, loopholes, super delegates, what?
>
> John R. Reilly [senior adviser, Mondale for President]: All of the above. . . . Probably the most important thing that we were able to do was enable the states to hold their primaries as early as they chose, because we felt that a national candidate or one that was known better than others had an opportunity to step out early. [1]

---

1. Jonathan Moore, ed., *Campaign for President: The Managers Look at '84* (Dover, Mass.: Auburn House, 1986), p. 3.

It is no great revelation, of course, to learn that candidates have a strong interest in being elected and that their operatives will do all they can to help them achieve that objective. For architects of electoral institutions, what is important is the *context* in which this aim is pursued. The situation has now developed in which an overt politicization of the system's rules is regarded as politics as usual, and many political scientists have implicitly acquiesced in this view by equating serious scholarly analysis with a sophisticated understanding of the politics of manipulating the process. What is at risk is not just a breakdown of an institution, but a loss of the idea that nominating candidates is properly a function to be institutionalized.

To claim that institutional instability is a problem, without specifying who or what is damaged, may seem like an abstract proposition. But the costs have been real enough. First, the Democratic party has suffered greatly from increased factional strife. Struggles over the rules have become a regular part of nomination contests since 1968, with losers claiming they were dealt with unfairly, especially in cases where the victorious candidate played a role in devising the rules. As the objective criteria of fairness grew more elaborate with each successive reform, complaints that the system was unfair became more widespread. Instead of helping to promote party unity and harmony, the rules became a continual source of discord. Second, even if Republicans could temporarily take solace in the discomfiture of the Democrats, everyone has been aware that what threatens the institutional health of one party threatens the entire two-party system. The struggles over the rules have kept the nominating process under constant scrutiny and have intensified demands for more change, including calls for Congress to take control of the process. Finally, instability detracts from the selection of a qualified candidate. Whatever attributes define a good candidate, it strains credulity to think they are closely associated with the tactical sense—or more likely the luck—to discern which strategy best fits the latest wrinkle in the rules.

Accordingly, anyone who dismisses the instability of the nominating process as a minor problem of a private institution (a political party) greatly underestimates its significance. The nominating system is a major *constitutional process,* using that term in its broad sense to refer to any process that bears significantly on a regime's arrangement of offices and the mode of elevation to them. The plain fact is that this generation has failed to institutionalize the process of selecting candidates for the most important office in the West.

Besides stability, the other standard for assessing the condition of an institution is quality. Assessments of quality are bound to generate controversy, as they depend on difficult value judgments. It is thus hardly surprising that two well-known presidential scholars, Erwin Hargrove and Michael Nelson, added a theological dimension to the polemics by labeling those critical of the post-1968 system as "counter-reformationists," implying perhaps that critics have been planning an inquisition against reformers.[2] Setting aside for the moment a discussion of the standard of quality, it is at least fair to say that the system has generated more dissatisfaction among political analysts than any other major American institution. If there is something to these criticisms—and I believe there is—then the nominating process today begins to fit the profile of the situation identified earlier as least desirable: an institution that is unstable and deficient. But is there any prospect for its improvement?

A Preliminary Diagnosis

It is on the ground of possible improvement that today, unlike a decade ago, there may be some basis for optimism. Among an influential group of political analysts and party leaders concerned with the long-term character of the institution, there has been an important change of opinion since 1980. The philosophy of reform that dominated in the 1970s, which touted the virtues of greater "fairness," "democracy," and "change," has yielded to a very different philosophy concerned with maintaining and strengthening political parties. To see the differences between these two philosophies, one need only compare the views of the McGovern-Fraser Commission (1969–72) with those of the Hunt Commission (1981–82). Whether one describes this new postreform effort as an attempt to modify the existing system, to transform it dramatically, or to begin a process that could lead to a transformation down the road, it is clear that reform principles have begun to be called into question.

Conflict between these two philosophies became public at the 1984 Democratic convention. Followers of the Reverend Jesse Jackson and Senator Gary Hart, appealing to reform ideas, very nearly succeeded in having the convention establish a commission that would have *mandated* a

2. Erwin C. Hargrove and Michael Nelson, *Presidents, Politics, and Policy* (Johns Hopkins University Press, 1984), pp. 163–65.

return to many of the practices of the 1970s. It was only by some smart politics that this proposal was sidetracked and eventually replaced by a commission under the control of the Democratic National Committee and the national party chairman. This commission, called the Fairness Commission, made only slight modifications in the 1984 rules and did so early enough to preclude participation by any of the candidates.

This near escape at the 1984 convention shows the precarious hold that proponents of the postreform philosophy have on the Democratic party. They did, nevertheless, manage to withstand a fundamental challenge and now have a chance to bring stability to the national party rules, while leaving the door open to modification of the system by action chiefly at the state level. Their victory was significant because in a decisionmaking process of this kind one of the strongest arguments for stability is, paradoxically, the fact of stability. Once a cycle of constant change is broken and the rules are kept substantially intact for one round, it becomes more difficult to change them.

For those, accordingly, who thought that the reform philosophy of the 1970s virtually excluded the possibility of improvement, the situation today is likely to appear more hopeful. At the same time, the temptation must be avoided to exaggerate the influence of the postreform philosophy. Proponents of the new philosophy can be compared with a new team of medical consultants called in, rather late in the day, to treat a severe case. Treatments given in the past have set in motion conditions that cannot be easily reversed or controlled, and the new consultants have been given authority to prescribe only certain remedies. Even if their diagnosis is correct, it is far from certain whether they have proposed the right cure.

Devising a strategy for improving an institution requires considering not just what constitutes health, but also how to act in a particular context to move from a worse to a better arrangement. As it is unclear what will happen in 1988, the "legislators" of the system—meaning those people in a position to influence its development—must be prepared to adjust their strategies to specific developments. In the event there is a breakdown in the current system and a public demand for a fundamental restructuring, legislators should be ready with a general plan for redesigning the system. Even if the problems of 1988 do not objectively merit scrapping the system, the cumulative effect of past instability has undermined respect for the system and prepared the way for dramatic gestures. Without a real crisis, however, legislators would be unwise to add their weight to these demands.

The preferred strategy is to build on the ideas of postreform. Under this strategy, legislators no longer should be thinking in terms of a single plan to redesign the entire system, but of a process of adjustment at a level below the national party rules. This strategy is consistent with the plural character of current arrangements. There are two political parties that have by now adopted quite different approaches, and there are different decisionmaking authorities (the states and the national parties), aligned in a nonhierarchic relationship, whose interests must be brought into equilibrium. Attempting to impose a single plan on this system is unrealistic, as the very idea presupposes a central point of authority at odds with its character. If change is conceived as an evolutionary process, it can take the form of promoting a deepening awareness of certain goals, leaving to a large number of decisionmakers the means by which to achieve them.

This approach, it must be emphasized, does not necessarily mean keeping the current system, for there are tendencies operative today that could modify it profoundly without the imposition of a new plan from the center. Indeed, if certain accidents occur, such as the failure in 1988 of any candidate to emerge as a clear winner in the primary contests, general expectations about the nominating system could change and steps could then be taken that could enable it to evolve very quickly into something quite different.

What is needed, accordingly, are not gratuitous exercises in offering yet more plans to scrap the system and redesign it anew. Such proposals are often little more than displays designed to convince audiences of an author's intellectual originality or to give the illusion of solving a problem within the confines of a single op-ed article. To meet today's political realities, it will be more helpful to offer a series of reflections on the nominating process that can assist legislators in improving it and enable them to take advantage of any fortuitous developments.

Character of the Current System

Scholars generally classify presidential nominating systems according to the "selectorate" empowered to choose the nominee and decide other matters, such as the platform, that are resolved in the same process. Political scientists have the additional concern of analyzing how the nominating system affects the performance of certain important tasks or functions, such as elevating political leaders and accommodating demands for political change. Changes in the selectorate, it turns out, have important consequences for the performance of these functions.

The changes in the selectorate yield the following familiar historical division: (1) the electoral college (1789–92), (2) the congressional caucus (1800–20), (3) the "pure" convention system (1836–1908), (4) the mixed system (1912–68), and (5) the plebiscitary system (1972–84). The change from one system to another has usually been preceded by a concerted public effort to justify a new selectorate. Each change has also been marked by the development (or extensive use) of a new instrumentality: the party caucus, the convention, the primary, and the national rulemaking process.

The current system has the following three properties with regard to the selectorate. First, the majority of the delegates are chosen or mandated in primaries according to their explicit candidate preference; in effect, the real selectorate has been the public, or at least that part of the public that votes in the primaries. Second, the choice of the nominee is nevertheless still made formally by the convention, which has not yet lost all discretion. In the event that the public does not mandate a winner through a popular choice in the primaries and caucuses, the existing system provides for selection by the delegates, whether before or at the convention, as the auxiliary method of decision. If, for whatever reason, this method should become the actual mode of selection, there would be a de facto modification of the system. Who the delegates are would then become crucial in characterizing and defining the system. (This is not the case where the delegates merely register the preferences of voters.) Third, the other business conducted during the nominating process—writing the platform, approving the rules, and presenting the party to the national electorate—is controlled by the delegates, who act without being bound by the public, though most of them follow the dictates of their respective candidate organizations.

Notwithstanding the instability in the rules since 1968, there has been no *essential* change in the system during this period. All along the public has had the effective power to choose the nominee. The races have displayed the same basic characteristics associated with a general popular contest, influenced by certain peculiar dynamics set in motion by the modern mass media. Indeed, many strategists during the period erred by overinterpreting the possible effects of marginal changes while losing sight of the persisting tendencies of the system. There have been, however, second-order changes that have affected the conduct of convention business and that could have a bearing on the probability that the nomination decision will be made by the delegates, thus conceivably changing the system. These changes have affected the way delegates are selected or mandated and the schedule of delegate selection contests.

Methods of Delegate Selection

The selection and mandating of delegates is determined by state law, state party rules, custom, and national party rules. Perhaps the most important consideration is whether delegates are mandated by a primary or a caucus. The authority to make this decision has remained the prerogative of the state governments, although their choice has been greatly influenced, in very different and complex ways, by national party rules. Since 1968, the number of primaries has waxed and waned, but no discernible trend has yet developed to alter the selectorate.

National party rules have affected other aspects of the choice of delegates. Before 1980 the major aim of the Democratic party's rules was "fairness," which the national party sought to enforce by ever more exacting regulations on the states and state parties—for example, proportional representation, a ban on the selection of ex officio delegates, and candidate approval of the delegates. One result of the emphasis on candidate preference was to solidify the plebiscitary system by reducing the number of uncommitted delegates. Since 1980 the emphasis has shifted. There has been some relaxation in efforts by the national party to dictate practices to the states, in particular where national rules sought to ban state practices aimed at building consensus. More striking, national rules now seek directly to aid the party as an organization, requiring the selection of ex officio delegates (a practice the rules only recently forbade to the states) and creating a category of legally uncommitted "superdelegates," all of whom now are chosen outside the control of the states or state parties.

These changes have increased the percentage of delegates at the Democratic convention with a "party" orientation. Democratic conventions from 1972 to 1980 were dominated by candidate enthusiasts and representatives of interest groups acting under the umbrella of candidate organizations. By 1984 party people had slightly more influence, which by some accounts helped promote consensus in the platform-writing process and may have proved decisive in blocking the establishment of an autonomous new reform commission. The addition of the superdelegates has also created a large bloc of formally uncommitted delegates, which increases the probability of a decision being made by the delegates.

For the Republicans, a modest degree of party influence has been

retained throughout the reform era. For example, in caucus states delegates are not formally chosen according to candidate preference, and
custom has ensured the choice of important party leaders. The fact that
Democrats have looked on occasion to the Republicans has proven an
embarrassment to much of the scholarship of the last generation, which,
when it did not ignore the Republican party altogether, treated it conde-
scendingly for its failure to adopt all the reforms of the Democratic party
or make use of the new instrument of national party rulemaking. In certain
respects, Democrats are now using national rulemaking to reinstitute what
their own prior rules destroyed and what the Republicans have to some
extent maintained.

Scheduling

The other major area of change has been in the scheduling of the
delegate selection contests. The sequence was far less important under
previous systems when the nominating decision was made by the delegates, often at the convention. Under the current system, in which the
public selects the nominee in the primaries, the position of a state's contest
in the schedule is arguably very important. The best predictor of how
candidates do in a particular primary is how well they did in the preceding
round of primaries. This seems to give more influence, all things being
equal, to states that schedule their primaries first or early.[3]

The tendency of the states to "frontload," or move up their contests,
cannot be explained completely by a desire to increase influence. Background factors are just as important. Because of instability in the rules, the
states have constantly had to change their laws and have become used to
the idea of making changes, a practice now abetted and encouraged by
candidate organizations. Moreover, many state Democratic legislative
leaders feel no responsibility for a system that they had little part in
creating and that they think may endure for only one election. The absence
of institutionalization has led states to behave as short-term "rational
actors" in a contest of each against all.

3. This logic is obviously open to question. As more states move their primaries to the
beginning of the campaign season, the influence any single state hopes to have over the
outcome is bound to diminish. In past years, moreover, primaries in the middle of the
campaign often became pivotal to the outcome of the race. Such was the case for Illinois, for
example, in the Democratic race in 1984. With so many states now bunching up at the
beginning, it would not be surprising if some states now decided that they might have a
better chance to influence the result by scheduling their contest on a lonely Tuesday in April.

Democratic party rules after 1980 attempted to regulate the timing of the delegate selection contests, with the objectives of shortening the process and making it fairer by removing the privileged positions of Iowa and New Hampshire. The first objective may have been partially attained by rules creating a delegate selection season or "window." But the second was not, for the Democratic party either would not, or could not, compel Iowa and New Hampshire to yield their positions. The Hunt Commission discussed the possibility of freezing the dates of all the state contests to avoid further frontloading, but took no action.

After 1984 there was a coordinated effort by southern party leaders to move state contests in their region to the earliest date allowable under the party rules. What analysts consider to be the most significant change for 1988 was thus made, not by national party rules, but by actions of the states. The political implications of this schedule naturally excite great interest, but the focus of this chapter is on the possible consequences for the institution, which for now can only be matters of speculation.

Three possible responses merit attention. First, there may be a general determination that the schedule is somehow unfair or unwise. The system will be depicted as chaotic, and the demand will grow for someone—presumably Congress—to step in and rationalize the process. Second, many state legislators may become disillusioned if the change of date does not produce the anticipated political result. They may then move to reposition their primaries for 1992. Thus the problem of frontloading, for those who find it a problem, may resolve itself. Third, with a large number of delegates selected so early, before many candidates have dropped from the race, there may be a great dispersal of the vote. This could have the effect of giving the nominating decision to the delegates, who could even select a nominee from outside the ranks of the early active candidates. A recourse to the auxiliary method for 1988 might change everyone's expectations for 1992. Candidates might orient their campaigns far more to party leaders, and some candidates might give up pursuing active campaigns in the primaries. Such changes would in turn force shifts in strategy by all participants in the process, from interest group leaders to party officials, initiating a de facto modification of the system. Indeed, there are signs that this kind of shift could be occurring for 1988, with some strong candidates choosing to sit on the sidelines.

A transformation along the lines sketched by this third possibility could occur, in contrast to system changes in the past, without a de jure change or a major new development in the institutional machinery. The character of the present system already gives the formal choice of the nominee to the convention, and an evolution of the system in the direction of a choice by the delegates, not necessarily at the convention, could be accommodated with little difficulty. Under such a transformation, no action by Congress or the national parties would be required, although certain changes in state laws and a few changes in party rules could help solidify the development. The aim or objective would be a system in which party leaders and political peers had a much greater say in selecting the nominee, especially in those cases where there is no clear public favorite. Just as important, the aim would be a change in the incentive structure under which candidates pursue the nomination. Of course, the introduction of such a system seems now to owe much to chance, while its survival would depend on whether this method of choosing the nominee could win general acceptance.

Criteria for Judging the System

The quality of a nominating system can be assessed by considering how it affects the performance of five major "functions" of the political system that are significantly influenced by the nominating process. These functions are maintaining democratic legitimacy, selecting qualified candidates, promoting effective governance, structuring healthy candidate behavior, and regulating political change.

Legitimacy

Major political institutions must enjoy a reasonable degree of public support to ensure their legitimacy. For the nominating process in the United States, legitimacy has traditionally required that the system should be fairly broad based and take seriously public preferences for the nominees. But before 1968 it was not widely held to require a system based on the principle of direct popular choice. This understanding of legitimacy, which reformers argue is essential for maintaining a democratic form of government, may for the moment be generally accepted by the American people. But in looking to the future, one may ask whether direct democracy in presidential nominations is really a prerequisite for maintaining a democratic regime.

At the outset of the reform period, the case for direct democracy was often linked to arguments about the concrete benefits it would produce, such as promoting change or destroying corrupt party organizations. Very quickly, however, these justifications were separated from the defense of direct democracy, which was then promoted as a worthwhile goal in and of itself because it stimulated citizen participation. The preoccupation with participation is confirmed in scores of social scientific studies, which dutifully seek to measure rates at which people vote in primaries. These studies, which sometimes dazzle the reader with their displays of statistical acrobatics, have produced many interesting findings, including an entire literature on whether participation is genuinely representative of party members or the public. But one may ask whether too much energy has been devoted to such matters, especially in view of the fact that proponents of direct democracy have never established that mass citizen participation in presidential nominations is necessary to ensure a bona fide republican form of government. Other Western democracies, after all, survive quite nicely without employing a plebiscitary principle of legitimacy in their executive nomination processes.

As to the argument that citizen participation is a good thing, this is doubtless true. But it in no way follows that the nomination process is the proper place to stimulate mass citizen participation or that pulling a lever in a closed voting booth constitutes a very significant or healthy form of participation. Reformers have clearly been indulging in a rhetoric designed to create their own reality, first flattering populist sentiments, then asserting that direct democracy is necessary to maintain legitimacy. The claim on behalf of direct democracy may now need to figure importantly in pragmatic calculations, but this requirement should not earn it respect as a worthwhile principle that legislators are obliged to promote.

Candidate Selection

Analysis of this function subdivides into two questions: Does the system expand the pool of able candidates who are considered? And does it help select from that pool an effective and highly qualified leader? The current system has been highly praised for its openness, but in truth it is open only selectively. It enables candidates to be self-starters, allowing serious candidacies by a Jimmy Carter, a Jesse Jackson, a Richard Gephardt, or a Pat Robertson—none of whom probably would have been part of the pool under previous systems. On the other hand, the system excludes those who, for whatever reason, are not in a position to run in an extended series of primaries. This could be an individual whose current responsibilities make active campaigning difficult or potential candidates who do not want to risk being politically "used up" by the system. In fact, the day may already have arrived when certain potential candidates are picking their occasion to run very carefully. This kind of calculation may represent prudent management of their own careers, but it limits the choices available to the nation.

Whether the current system encourages a wise selection from the pool is another question. In comparison with past systems in the United States or those in most other democratic regimes, the current system gives an unusual opportunity to an "outsider," that is, a candidate enjoying minimal support from other political elites. Reformers regard this as a strong point in favor of the system and have resisted changes that might make it more difficult for outsiders. Their view is apparently based on a notion of fairness, under which it is thought important to give an equal opportunity to every candidate who chooses to enter the race. In other systems such a notion has figured very little, as it is seen to have no connection to promoting the choice of a good person. Other systems are predicated on the idea that the nomination decision should be based on a judgment of what individuals have *already* done, whereas the current system is based on the idea that the nomination decision should be viewed as an award for performance *during* the nomination campaign.

The distinction between a retrospective and a prospective orientation is essential for understanding the current system and the claims made on its behalf. Under past systems, even allowing for all the robust politicking that took place, it was not considered the chief task of the nominating process itself to display, measure, or test the qualities of the candidates, nor were the decisions based primarily on what candidates did during the process itself. By contrast, proponents of the current system view the nominating process as a sort of trial run to test certain qualities immediately relevant to being a successful president, above all the skills of divining the public mood and displaying rhetorical prowess.[4] By this argument a plebiscitary system—whether the current variant or, better still, a national primary—should continue to produce the best presidents possible, with allowances made for the fact that no system is flawless.

Whatever the merit of the view that the nominating process should be arranged to "test" presidential qualities, there is a problem with the argument as it is applied today. Although the skills of reading the public mood

4. Hargrove and Nelson, *Presidents, Politics, and Policy,* p. 166.

and engaging in public persuasion are surely important qualities for a president—and ones that could not be ignored under any alternative system—they may not be as important for governing well as they are for getting nominated. Moreover, the lines of causality for determining the qualities needed do not run exclusively from the presidency to the nominating process, but in the opposite direction as well. By putting a premium on the techniques of popular persuasion in the nominating process, the current system has inflated the importance of these attributes for presidential leadership and given to them a distinctive character that pushes presidential leadership toward the style of political campaigning. A rhetorical presidency is in part the result of a rhetorical nominating process.

Governance

The current nominating system has been held responsible for virtually every failure in Washington over the past two decades, from Watergate to the budget deficit. This kind of *reductio ad reformism* overstates the nominating system's effect on governing, but there can be no question that the system, especially the Democratic party variant of the 1970s, weakens the connection between the president and party members whose support is needed for establishing a solid political base in Congress and in the states. A presidency whose main constituency is public opinion may well be able to ride high when popularity is on the president's side, but party support is what helps to sustain a president in leaner seasons.

Of course, the nominating system is only one factor, and by no means the most important one, that accounts for the degree of cooperation between presidents and fellow party members in Congress. But to the extent that it has an influence, experience with the Carter presidency demonstrated its adverse effect on legislative-executive relations. For those who espouse governance by European-style parties, discussion of the effect of the nominating system on party unity is apt to appear ludicrous. Still, the difference between slightly weaker and slightly stronger instruments of cooperation can have very important consequences for the governability of the American political system.

Candidate Behavior

A nominating system not only screens potential candidates and selects a winner; it also marks out a course of political behavior by which prospective candidates are led to seek their goal of becoming president. The selection system thus works to form the "public character" of prominent politicians. Furthermore, since presidential campaign politics set the tone for other campaigns, the nominating system shapes the general style of American politics.

The method of solicitation that candidates currently employ to seek the nomination relies heavily on the arts and techniques of mass persuasion. According to classical analyses of democratic politics, any broad and unstructured process of popular solicitation risks encouraging charlatanism or demagogy, not only in its harsher sense as excessive appeals to fear, nationalism, or class resentment, but in its softer sense as indulgence of sentiments of compassion, harmony, and peace. Certain of the popular arts have clearly been stimulated by conducting campaigns through the mass media. Reporting on the campaigns has been found to play up the quick, the new, and the horse-race elements of candidate competition. While this emphasis sometimes reflects poor reporting, it is a failure of institutional analysis to blame everything on the influence of current practices of journalism. The values of journalism cannot be the same as those that a political institution should promote, which in this case includes fostering behavior that encourages moderation and the conciliation of different elements of the party.

Political Change

One of the main points of access for demands and pressure for political change is through the nominating process. Traditionally, the party system has been viewed as one of the key institutions that regulate and control the pace of change, usually in a way that dampened too quick and reflexive a response to transient currents of opinion. Party leaders performed this function partly from interest, to maintain the party coalition, and partly from an understanding that parties had this responsibility. Party control of the nomination system provided an auxiliary barrier to dangerous short-term pressures for change. This barrier has been removed under the current system, which relies exclusively on the good sense of the American people to resist candidates and movements that might flatter prejudices to betray long-term interest.

The current system was instituted to encourage more rapid political change in a political regime that reformers viewed as blocked and resistant to popular pressures. It seems to have lived up to this expectation, at least in the superficial sense that candidates often seek to win the nomination by appeals to the new and the different—new faces, new coalitions, new beginnings. There is a constant search for new ideas before any need for them is evident. The current system would thus seem to be profoundly anticonservative except that by requiring change all the time it trivializes the notion of change. Fundamental change becomes more difficult when all changes are advertised as fundamental.

The System as a Whole

In evaluating nominating systems, it is important to avoid a simplistic kind of reasoning that isolates one function and judges the system by how well it performs this function as measured against some ideal standard of perfection. Reasoning of this kind is worse than useless, it is destructive of any kind of sound institutional analysis. The pertinent consideration for institutional analysis is how well different systems, taken as wholes, perform on balance all of the functions. Considering systems as wholes, moreover, means taking into account those things that serve to maintain them, even when such supports may not by themselves contribute directly to a positive result.

The major alternative today to the plebiscitary system is a system that would give more control over the nominating process to the ongoing party organizations and to party leaders. Delegates, representing state party interests as well as preferences for specific candidates, would regain much of the effective power to choose the nominee, although there is no question today that popular preferences as measured in primaries and caucuses would have to be accorded great weight.

In the literature of political science, party control has been criticized for two very different reasons: corruption or resistance to change, and ideological rigidity. The first has been the charge traditionally made against American parties, the second against many European parties, though it could at some point become as relevant as the first to the United States. The general problem is this: party control risks either bargained politics or ideological rigidity; popular control risks demagogy and programmatic instability. The best solution is a balance. The current system has tipped so far in the direction of popular control that there is now little danger in exploring every reasonable mechanism for moving toward greater party control. Depending on specific circumstances in each party and each state, this change could be achieved by such means as reinstituting caucuses, increasing the number of ex officio delegates, and encouraging an early selection for some of the delegates. How the shift to greater party control can be achieved is likely to be a matter of trial and error.

Mechanisms for Changing the System

Analysts of the nominating process generally focus on *what* the system should be rather than on *who* should have the authority to change it. There are at least two reasons, however, for giving the latter question equal attention. First, the character of the present system cannot be understood without considering the effect of the power structure that framed it. Throughout American history, no single agency has possessed the full authority to alter the system, and results have therefore always been generated by the interactions of different agencies (national parties, states, state parties, Congress, and the courts). Misunderstanding the power structure can lead to attempts to reconstitute the system through an agency that lacks sufficient power to do so, setting off a chain of unintended results.

Second, the source of change is nearly as important to the long-run well-being of the nominating process as the specific character of change. Any particular reform, however well conceived, is unlikely to represent the final effort at institutional transformation. But the agency given the authority to enact the reform will probably continue to control the process well into the future. Authority structures endure longer than specific plans. Thus the hidden element of any reform is the determination of who is to be invested with the power to constitute the system.

Analysis of these issues requires a constitutional logic that focuses not on specific plans, but on the alternative procedures and results likely to be favored by different power structures. History can serve to elucidate the important themes.

The Founders designed the original electoral college to serve as a mechanism both for nominating and electing. Its complex authority structure was intended to protect the principles of separation of powers and federalism. The Constitution itself specifies certain aspects of the system, while directing or permitting other aspects to be constituted by the states or by Congress. Specifically, the Constitution (Article II, section 1) directly establishes the legal qualification for the office of elector—no member of Congress or other national officer may serve—and dictates the apportionment of electors and the basic rules governing their voting. The Constitution goes on to give the state governments the general authority to determine the method of selecting electors, while reserving to Congress an option to set the dates on which electors may be chosen and vote.

When political parties emerged in the 1790s, the power to shape the nominating process escaped from the public jurisdiction of the Constitution and the states and was assumed by a "private" authority, the party caucuses in Congress. But the legal distinction between public and private does not do justice to the broader reality that operated at the time. The caucus system was debated on constitutional grounds, with critics ultimately charging that it jeopardized the separation of powers, neglected state prerogatives, and ignored the popular will.

When parties were reconstituted in the 1830s, proponents argued that the new nominating institution—the party convention—overcame the principal constitutional deficiencies of the caucus system. The party convention respected the separation of powers, was federal in character, and was broadly based and popular. In addition, party officials may also have felt obliged to imitate other constitutional arrangements in establishing their power structures. Paralleling the national elements of the Constitution's arrangement, the national parties established the apportionment scheme (adopting until 1916 the Constitution's formula) and determined the voting rules for deciding the nominee. Following the Constitution's federal elements, both national parties left the determination of the methods of selecting convention delegates to the state parties, with the convention having the ultimate right to determine credentials.

This power structure remained intact until the Progressive era, when reformers charged that parties had abused their trust by ignoring the public interest and serving the needs of corrupt organizations. Reformers divided, however, over who should supervise the nominating process. One group favored national control, whether by a constitutional amendment or, as some thought possible, by a simple assertion of congressional jurisdiction. Another group was content to modify the convention system by having the state governments take control of the selection of delegates. The latter approach won the day, and by 1916 the national parties recognized the authority of state law over delegate selection where states chose to exercise it.

The modern reform period began in 1968 amid many of the same charges against the evils of party control heard during the Progressive era. To resolve the problems, reformers developed the new instrument of national party rulemaking. This development has depended first on a willingness to assert national control, which has been limited for the most part to the Democratic party. Within the Democratic party, the nationalizing impulse has varied according to the respect for federal arrangements shown by different groups. Reformers have sought to work through the national convention and give direct mandates to autonomous commissions, while defenders of state party interests have favored commissions operating under the jurisdiction of the Democratic National Committee.[5] More important, the rulemaking authority has depended on the national party's legal authority, which is still misunderstood. Many early enthusiasts of reform imagined the national party's new authority to be comparable in scope to a plenary legislative power. This broad interpretation, which has proven to be exaggerated, flowed in part from the way the legal issues were initially framed. In the two major test cases—one in 1972 involving Illinois' primary law and the other in 1980 involving Wisconsin's famed open primary—it was supporters of the power of the *states* who brought action, arguing that state law for the selection of delegates should be binding on the national parties. In rejecting the states' claim, the Supreme Court emphasized the prerogatives of the national party, establishing, sometimes in very broad language, its power to decide who would be seated at the national convention.[6]

Yet this power, impressive as it is when viewed against the backdrop of the previous federal structure of the parties, falls well short of being a true legislative power. The national party has only a negative power in relation to the state governments—a power to refuse to seat delegates. This power, it is true, can be converted into a positive instrument to the extent that the states, in seeking to ensure seating of their delegates, comply with the rules. But the national party cannot write state law. This fact has given the states great political leverage against the national party. If a state refuses to comply with a national party rule, the party's only method of enforcing its will is to threaten to disregard state law. So extreme a mode of enforcement is difficult to employ, especially for those who continue to think that the purpose of a political party has more to do with winning elections than with legislating rules.

Over the past decade the relationship between the national party and the

5. For accounts of developments in the Democratic party during the reform period, see Nelson Polsby, *Consequences of Party Reform* (Oxford University Press, 1983); and Byron Shafer, *Quiet Revolution* (New York: Russell Sage Foundation, 1983).

6. See *Cousins* v. *Wigoda,* 419 U.S. 477 (1975); and *Democratic Party of the U.S.* v. *La Follette,* 450 U.S. 107 (1981).

states has been shaped by power struggles, reminiscent of games of political chicken, testing who would flinch first. The national party gained power until 1980, but since then the states have fought back. The battle over the open primary in Wisconsin is indicative of this change. Although the national party won the legal battles against the state in 1980, it has since conceded the war, dropping its ban on the open primary for 1988. A full evaluation of the consequences of the legal struggles over national rulemaking must also include consideration of the spirit, often adversarial, in which the different authorities have interacted with each other. Many state legislatures and state parties have felt themselves to be pawns manipulated by an alien national party. The creation of the unified Southern delegate selection primary for 1988 was fueled in part by this resentment, as many southern Democrats saw this step as one they could take on their own without interference from the national party.

The era of further national party efforts to dictate delegate selection procedures to the states seems to have come to an end. Only if national rulemaking is needed to forestall a congressional takeover of the nominating process is it likely to reappear, and in this case the Democratic party would probably have the support of many states and the Republican party. Unless this situation develops, the power structure for framing the nominating process will retain its present complexity. Even though the boundary lines among the various authorities involved have not been precisely settled, there are limits to the power of each authority. Achieving stability for this system will require establishing an equilibrium among them.

Should Congress Legislate a National System?

Given the inability of the present power structure to impose any particular system, many have wondered whether it can or should be maintained. This concern has led to calls for a national "takeover" of the nominating process. A takeover could obviously be accomplished by a constitutional amendment, although it would almost certainly be difficult to secure ratification. Most analysts, however, believe that Congress already possesses the authority to change the system by ordinary legislation and that a constitutional amendment is thus unnecessary.

But is a congressional assumption of jurisdiction over the nominating process actually constitutional? It may, of course, be perverse in this day and age to introduce the text of the Constitution into a discussion of constitutional law. But it should be recalled that the national government is in principle a government of limited powers. In this case, the grant of jurisdiction to Congress is quite specific and limited, in marked contrast to the broader jurisdiction granted for regulating congressional elections. This difference cannot be attributed to a mere accident of expression, for some of the Framers were explicit in their intent to limit direct congressional control of the presidential selection process in order to safeguard executive independence.

A second question is whether Congress's authority, even if broadly constitutional, is limited by competing rights of political parties. Until recently, legal analysts generally held that Congress had a free hand to structure the nominating process as it wished. But a growing body of case law has begun to apply a right of free association to the parties in a way that limits state regulation of parties and of primaries. This right might be invoked in a similar way on the national level, placing important constraints on the kind of plan Congress could devise.[7]

A final question is whether an assumption of jurisdiction by Congress would be wise. Of course, to discuss the power without the plan abstracts from the way people ordinarily think. Plans differ greatly in their objectives, and some ingenious suggestions have been proposed—most notably a plan offered in 1980 by Everett Ladd.[8] But much of the recent talk about a congressional takeover has viewed it virtually as an end in itself that

7. See Thomas Durbin, "Presidential Primaries: Proposals before Congress to Reform Them and Congressional Authority to Regulate Them," *Journal of Law and Politics,* vol. 1 (Spring 1984), pp. 381–401. The dominant scholarly view of how the Constitution applies to the presidential selection process recognizes a general congressional jurisdiction to legislate, which is subject to limitations coming from a right of association. This view, I believe, is misguided not just on the issue of jurisdiction, but on the issue of limitations as well. As a practical matter, it would mean that the agencies controlling the structure of the nominating process would be Congress and the Supreme Court.

The Framers regarded presidential selection as an area of political activity important enough to be governed by a fundamental institution of government. To introduce into the construction of an institution a logic based chiefly on a calculus of rights, determined by courts claiming a power to perform a balancing test between private rights and state interest, represents a legalistic orientation at odds with the Framers' approach. While there is much to be said today for public authorities giving great latitude to parties in performing the function of presidential nomination, this grant of discretion should flow from a logic of institutional reasoning, not a logic of rights. Friends of parties today who attempt to use the courts as the principal source of institutional protection may yet rue the legal straitjacket they will create.

8. Everett Carll Ladd, "A Better Way to Pick Our Presidents," *Fortune* (May 5, 1980), pp. 132–42. Ladd has since had second thoughts. See chap. 10 of this book, p. 229.

could eliminate the jurisdictional chaos of the current authority structure. A congressional takeover, however, is not a panacea; indeed, it is not even a plan. If there were agreement about what specifically was wanted from a congressional takeover, there might not be any reason to do it, for it is quite possible the same thing could be accomplished without action by Congress. The danger is that, lacking agreement, there will be pressure to turn to Congress merely from an abstract impulse to "rationalize" the process.

There is every reason for hoping that an assumption of congressional jurisdiction can be avoided. Once the principle of congressional jurisdiction is admitted, there is no guarantee that any particular plan will be adopted or maintained. Over the long term, congressional involvement could threaten the separation of powers and open the door to the spectacle of the candidates and parties seeking to change federal law to enhance their electoral prospects. There is, moreover, no avoiding the fact that a congressional takeover of the nominating process from the parties, even if it is represented as a "friendly" takeover, would constitute a loss of power for the parties and the states. The means—the use of national statutory power—is contrary to the end of stronger, federally oriented parties.

Stability and Constructive Change

An improved nominating system would be characterized by either greater stability or enhanced quality (or both). Given the serious problems raised about the quality of the current system, it might reasonably be argued that enhancing stability alone is too modest a goal and that, since the only way to enhance quality is at the cost of stability, stability should be sacrificed for a fundamental and comprehensive effort at reform.

Enhancing stability cannot, quite rightly, be the only goal. But in the present context stability is not in tension with quality. Strategies that demand scrapping the current system and starting anew would probably further undermine rather than enhance quality. The best hope for improving the nominating system under current conditions is to endow the system with a reasonable degree of stability at the top, while encouraging a process of evolutionary change at the state level. Much that is deficient in the current system has been exacerbated, if not caused, by instability at the national level. Constructive change through evolution is not likely to proceed if the overall stability of the system is now placed in doubt.

CHAPTER THREE

The Media
and Presidential Campaigns

ALBERT R. HUNT

IN THE spring of 1987, Gary Hart's second campaign for the presidency ended abruptly when the *Miami Herald,* responding to a tip, staked out the Democratic front-runner's Washington home and reported he had spent the weekend with a young Miami woman. The media jumped on the story, and Hart—who ironically over the same weekend was quoted in another newspaper as challenging reporters to follow him to check out rumors of his womanizing—was forced out of the presidential contest within four days.

Hart in a sense was politically destroyed by the media—or, perhaps more properly, was given the opportunity to destroy himself. At an earlier stage in his career, it has been argued, the media helped make him a viable candidate for the presidency in the first place.

In January and the first half of February 1984, Hart's nascent presidential campaign still was floundering in the South. During the last five days of January, the Darden Research Company of Atlanta surveyed 1,000 voters, 575 of whom were Democrats and independents, in nine southern states and found that only 2.4 percent of the respondents preferred Gary Hart, while 44.5 percent were for front-runner Walter Mondale. In the first week of February, before the Iowa caucuses, Gary Hart's prospects looked even more bleak in Florida: a *Miami Herald* poll measured his Florida support at less than 2 percent.[1]

1. Richard Morin, "Mondale Leads Closest Rivals 2-1 in State; Reagan Shows Appeal in Poll of Democrats," *Miami Herald,* February 19, 1984.

This was not surprising. Gary Hart once was George McGovern's campaign manager, he had a decidedly liberal voting record in the Senate, and he had devoted little of his campaign time, effort, or resources to the southern states. "Our campaign in Georgia, Florida and Alabama is nonexistent," a Hart supporter lamented at the time.

But a little more than a month later, on March 13, it was a different story. That day Gary Hart swept the Florida primary, defeating former Vice-President Mondale by almost 70,000 votes, nearly won the Georgia primary, virtually tied John Glenn for second in Alabama, and won the Oklahoma caucuses.

Two phenomena changed the climate during those weeks. First, Hart finished second in the Iowa Democratic caucuses and, a week later, upset Mondale to capture the New Hampshire primary. Second, he dominated news coverage, especially television, for the two weeks leading up to the southern primaries on March 13. In January most of the media focused on Mondale and Glenn and Jesse Jackson; the rest of the Democratic field, including Hart, was largely ignored. In the two weeks preceding New Hampshire, according to John Merriam, head of the Conference on Issues and Media, Inc., a research organization that measures media coverage and impact, Hart received approximately 20 percent of the media coverage accorded Mondale and only half of that given Glenn. But Merriam found the coverage of Hart increased tenfold in the first two weeks of March, after New Hampshire.[2]

"After the media event that is New Hampshire, Hart was, for a time, capturing three million supporters a day, most of whom did not know why he had become their man," writes Michael Robinson, who has studied and written extensively on media coverage of politics and government. "In light of Hart, it makes about as much sense to argue that the media are impotent as to argue that Ronald Reagan is a devoted grandfather."[3] Peter Hart, Mondale's poll taker during that time, goes a step further: "A campaign is not played out anymore so much for people or voters; it's played out for the media."[4]

This problem is said to be systemic. Nobody articulates this better than

2. Interview with John Merriam, July 9, 1987.

3. Michael J. Robinson, "Where's the Beef? Media and Media Elites in 1984," in Austin Ranney, ed., *The American Elections of 1984* (Duke University Press, 1985), pp. 166–202.

4. Interview with Peter Hart, February 19, 1987.

John Sears, the insightful political practitioner who was a top strategist for Richard Nixon's 1968 campaign and who ran Ronald Reagan's 1976 quest as well as the first part of his 1980 bid:

> The media stand in a position today, especially in the nomination phase, where the old party bosses used to stand. The people who were interested in who was going to get nominated made their feelings known or asked questions to their local leaders. This provided some opportunity for peer review. Today, however, without meaning to, it's the press who first decides who's ahead and who's behind on the basis of public opinion polls. Before, the party boss also knew who might be ahead but he might ask more questions about the fellow.[5]

How Much Influence?

The contention is that the media pick and choose which candidates are considered seriously by the voters, reinforce the momentum of early decisions, tilt to the most telegenic, and magnify mistakes. It is a compelling case until one looks at the last few elections.

In 1980 the most charismatic candidate was Ted Kennedy, who was trounced by the "dull" Jimmy Carter. On the Republican side, George Bush became a media darling with his "momentum" after winning the Iowa caucuses. Five weeks later he was routed by Ronald Reagan in New Hampshire. Reagan, during both the primary and general election, made more gaffes than any contender since George Romney; he also easily won both the nomination and the presidency.

In 1984 few candidates got a more massive pre-primary buildup than John Glenn. The movie *The Right Stuff* came out only months before the first primary and resulted in a favorable *Newsweek* magazine cover piece.[6] John Glenn finished a dismal sixth in the Iowa caucuses with only 5 percent of the vote.

While Michael Robinson recognizes the media's impact, he dismisses notions that the media are omnipotent: "Bad press is not necessarily fatal, or even debilitating, to strong candidates. News agendas are very much

5. Interview with John Sears, February 26, 1987.

6. David Ansen with Katrine Ames, "A Movie with All the Right Stuff," *Newsweek*, October 3, 1983.

overrated as a force in public opinion; the public influences the news about as often as news influences the public."[7]

Jeff Greenfield, in a provocative book on the 1980 election, suggests not only that the media's influence is exaggerated, but also that the public was well ahead of the media that year. "Convinced that the 'real' story was behind the scene, the press as a rule spent tens of millions of dollars covering events that were supposed to provide Delphic clues to the unseeable future ('who's going to win?'), while giving short shrift to the flow of ideas and the underlying political terrain that—as it turned out—provided important clues about the nature of Campaign '80."[8]

Gary Hart's 1984 campaign can be used to marshal arguments either way. The media were the catalyst for Hart's mercurial rise after Iowa. His showings in the southern primaries, in particular, would not have been possible without the favorable saturation coverage on the networks, news magazines, and newspapers. Yet *before* the Iowa caucuses John Glenn and Jesse Jackson got far more coverage than Hart. Nevertheless, it was the Colorado Democrat who, surprising much of the press corps, finished second in Iowa to launch his rise. It is true that Hart began to drop around mid-March when coverage got much tougher. But Hart still won more votes than Mondale in the final month of the contest.

A few conclusions seem fair:

—A dark horse can emerge in the presidential nominating system (Jimmy Carter in 1976), especially if he or she can attract press attention early enough to be positioned to take advantage of it.

—A front-runner can take bad press (Reagan in 1980) if his political base and political rationale are sufficiently strong. And a front-runner whose base and persona cannot take that scrutiny (Kennedy in 1980) will be crippled by bad coverage.

—The shorter the time frame between important events, the greater the media power. When Gary Hart won the New Hampshire primary in 1984, there were fourteen more contests coming up in the two following weeks, creating a political blur dominated by press coverage. Yet in similar circumstances in 1980, following George Bush's surprise Iowa win, there were four weeks until the next opportunity for voters to reflect and to soften the follow-the-pack mindset in press coverage.

---

7. Robinson, "Where's the Beef?" p. 195.

8. Jeff Greenfield, *The Real Campaign: How the Media Missed the Story of the 1980 Campaign* (Summit Books, 1982), p. 25.

The Charge of Liberal Bias

One of the most common charges against the national press is that it reflects a decided liberal ideological bias. There is little doubt that senior national political reporters are more likely to be liberal than conservative on most issues and probably vote disproportionately Democratic. That is partly because most of them spent their formative professional years during a time when the liberal agenda—civil rights, opposition to the Vietnam War, fighting poverty—had strong moral attraction and political glamour.

But many of the younger political journalists, reflecting the more conservative mood of the 1970s or early 1980s, are politically agnostic or even a bit conservative. The bottom line, however, is, as Stephen Hess notes: "Having said that [most reporters are liberals], so what?"[9] All that matters is whether their ideology affects coverage, and there is little evidence to suggest that it does.

One does not need studies to prove this case. For starters, there is an inherent contradiction in the argument that the powerful national media are promulgating their left-wing causes: for the past two decades conservatives have dominated not only presidential elections—capturing four of the past five, three by landslides—but also the national agenda. These ideological critics are left with one of two possibilities: either the press is not so powerful, or it is not so biased. Certainly, few would deny that Jimmy Carter got a rougher press than Ronald Reagan and that no recent candidate has been treated more harshly than Ted Kennedy.

This is not because the press is moving to the right; it is because ideology is not a major consideration in how the national press operates. The problem with spending so much time on this largely irrelevant question is that it distracts from the more serious media issues.

And there is no doubt that the media, over the past two decades, have significantly changed the ways campaigns are conducted and covered. There are a number of important causes.

The first is Theodore H. White's pioneer *Making of the President* books. Starting with his celebrated 1961 work, Teddy White captivated voters, politicians, reporters, and editors with the dynamics of the presidential quest. The politics and personalities inside the campaign were so forcefully and brilliantly depicted that the book became the staple of

---

9. Albert R. Hunt, "Media Bias in Eye of the Beholder," *Wall Street Journal*, July 23, 1985.

subsequent campaign coverage, though no one ever has replicated the grace and style of the late Teddy White.

Before White, major candidates used to give important speeches, shake hands at a few rallies or parades during the day, and occasionally chat off the record with the small entourage of traveling reporters, mainly from newspapers. Usually those speeches and other remarks were reported dutifully, with little effort to get inside a campaign.

For the most part White made a positive contribution to political reporting, expanding the understanding of and interest in this fascinating process. But, unintentionally, there has been at least one negative by-product: the press gets so caught up in trying to report the story behind the scenes that major speeches or position papers or the substance of a campaign receive relatively little attention.

The Awesome Power of Television

When Teddy White began writing about political campaigns, an even more profound change was occurring. Although television started in the 1940s, by 1960 it only had begun to approach maturity. By 1984 it was abundantly clear that American political elections were driven by television.

Any modern presidential campaign is dominated by the awesome importance of television coverage. Days are scheduled and shaped with this in mind. Campaign appearances are held with an eye to visuals; speeches are designed to provide thirty-second snippets; groups are addressed that will play well on television. After Hart's upset New Hampshire win, he spent much of the next several weeks dashing from airport tarmac to airport tarmac looking for television opportunities.

To be sure, television has made some important contributions to the political system. Millions of citizens have been made more knowledgeable about politics. Regional and geographical differences have narrowed; the evening news programs make it difficult for a candidate to conduct one type of campaign in Massachusetts and another in Mississippi.

But, as David Broder argues, the "biggest effect television has had on our politics has been to lessen the substance of the campaign itself. And its consequences are not less serious because they are inadvertent."[10] A seri-

10. David S. Broder, *Behind the Front Page: A Candid Look at How the News Is Made* (Simon and Schuster, 1987), p. 216.

ous discussion of an important issue rarely will get much air time. Network television producers' eyes glaze over at the mere mention of a proposal to address the international debt situation or a welfare program or military reform.

The strictures of television create problems, for one, the inability, especially during a general election campaign, to say there is no story that day. Former CBS News president Richard Salant once ventured: "I wish we had the guts to say that 'today, candidate X campaigned at six stops and didn't say a goddamn thing.'"[11] But, particularly if there is a good visual, as the Reagan campaign demonstrated in 1984, television is incapable of saying no. Finally, the competition to get on those few precious moments of air time breeds a macho form of cynical reporting. When a correspondent draws a parallel between the candidates and the animals at the zoo, it is usually sure to get on the air—which may produce entertaining television but is not very enlightening about the political process.

Some television programs avoid these pitfalls. The "MacNeil-Lehrer NewsHour," "Nightline," some of the features on the morning shows (especially NBC's "Today" show and the CBS "Sunday Morning News"), and occasional specials offer first-rate political interviews and insights. But these programs usually involve 2 million to 8 million viewers. When 13 million to 15 million Americans are watching the networks' evening news programs, the medium is at its most superficial.

Ironically, it is television's own insecurity that enables the newspapers to set the media agenda of campaign coverage, especially in the initial phase. Television producers and correspondents scour the newspapers for political insights; the reverse rarely occurs. The 1984 election is instructive. Virtually all of the unfolding stories—Mondale's links to special interests, Hart's character as called into question by changes in his age and name, Jackson's ties with black extremists, tensions between Jews and blacks, Reagan's age problem—as well as efforts to explore the candidates' substantive views and inclinations, were initiated by the press. Once that agenda was on the table, television dominated the dialogue.

The campaigns' more vehement reaction, nonetheless, is directed at the subsequent television coverage. Questions about Gary Hart's character were first raised seriously by George Lardner in an in-depth January 17 front-page profile in the *Washington Post*.[12] It took the TV networks

11. Greenfield, *The Real Campaign*, p. 31.
12. George Lardner, Jr., "'New Ideas' Democrat Has Long Had His Eye on the Presidency," *Washington Post*, January 17, 1984.

weeks to pick up on these issues, but some of the Hart entourage still blame television for their candidate's March and April defeats that cost him the 1984 nomination. Two days after the first Reagan-Mondale debate in which the president stumbled badly, the *Wall Street Journal* wrote a tough front-page analysis of Reagan's age as an issue.[13] That night the story was picked up by the networks. The White House privately complained to the networks; the *Wall Street Journal* never heard a word.

Filling a Vacuum

Television does not assume its dominant role until the campaign is well under way. In the current presidential election system, full television coverage usually starts a few weeks before the Iowa caucuses. Thus most of the preseason skirmishing to determine the initial agenda is played out in print.

Here technology, specifically public opinion polls, takes on a key effect. Twenty years ago the top political reporters, such as David Broder of the *Washington Post,* Alan Otten of the *Wall Street Journal,* Jack Germond, then of Gannett newspapers, Tom Ottenad of the *St. Louis Post-Dispatch,* syndicated columnist Robert Novak, and NBC's John Chancellor, went out and interviewed scores of voters. Although some of these reporters and a few of their successors still patiently pursue actual voters, most political journalists today rely on the polls, conducted by newspapers or candidate organizations, many done nightly. These polls, in the early stages, determine which contender gets the most coverage, who are the most serious challengers, and who are the also-rans.

At the same time, over the past four elections the nominating process has been taken away from party leaders and turned over to popular election. In 1960 there were only sixteen Democratic primaries and only 19 percent of the pledged delegates to the party conventions were elected in those contests.[14] The rest were party officials and functionaries, elected officials, and key party supporters. Abuses of this system in the turbulent year of 1968 led the Democratic party to initiate a series of "reforms" that by 1984 had resulted in more than thirty primaries and the selection of

13. Rich Jaroslovsky and James M. Perry, "New Question in Race: Is Oldest U.S. President Now Showing His Age?" *Wall Street Journal,* October 9, 1984.

14. Elaine Ciulla Kamarck, "Structure as Strategy: Presidential Nominating Politics Since Reform" (Ph.D. dissertation, University of California–Berkeley, 1986), p. 77.

more than 54 percent of the pledged delegates on the basis of primary results.

The upshot is that party leaders, with a few exceptions, play a much smaller role in the whole process. It is this loss of "peer review" that John Sears thinks has hurt the system. And, as he says, since the voters get their information from the media, the media have largely jumped into the vacuum.

There has recently been some effort to modify this participatory democracy. About 15 percent of the delegates to the Democratic convention are now elected officials and party leaders. But this group so far has not assumed much of a leadership role. "It used to be that we paid some attention to the media because political leaders read the papers too. But we didn't share everything with the media," recalls John Sears. "That has changed now."[15] Thus any smart campaign strategist spends considerable time plotting not only a candidate's paid media—that is, commercials and advertisements—but also what practitioners call "free media"—namely, newspaper, magazine, and television news coverage.

Consideration of the press ranges from the routine—providing telephones and typewriters or word processors, submitting advance texts of speeches and helpful background information—to the more profound and calculated—scheduling speeches and statements so they will receive maximum coverage, especially on television, tailoring activities to how they will play on the news. In any event, campaigns today spend far more time thinking about the media than they did two decades ago and correspondingly less time thinking about other matters.

A discussion of the ways campaigns seek to manipulate coverage leads back to a remarkably prescient memorandum that Hamilton Jordan wrote in late 1972 mapping the way to the White House for the then relatively obscure governor of Georgia, Jimmy Carter. Press coverage was a paramount concern, and Jordan counseled that it would have to be finely tuned: "Stories in the *New York Times* and *Washington Post* do not just happen, but have to be carefully planned and planted."

Jordan cited the campaign's goals: one, to "generate favorable stories in the national press" about Carter; two, to "develop and/or maintain a close personal relationship" with important columnists and reporters; and three, to "take full advantage of every legitimate opportunity for national exposure." Jordan went on to list eighteen journalists who should be care-

15. Interview with John Sears.

fully cultivated. He suggested that some "like [*New York Times* columnist] Tom Wicker and [*Washington Post* publisher] Katharine Graham are significant enough to spend an evening or leisurely weekend with." Jordan continued in this memo:

> The views of this small group of opinion makers and the papers they represent are noted and imitated by other columnists and newspapers throughout the country and the world. Their recognition and acceptance of your candidacy as a viable force with some chance of success could establish you as a serious contender worthy of the financial support of major party contributors. They could have an equally adverse affect, dismissing your effort as being regional or an attempt to secure the second spot on the ticket.
>
> Fortunately, a disproportionate number of these opinion makers are Southerners by birth and tradition and harbor a strong, subconscious desire to see the South move beyond the George Wallace era and assert itself as a region and as a people in the political mainstream of this country. It is my contention that they would be fascinated by the prospect of your candidacy and would treat it seriously through the first several primaries.[16]

One interesting facet of this insight is the importance Jordan attached to newspaper reporters and editors rather than television. To be sure, fifteen years later, this probably would change some, but it underscores the more important early role the press plays in setting the political agenda.

The Carter camp followed this advice almost perfectly and much of what Jordan sought was achieved. If Carter had been a bad candidate, such manipulation no doubt would have failed. The major newspapers play a key role in setting the political agenda, but shrewd, resourceful politicians can shape their thinking significantly.

Iowa and New Hampshire

Most considerations of the media's impact on presidential campaigns focus on the national press, consisting of the three TV networks, the three weekly news magazines, the two wire services, the *New York Times,*

---

16. Memo from Hamilton Jordan to Jimmy Carter, November 4, 1972.

Washington Post, Wall Street Journal, and key reporters from large regional newspapers such as the *Los Angeles Times, Chicago Tribune,* and *Boston Globe.* But, as Hamilton Jordan learned, in the critical early stages of the nominating process the local media in two states, Iowa and New Hampshire, take on huge importance.

In Iowa the dominant paper is the *Des Moines Register.* It circulates statewide with 233,000 papers during the week and 375,000 on Sundays. Its influence is enormous, and although its editorial page is moderately liberal, the news pages are as straight as rows of Iowa corn. Editor James Gannon is one of the top newsmen in America, and his clout is enhanced every four years by his paper's coverage and by the all-important initial presidential campaign debate that he conducts.

The *Register*'s top political reporter is much sought after by aspiring presidential candidates. The current incumbent is David Yepsen, a thirty-six-year-old, self-described political agnostic. For the year before the election and the first six weeks of election year, prior to the Iowa caucuses, Dave Yepsen's calls will be returned sooner than most of the big-time national press figures.

Indeed, much of the national press corps follows the *Register*'s lead in this influential first caucus. Yepsen's predecessor, James Flansburg, arrived at work early one morning in 1980 to find the top political correspondent of the *New York Times* camped at his desk. In 1983, when Yepsen wrote about the disarray of the Glenn campaign in Iowa, stories in much of the national press soon followed. There are other newspapers and numerous television and radio stations in Iowa, but even combined they lack the influence of the *Register.*

The New Hampshire press situation is dramatically different. The only statewide newspaper is the *Manchester Union Leader,* whose publisher, the late William Loeb, used to terrify political opponents, once even bringing Senator Edmund Muskie to tears. The *Union Leader* runs biting front-page editorials daily, and its news pages rarely stray from the conservative line.

The paper's impact is heightened by its persistence. It gets behind its favorite conservative contender and never lets up on its enemies. In 1980, for instance, in the month before the GOP primary there were no fewer than a dozen front-page stories attacking George Bush as a closet moderate or lauding Ronald Reagan. One "news analysis" warned that "just because the Texas millionaire Bush walks, quacks, swims and looks like a duck, he ain't." On the other hand, a columnist wrote an open letter to

Ronald Reagan declaring that he had a "red-white-and-blue desire to call you 'Mr. President.'"[17]

The newspaper has lost some of its bite since Loeb died in 1981, but Republicans still spend considerable time courting the *Union Leader.* Democrats are affected only if they react to the paper. Indeed, the influence and reach of the *Union Leader* are exaggerated. The combined New Hampshire Sunday circulation of the *Boston Globe,* the *Nashua Telegraph, Foster's Democrat,* and the *Concord Monitor,* all of which are ideological foes of the *Union Leader,* is almost 50 percent larger than the 70,000 circulation of the Manchester paper. But the *Union Leader's* special brand of invective makes it a key force in the nation's first presidential primary every four years.

The Horse Race

During this early phase, the national press and television devote much of their efforts to reporting on what George Bush called the "big mo," as in momentum. This produces snowball coverage of the hottest candidate. In 1976, for example, after Jimmy Carter won in Iowa and the next month in New Hampshire, he was on the cover of the news magazines, dominated the network evening news programs, and received more coverage from major newspapers than the other contenders combined.

Much of the coverage centers on the horse race and why the top contender is winning, coverage that has caused more than a little grief for the press. The day of the 1984 New Hampshire primary, a *New York Times* front-page story said, "Walter F. Mondale now holds the most commanding lead ever recorded this early," citing his national standing.[18] The same day readers of *Newsweek* magazine were assured that the former vice-president's "lead in New Hampshire appeared unassailable."[19] Mondale lost by nearly ten points.

In both 1980 and 1984 NBC misread the Iowa caucuses: in 1980 an NBC correspondent said the Iowa results sounded the death knell for

17. Albert R. Hunt, "Subtlety Isn't One of Mr. Loeb's Strengths," *Wall Street Journal,* February 12, 1980.

18. Hedrick Smith, "Mondale Lead Over Nearest Rival in Poll Sets Nonincumbent Record," *New York Times,* February 28, 1984.

19. Walter Shapiro, "Countdown to Super Tuesday," *Newsweek,* March 5, 1984, p. 22.

Ronald Reagan, and in 1984 another NBC correspondent suggested that the caucuses were a tremendous boost for Walter Mondale.

This vulnerability affects even the very best political reporters. In late December of 1983, the *Washington Post*'s David Broder, the most respected political reporter in the business, suggested that Mondale held such an overwhelming advantage that the Democratic presidential contest would be dull. Two and a half months later he said the Maine caucuses had dealt a "serious and possibly fatal" blow to the Mondale candidacy.[20]

Nevertheless, campaign strategists spend a lot of time figuring out how to ride, or in some cases try to deflect, media-induced momentum. Often these efforts are futile; attempts to interpret a "respectable" third place finish or a "close fourth" are dismissed, rightly, by most of the press.

A classic example of getting a beneficial "spin" on a story, however, occurred after the March 13 Super Tuesday Democratic contests in 1984. There were nine primaries or caucuses that day. This was right after Gary Hart's stunning New Hampshire upset, followed by decisive victories in the Maine and Wyoming caucuses and in a nonbinding Vermont primary. Mondale was on the ropes. The Mondale campaign zeroed in on the Georgia primary where, despite Hart's momentum, they felt they had a good shot at winning. During the days before the primaries, the Mondale campaign, in a surface display of candor, acknowledged that if they lost Georgia they were gone.

That election night hardly could have been better for Gary Hart: he won six of the nine tests and held his own in the South, his weakest region. But Mondale won Georgia, and with a few exceptions, such as the *Baltimore Sun*'s Jack Germond, most of the press greeted the results as a comeback for the former vice-president. When Mondale campaign manager Robert Beckel went on NBC's "Today" show the next morning, he was congratulated on the air for the Mondale "victory." A nonplused Gary Hart looked on in amazement. This successful "spin" clearly played a role in the more substantive comeback that Mondale made over the ensuing few weeks.

The "big mo" phenomenon makes it very difficult, if not impossible, for aspirants to pick and choose which early contests they enter. In 1976, for example, Senator Henry (Scoop) Jackson of Washington decided to skip the New Hampshire primary and focus instead on Massachusetts,

20. David S. Broder, "Jane Byrne Reelected? Oh C'mon, Broder," *Washington Post*, December 21, 1983; and Broder, "Hart Defeats Mondale in Maine Party Caucuses: Serious Blow to Loser's Prospects," *Washington Post*, March 5, 1984.

where he believed his prolabor and traditional Democratic economic views, along with a tough defense posture, would play well. In a narrow sense he was right; he won the Massachusetts primary. But by ceding New Hampshire to someone else, in this case Jimmy Carter, the media momentum already was going the other way by the time Jackson won Massachusetts a week later.

Jackson's experience certainly should be a consideration in 1988 for any hopeful who considers waiting until the southern or the midwestern primaries to enter the fray. By then someone will have won a sweeping victory or victories in Iowa and New Hampshire, appeared on the cover of the news magazines, and dominated the network news programs. The late entry, no matter how attractive, is not likely to be able to compete for press attention.

Between mid-February and mid-March of a presidential election is a time when the quantity of coverage is more pronounced than the quality. It is not uncommon to see more than a dozen political stories in some major papers on any single day. The weekend before the 1984 New Hampshire primary, the *Washington Post* had more than twice as many reporters in New Hampshire as there were serious candidates. Even the time-pinched networks sometimes run three or four political pieces at this time. Most of the stories focus on who is going to win, who has the momentum, and who does not. This puts strains on reporters assigned to specific candidates.

Reporter-Candidate Relationship

The relationship between a presidential candidate and a reporter who covers the candidate is awkward at best; it is part adversial, part symbiotic. As the *Washington Post*'s veteran political editor, James Dickenson, notes: "All too often, reporters fall in love with the candidate they're covering."[21] The success of the candidate and the correspondent often seem linked. The television networks, in particular, usually assign a reporter already on the fast track to success to the leading contenders. If the candidate is successful, the reporter expects to follow the victor to a White House beat. When that reporter realizes that Dan Rather and Tom Brokaw used the highly visible White House assignment to catapult to their current status, an inherent conflict is apparent.

21. Jane Mayer, "The Press Bus Blues: Hitching a Wagon to a—Loser?" *Wall Street Journal*, February 24, 1984.

The distortion can be just as great for reporters covering candidates who do poorly. They worry that both careers may be headed downward. "Reporters start to think, 'Hey, I was going to be Sam Donaldson,'" notes political columnist Mark Shields. "On a loser's bus, resentment starts to build up."[22]

That resentment is fueled by the reporter's inability to get on the air or the front page. By the time the primary season starts, news coverage is for front-runners; even if second-tier candidates have interesting ideas, the public is not likely to find out unless the candidate is in a special situation, such as Jesse Jackson or Pat Robertson.

In his new book, *Behind the Front Page,* David Broder notes the conflict between covering candidates on the basis of their substantive qualifications and on how they stand in the polls. "I thought two of the men eliminated early from the Democratic field in 1984—Governor Reuben Askew of Florida and Senator Ernest F. Hollings of South Carolina—should have been seriously considered for the presidency. As a columnist, I freely made that point—but as a reporter, I felt obliged to report what I saw—that their campaigns were falling flat—even though such reporting further burdened their candidacies."[23]

As usual, David Broder is right; the campaign is, after all, a horse race, and people do care who is going to win. The problem, however, is that often when that collective, conventional wisdom of the media sees a candidate going nowhere, it becomes a self-fulfilling prophecy.

Coverage of Issues

What candidates are saying or what issues are drawn gets secondary attention at these critical junctures. Thomas Patterson surveyed the 1976 campaign coverage of the networks, news magazines, and major papers and found that the horse race (who is winning and who is losing) received twice as much attention as issues and policies.[24]

This is true of newspapers as well as television, although the problem is more acute in the latter. On occasion, television programs do a superb job

22. Ibid.
23. Broder, *Behind the Front Page,* p. 272.
24. Thomas E. Patterson, *The Mass Media Election: How Americans Choose Their President* (Praeger, 1980).

in crystallizing the substance of the elections. But for the most part television journalism in the early primaries—when not only are candidates being weeded out but also much of the agenda for the election year is being fashioned—alternates between the horse race, a video version of *People* magazine, and follow-ups on negative newspaper stories. Serious discussions of what the candidates are saying and the differences between them are submerged.

There is substantive coverage before the primaries get under way. Newspapers invariably do long profiles on each of the candidates detailing their views and records. They often focus on a handful of the most important issues and compare and contrast the various contenders. Although less than in newspapers, there is some substantive coverage on television.

The difficulty, however, is that some of the most substantive reporting takes place at a time when the public is paying the least attention. That rankles political operative John Sears: "Every time someone criticizes the media for not covering more issues, they say 'we did that.' And they have, but at a time when people aren't ready to make a decision. It's true that once the race starts readers and viewers probably are more interested in who's winning and who's losing. But it doesn't do much good to say you covered something when people are not interested."[25] Broder makes a similar point by noting that early in the process "we reporters get our first extended exposure to the candidates and may write in a fresh, insightful way about the contenders and their positions. But the attentive audience for such stories is small."[26]

The massive favorable coverage John Glenn received after the movie *The Right Stuff* came out in the fall of 1983—and the small effect it ultimately had on his campaign—dramatically illustrate the importance of timing. The Ohio Democrat was enjoying the best coverage of the field at a time when the Glenn forces thought it was most propitious. But within months Glenn's candidacy was dead. There were countless explanations, including the fact that the movie was a box-office bomb, but the most persuasive was that voters were not yet tuned into presidential politics. "You can't move people when they aren't paying attention," says poll taker Peter Hart. "Favorable media coverage can enable a candidate to set up the ability to get those votes when people start paying attention. But the coverage itself, whether it was John Connally in 1979 or John Glenn in

25. Interview with John Sears.
26. Broder, *Behind the Front Page,* p. 237.

1983, counts for very little. Off-year cover stories don't produce votes or even movements in the Gallup poll."[27]

As the primary season unfolds, television becomes more and more important, and by the time of the party conventions, it is dominant. Some of that is good. Millions of Americans understand politics better and think it more interesting because of such saturation coverage. But the networks become such an awesome presence at the party conventions that some of the important functions of these sessions get overlooked. Although few politicians are willing to risk the wrath of television by complaining about its intrusiveness, the legendary Walter Cronkite once said that if he were running a political party he would ban television from the convention floor.[28]

For economic reasons, the networks are moving away from gavel-to-gavel coverage of national conventions, which may be a blessing in disguise. Cable television still probably can offer that service for political junkies. And if the networks utilize their more selective coverage, not to smother both viewers and the party with a poor imitation of sports reporting, but to focus on the important substantive and political developments inherent in any convention, it would mark a real improvement.

White House Glamour

In a general election, when there are only two or three candidates, the Democratic and Republican nominees, at least, always receive almost equal coverage. A strong media tendency in this phase of the campaign is, as Jeff Greenfield says, "a fascination with the question of who screwed up."[29] This produces a gaffe watch, waiting for one candidate to make a misstatement and then seizing on it.

It is the absolute duty of the press to report on mistakes, but an unfortunate by-product is that this encourages campaigns to shelter their candidate and try to manipulate the agenda to an even greater extent. Most of the campaigns' efforts are aimed at television. Print is dominant in the early stages of the primaries; by the general election it is a television show with built-in advantages for incumbents.

27. Interview with Peter Hart.
28. Martin Schram, *The Great American Video Game: Presidential Politics in the Television Age* (William Morrow and Co., 1987), p. 112.
29. "The Press and the Election," *Brookings Review,* vol. 3 (Winter 1985), p. 39.

The campaigns of both parties jockey to manipulate the agenda and coverage to their advantage. Incumbent presidents have lost two of the past three elections, but the Reagan forces amply demonstrated in 1984 that an incumbent president, skilled at media manipulation, is virtually unbeatable, unless there is a war or economic catastrophe. Reagan would have won the last election even without his imagery team, but not as easily. He dominated the television networks. A top CBS producer was not far off the mark when he ventured that "Michael Deaver was the executive producer of the evening news broadcasts."[30]

There are two major reasons. One is the networks' preoccupation with the White House in general. All three commercial networks devote more time, personnel, and effort to covering the White House than the whole of Congress or national security or all domestic policies. Anytime television commits such resources, air time is virtually assured, regardless of journalistic merit. The networks believe that the correspondent standing in front of the White House or traveling with the president lends panache and prestige to the news programs. "Television news loves the presidency," notes Michael Robinson. "It may not like the incumbent; it may not like any incumbent; but the office of the president has become the *sine qua non* of network journalism."[31]

Unlike Jimmy Carter, Reagan or his people fully understood the frailties of television, especially the irresistible lure of good visuals. Thus, throughout 1984 Ronald Reagan was pictured on charming whistle-stop trains, before patriotic, adoring audiences with colorful balloons and banners. (After the first debate the networks showed deflated balloons for a day or two but the Reagan forces quickly turned that around.)

John Reilly, senior counselor to Walter Mondale in the 1984 election, sums up the impact:

> The Reagan people produced these scenes—what Mondale called the "puppy dogs, picket fences, and morning in America"—and that's all people saw. It didn't make any difference that Sam Donaldson was standing under a plane wing and reporting that for the 43rd straight day President Reagan refused to talk to the press. People loved the visuals. By contrast, Susan Spencer [of CBS] might report that Mondale said the

30. Schram, *The Great American Video Game,* p. 33.
31. Michael J. Robinson and Margaret A. Sheehan, *Over the Wire and on TV: CBS and UPI in Campaign '80* (Russell Sage Foundation, 1983), p. 191.

following seven substantive things today but we weren't as good with the visuals so the public tuned out.[32]

A major miscalculation, Reilly said, was "we thought television would force the candidates to talk about substance. They didn't." The lesson drawn by Reilly: "You're wasting your time to talk about substantive issues until you're forced to."

Television sometimes does cover substantive issues in the general election, doing long takeouts on economic or national security matters. But these are separate from the everyday coverage and become blurred in the minds of voters who do not see the connective analysis.

When TV does do the job well, it is impressive. About a month before the 1980 election, for example, CBS correspondent Bill Plante did a lengthy analysis of candidate Ronald Reagan's shift to the center. It was full of specific facts, used attractive visuals, told people something about the candidate but, unlike many so-called "negative" TV pieces, was not snide or vituperative. It was fair and informative, and the pictures as well as content were determined by the correspondent and not the campaign.

Debates: The Importance of Spin Control

The most intense media coverage in the general election involves the now almost automatic TV debates. A major question is whether journalists should participate in these events. In 1984 the League of Women Voters, the sponsoring organization, gave the two candidates veto power over participating journalists.

The press rarely distinguishes itself in covering debates. The tendency to jump to sweeping conclusions often ignores underlying realities or misses important factors. "On the basis of our scant national experience with this art form, instant analysis of it usually is worthless," Robert Kaiser of the *Washington Post* wrote in 1980. "After the Reagan-John B. Anderson debate [in 1980] the analysts said Anderson held his own, but within days the polls showed Anderson sinking like a cold souffle. The instant analysts missed the significance of Nixon's makeup and misread the electoral consequences of Ford's Polish slip."[33]

32. Interview with John Reilly, February 27, 1987.
33. Robert G. Kaiser, "Looking for Old Ghosts; Perhaps You Thought Instant Analysis Couldn't Get Any Shoddier; The Wise Ones of the Mass Media Keep on Looking for the Old Ghosts," *Washington Post,* October 30, 1980.

From the candidates' perspective, "spin control"—putting the most favorable perspective on the event—is in full force after every debate, and some of it results in inane observations appearing in newspapers and on television. Sometimes the media themselves compound the problem. One such case was after the 1980 Reagan-Carter debate when ABC conducted a call-in poll; for fifty cents viewers could vote on who won the debate. Instant polls may be questionable; this was outrageous. The results clearly were skewed to Reagan since more Republicans have phones and the poor, some of whom cannot afford the luxury of a fifty-cent phone call, are mainly Democrats. Nevertheless, this gimmick had a real impact. Although at first most analysts thought the debate was pretty much a draw, the next day numerous newspapers were headlining that Reagan won two-to-one, reflecting the ABC telephone call-in poll.

Superficial coverage of debates may be endemic. Equally unavoidable, as the campaign draws to a conclusion, is the role public opinion polls play in shaping coverage for both television and newspapers. It is very tough to justify a piece on Walter Mondale's plans for the defense budget when reliable surveys show him losing every state in the Union.

Less defensible is the networks' penchant for sometimes revealing results of election-day exit polls before all Americans have voted. In 1980 Jimmy Carter's early concession, spurred on by the networks' polls, meant that millions of West Coast voters went to the polls knowing who had won. Studies on how this affects voting behavior are imprecise. But it is journalistically irresponsible and unnecessary.

How Coverage Can Be Improved

Even if attention were more properly focused, change would be slow. In his classic book on campaign reporters, *The Boys on the Bus,* Timothy Crouse noted that "journalism is probably the slowest-moving, most tradition-bound profession in America. It refuses to budge until it is shoved into the future by some irresistible external force."[34] There are no such powerful external forces, other than increased competition, particularly from cable television and local television stations, so any change is apt to be moderate.

It is an exaggeration to say that the media manipulate the presidential

34. Timothy Crouse, *The Boys on the Bus: Riding with the Campaign Press Corps* (Random House, 1972), p. 303.

election system; similarly it is an exaggeration to assert that media coverage is totally manipulated by scheming politicians. In many ways the system's untidiness is a strength. But there emerges sometimes a thoughtlessness to the media's role that produces unintended and negative consequences.

In part, it is up to the political parties to consider these effects. My specific suggestions include:

—Stretching out the primaries over a slightly longer period. For all the complaints about the lengthy process, over half of the pledged delegates to the 1988 conventions will be determined in a six-week span (from mid-February to late March) covering almost thirty primaries and caucuses. By the end of April, this figure will increase to 75 percent. This is when horse-race journalism is in full practice, permitting little time for reflection. Since most primary voters do not think seriously about candidates until shortly before the actual contest, they would be better served by a little longer time to consider the choice. Then they might not be so affected by fleeting passions of the moment.

—Continuing the political parties' constructive step of taking over and formalizing debates. Reporters' roles ought to be minimized and a format developed to display the candidates' own skills and maximize their participation in these important exchanges. (Media pressure, one may hope, will minimize the perils of not including legitimate third-party candidates.)

—Ensuring more "peer review" by both Democrats and Republicans—perhaps by requiring that at least one-third of national convention delegates automatically be elected politicians and party officials. Politicians can be stampeded by public opinion and media fervor as easily as voters. But they also have a better capacity to ask whether the particular front-runner of the moment seems to have political durability and how he or she might behave as president.

There are some important steps the media can take to improve their role, too. These include:

—Rotating reporters among candidates. Whatever gains are achieved by a more detailed knowledge of the campaign and candidates are more than offset by the distortions that occur when a journalist has a stake in how a particular candidate fares.

—Doing more pieces on issues when voters are paying attention. Both newspapers and television should seek ways to report on substantive differences in an interesting fashion right before and during the early primaries, as well as during the general election.

—Setting better priorities on coverage. For newspapers this means fewer stories but more comprehensive and thoughtful ones. For television this means ignoring even the president of the United States when there is no news. It also requires the discipline to resist the blandishments of great visuals that have little substantive significance. TV should worry less about the "puppy dogs and picket fences" and more about what is at stake. This can be interesting as well as informative.

In his book on television's coverage of the 1984 campaign, newspaper journalist Martin Schram concludes that the television news business "creates a sort of split professionality that turns its people into part journalist and part artist, and allows the politicians to play to the instincts of the latter." Those in the television news, Schram adds, "have failed to keep their eyes and minds on their role as journalists. It is often because they have allowed themselves to fall for the traps set by the best of the image-makers and manipulators, people such as Michael Deaver."[35]

Austin Ranney does not think the situation will get any better: "Television doesn't spend enough time on covering politics seriously and they knock themselves out to make it entertaining. With all the financial troubles the networks are going through, this will put the heat on them to be even more superficial." The best hope, Ranney argues, is more "narrow-casting—there will be more MacNeil-Lehrer NewsHours, C-Spans, Cable News Networks to provide substantive information."[36]

One suggested change that all the media should weigh warily is the notion of spending more time evaluating the character of the candidates. That way, it is suggested, the voters might have rejected a Richard Nixon or a Jimmy Carter or a Ronald Reagan. But that is a dicey proposition. Journalists are not trained in character assessments; one wonders what kind of character marks untrained journalists might have given Jefferson or Lincoln or Franklin Roosevelt.

Gary Hart's fate in the spring of 1987, with which this chapter began, brought to a head the issue of how far the media should go in examining the personal character of public figures.

Neither journalists nor the public indicated much sympathy for Hart, who seemed to have been asking for trouble. But the incident set off a heated debate over how much the media should pry into the private lives of politicians. Within weeks the *Cleveland Plain Dealer* ran a banner front-

35. Schram, *The Great American Video Game,* pp. 57, 308.
36. Interview with Austin Ranney, March 5, 1987.

page story suggesting that aides to Ohio Governor Richard Celeste worried that previous extramarital affairs might damage his chances of running for president.[37] *Newsweek* magazine reported that George Bush's son had asked his father about rumors the vice-president had committed adultery (he reportedly said he had not), and the *New York Times* asked all presidential candidates for their most confidential medical records and access to their raw FBI files.[38] Most sensible journalists felt all this was going too far—the editor of the *New York Times* subsequently admitted his paper had made a mistake—and would distort political coverage and distract both press and public from paying attention to serious governmental issues.[39] Indeed, while there is no doubt that a person's sexual behavior reflects on that person's moral character, there is no consensus that it says much about capacity for political leadership. No one ever accused Richard Nixon or Jimmy Carter of infidelity, but marital good conduct did not save them from erring seriously as president.

This does not mean that journalists should not more vigorously scrutinize the political character of presidential aspirants. Without becoming unlicensed psychiatrists or compulsive watchers of bedroom behavior, journalists need to think, write, and report more, not only on the skills required to get to the White House, but also on how these skills relate to what is needed once one is in the Oval Office.

37. "Celeste Womanizing Worries Aides; Links to Three Women May Imperil Presidential Ambitions," *Cleveland Plain Dealer,* June 3, 1987.

38. "Bush and the 'Big A' Question," *Newsweek,* June 29, 1987, p. 6; and Eleanor Randolph, "Quizzing the Candidates; Is Anything Off-Limits?" *Washington Post,* May 14, 1987.

39. Eleanor Randolph, "Questions Too Pointed, N.Y. Times Editor Says; Paper Backs Off from Request to Candidates," *Washington Post,* June 20, 1987.

CHAPTER FOUR

"Why Great Men Are Not Chosen Presidents": Lord Bryce Revisited

STEPHEN HESS

ON October 22, 1888, as voters were getting ready to decide whether Grover Cleveland should continue to reside in the White House or should be evicted in favor of Benjamin Harrison, the future Lord Bryce (he was made a viscount in 1913) signed off on what was to be the first edition of *The American Commonwealth.* This massive description of late nineteenth century democracy in the United States would have a profound influence on a generation of political scientists, but today it is recalled largely because of the name of its eighth chapter: "Why Great Men Are Not Chosen Presidents."

Although James Bryce was Regius Professor of Civil Law at Oxford when he wrote *The American Commonwealth,* his approach was journalistic, a reporting of data gathered largely by talking to politicians and others. As a conventional British gentleman, albeit one who loved America, he would probably have been offended by this classification; journalists were not gentlemen, of course. But in a sense Bryce was the Theodore H. White of his day and the impact of his book was not unlike that of the first *Making of the President* when it was published in 1961. Bryce and White were fascinated by the presidential nominating process. Bryce argued that party organizations largely controlled nominations and

The author is in the debt of the following thoughtful readers: David S. Broder, Robert A. Katzmann, Herbert Kaufman, and Paul E. Peterson.

preferred mediocre candidates. Process, too, is the theme of this essay, although I conclude that it does not determine who seeks the nomination, which is now the most important determinant of who ultimately becomes president.

While Bryce had high praise for presidents "down till the election of Andrew Jackson," he considered subsequent executives, with several exceptions, to be "personally insignificant."[1] It was apparently the presidencies up close that loomed largest on his canvas. (Even Oxford dons cannot repeal the laws of perspective.) When he first visited the United States in 1870, the White House was occupied by Ulysses S. Grant; the presidents on his next visits were Rutherford B. Hayes (1880) and Chester A. Arthur (1883). His low opinion of American chief executives, Bryce might have claimed, was based on personal observation.[2] Yet to have made his case for the debasing influence of parties on nominations, he would have had to prove that the parties pushed aside more distinguished figures. And this was not necessarily what happened. Should the Republicans have preferred John Sherman to Hayes? Should the Democrats have chosen Thomas Bayard over Grover Cleveland? There are times that seem to lack great men. Perhaps Bryce was merely observing one of history's troughs, regardless of how the candidates were chosen.

Bryce never felt the need to define greatness. He apparently thought that any intelligent person would recognize its presence or absence. This tends to turn the hunt for great men into something of a parlor game. Why, for instance, did Bryce not pay more attention to early twentieth century nominees? (The book was extensively revised in 1910 and 1914, with editions coming out until 1922, the year of his death.) During this period the Republicans and Democrats nominated what a British gentleman surely should have concluded were some of the finest candidates since the nation's founding generation. For sheer brilliance it would be hard to surpass Theodore Roosevelt, William Howard Taft, Woodrow Wilson, and Charles Evans Hughes. Also, while the populist William Jennings

---

1. James Bryce, *The American Commonwealth,* vol. 1 (Macmillan, 1888), p. 80. All references are to this edition unless otherwise noted. For biographical information on Bryce, see Robert G. McCloskey's entry in *International Encyclopedia of the Social Sciences;* and H. A. L. Fisher, *James Bryce* (Macmillan, 1927), vol. 1, especially pp. 222–42.

2. Similarly, James MacGregor Burns, apparently still entranced in the mid-1960s by a system that had selected John F. Kennedy, challenged Bryce in his essay, "Why Great Men Are Chosen President," in *Presidential Government* (Houghton Mifflin, 1966), pp. 295–303.

Bryan would not have appealed to Bryce, the Great Commoner was a person of extraordinary qualities as well. All but one of Bryce's revised editions contain a footnote stating that "of Presidents since 1900 it is not yet time to speak"; still, he did change the 1910 text to read, "Great men have not *often* been chosen Presidents."[3] (By leaving himself wiggle room to elevate his friend Roosevelt to the pantheon of greatness, Bryce also aided the cause of Anglo-American friendship, for which he had assumed some responsibility upon appointment as British ambassador to Washington in 1907.)

Necessarily, Bryce recognized that some great men would prove to be not-great presidents (Grant), and that others of more modest pre-presidential achievement (Lincoln) would become great presidents. There were bound to be surprises galore once a person entered the White House. What qualities or circumstances produce greatness is an interesting question.[4] But it is not the question that Bryce raises or that this centennial revisit addresses.

The title of Bryce's essay reflects historical fact: no major party has nominated a woman for president, which suggests the obvious: whenever an excluded group is allowed into the pool of presidential contenders there will be more possibilities, some of whom might be great. When a religious barrier came down—with the 1928 nomination of Alfred E. Smith, a Roman Catholic, and John F. Kennedy's election in 1960—the pool expanded, but not the type of contenders. Smith, the governor of New York, and Massachusetts Senator Kennedy were professional politicians, differing from the other contenders in their generation primarily in religious affiliation. The first woman presidential nominee most likely will have been vice-president, as the first woman vice-presidential nominee of a major party was a member of Congress.

Although Bryce's evaluation of the American system is tinged by a parliamentarian's preference for the way prime ministers are selected, his critique cannot be dismissed as mere chauvinism.[5] He argued that in the

3. Bryce (1910 edition), vol. 1, p. 83. Italics added.
4. For listings of so-called presidential qualities, see Clinton Rossiter, *The American Presidency* (Harcourt, Brace and World, 1960), pp. 172–74; Stephen Hess, *The Presidential Campaign*, rev. ed. (Brookings, 1978), pp. 27–38; and especially Hedley Donovan, *Roosevelt to Reagan* (Harper and Row, 1985), in which thirty-two "attributes of presidential leadership" are proposed, pp. 295–309.
5. For a more balanced and rigorous comparative examination of the two systems, see Hugh Heclo, "Presidential and Prime Ministerial Selection," in Donald R. Matthews, ed., *Perspectives on Presidential Selection* (Brookings, 1973), pp. 19–48.

America he had observed, great men were less drawn to politics than to "the business of developing the material resources of the country"; that compared with European countries, American political life offered "fewer opportunities for personal distinction"; that "eminent men make more enemies"; and that the American voter did "not object to mediocrity." The heart of Bryce's argument, however, was that great men were not chosen president because of the party system. Political bosses, he observed, gauged the strength of local organizations and the loyalty of voters and then calculated which candidate would add the right demographics to ensure victory. The objective was winning, not governing. He illustrated:

> On a railway journey in the Far West in 1883 I fell in with two newspaper men from the State of Indiana, who were taking their holiday. The conversation turned on the next presidential election. They spoke hopefully of the chances for nomination by their party of an Indiana man, a comparatively obscure person, whose name I had never heard. I expressed some surprise that he should be thought of. They observed that he had done well in State politics, that there was nothing against him, that Indiana would work for him. "But," I rejoined, "ought you not to have a man of more commanding character. There is Senator A. Everybody tells me that he is the shrewdest and most experienced man in your party, and that he has a perfectly clean record. Why not run him?" "Why, yes," they answered, "that is all true. But you see he comes from a small State, and we have got that State already. Besides, he wasn't in the war. Our man was. Indiana's vote is worth having, and if our man is run, we can carry Indiana."[6]

A Game of Musical Chairs

The paradox of revisiting Lord Bryce a hundred years after he said great men were not chosen presidents because of political parties is that political parties are in decline, and there is still no certainty that great men will be chosen president.

"The media in the United States are the new political parties," James David Barber contends. "The old political parties are gone."[7] Former

6. Bryce, vol. 1, pp. 74–75, 78.
7. Quoted by Gary R. Orren in "Thinking about the Press and Government," in Martin Linsky, ed., *Impact: How the Press Affects Federal Policymaking* (Norton, 1986), p. 10.

Democratic House Speaker Thomas P. O'Neill has said that members who entered Congress since the upheavals of Watergate and the Vietnam War "had no loyalty to the party whatsoever. They looked down on it. They said, 'The party didn't elect me, and I'm not beholden to the party.' "[8] Indeed, campaign consultant David Garth has noted that "the boss is a plus to have against you."[9]

Although some experts see new life in the old parties,[10] the way presidential candidates get nominated has irrevocably changed since Bryce's day. In 1901 Florida enacted the first presidential primary law, an invention designed to take nominations out of the hands of the party regulars. By 1980 primaries selected 71 percent of the delegates to the Democratic national convention. The number of primaries dropped in 1984, but by then the news media had turned important party caucuses, such as Iowa's, into quasi primaries. Accompanied by much greater voter independence and major technological changes, notably the coming of television, the new system was expected to produce a different type of presidential nominee. As one careful student of presidential politics wrote in 1981, "neither Jimmy Carter nor Ronald Reagan were unlikely nominees for the system under which we now choose our presidents, as Harry Truman and Thomas E. Dewey were not unlikely nominees for the system under which we once chose them."[11]

A tenet of political science and political journalism is that as the process changes so too do the outcomes. This notion is laudable and essentially optimistic. We are capable of changing the way we nominate presidential candidates, ergo we can improve the quality of presidents. Then if improvement schemes turn out otherwise, we can rail against the shortsightedness of reformers or the ignorance of those who fail to foresee unanticipated consequences—or both. Obviously the rules have affected some contenders' prospects in the past. Neither James K. Polk nor Woodrow Wilson, for example, would have been nominated had not Democratic

8. Quoted in Steven V. Roberts, "For New Speaker, New Role Is Seen," *New York Times*, December 8, 1986.

9. Quoted in Alan Eysen, "Tracking the Decline of Party Organizations," *Newsday*, April 23, 1981.

10. See David E. Price, *Bringing Back the Parties* (CQ Press, 1984); Xandra Kayden and Eddie Mahe, Jr., *The Party Goes On* (Basic Books, 1985); and A. James Reichley, "The Rise of National Parties," in John E. Chubb and Paul E. Peterson, eds., *The New Direction in American Politics* (Brookings, 1985), pp. 175–200.

11. Byron E. Shafer, "Anti-Party Politics," *The Public Interest*, no. 63 (Spring 1981), pp. 95–96.

conventions operated under a two-thirds rule, which was repealed in 1936.[12]

But do changes in process really result in different kinds of persons seeking the presidency? Following the 1968 and 1972 Democratic conventions, party commissions duly inflicted major changes on the demographic mix and selection of delegates. Analyses suggesting that subsequent nominees were different in kind because of these changes may simply be placing too much emphasis on too few cases. After all, there have been only eight major-party nominations in the past four elections, and four of them have gone to sitting presidents. For every obscure senator from a small state who has been nominated in recent times (George McGovern of South Dakota), one can find an earlier obscure senator from a small state (Franklin Pierce of New Hampshire, for example). An obscure governor (Jimmy Carter of Georgia) can be juxtaposed against an earlier obscure governor (Alfred M. Landon of Kansas). History is wondrously full of contrary examples to confound theories.

Observing the 1952 Democratic presidential convention, the *New Yorker*'s Richard Rovere compared contenders' activities with a game of musical chairs in which each chair represents an ideological position (liberal through conservative); if a chair is occupied when the music stops, the player is forced to seek a different chair. (Averell Harriman suddenly found himself in the liberal seat, Alben W. Barkley in the conservative seat.)[13] In terms of Rovere's formulation, when Hubert Humphrey, a lifelong liberal, entered the race in 1968, he discovered Robert Kennedy already sitting in the liberal chair and had to find another place to sit. This does not mean that Humphrey or Kennedy (or Mondale or Hart, Bush or Dole) as president would respond to similar pressures in dissimilar ways. Quite the contrary: professional politicians are more likely to have similar responses. They are not clones, of course, but they tend to weigh opportunities and constraints on the same scale. Hence, some of the claims that today's candidates are markedly more ideological than those in the past may be simply taking too literally the images that contestants have drawn of themselves (and of their opponents) during recent intraparty disputes.

12. At the Democratic convention of 1844, Martin Van Buren received 55 percent of the vote on the first ballot; on the tenth ballot at the 1912 Democratic convention Champ Clark had 51 percent of the vote. See Richard C. Bain and Judith H. Parris, *Convention Decisions and Voting Records,* 2d ed. (Brookings, 1973), app. C.

13. See Richard Rovere, "Letter from Chicago," *New Yorker* (August 2, 1952), pp. 58–59.

(Reagan was one of the most ideological candidates and Carter was one of the least.) The jury is clearly still out on this question.

Following his defeat in 1984, Walter Mondale publicly worried that television had changed the rules, that future presidential candidates would have to be masters of the "twenty-second snip, the angle, the shtick, whatever it is."[14] Having just been run over by a former actor, who also happened to be one of the great politicians of this century, Mondale commands sympathy. One could imagine Alf Landon making the same statement in 1936 after his landslide loss to Franklin D. Roosevelt, although Landon's concern would have been directed against the impact of radio. Politicians will adapt the technology at hand to their needs. For William Jennings Bryan in 1896, it was the transcontinental railroad. He logged 18,000 miles in quest of the presidency, thus ending the previous practice of candidates who stayed home and waged front porch campaigns.[15] What is most surprising about the TV age, however, is that besides Reagan and John Kennedy, the others who have won presidential nominations—Nixon, Johnson, Goldwater, Humphrey, McGovern, Carter, Ford, and Mondale—are no more telegenic than any cross section of middle-aged white males. Nor do the politicians who are presently at the starting gate for 1988 appear to have come from Central Casting. All of which suggests how little things change as the nation moves from party democracy to media democracy.

Throughout American history those picked to be major party presidential candidates, above all else, have been professional politicians. This is even more true today than it was in the nineteenth century. The reason is that "just wars" generate viable amateur candidates. Between 1824, when Andrew Jackson first ran for president, and 1892, when Benjamin Harrison last ran, persons who had been generals were nominated in all but three elections (1844, 1860, 1884). In this century only the Second World War yielded a nominee, Dwight Eisenhower.[16] The twenty-nine men nom-

14. Quoted in Elizabeth Drew, "A Political Journal," *New Yorker* (December 3, 1984), p. 174.

15. See Stephen Hess, "The Making of the President, 1896," in *The Nineties* (American Heritage, 1967), p. 133.

16. To date the only military men who have successfully used the Vietnam War as a political springboard in statewide elections have been two antiwar leaders (Robert Kerrey and John Kerry, both of whom served in Vietnam) and two former prisoners of war (Jeremiah Denton and John McCain); the war's premier general, William Westmoreland, was defeated in his attempt to become a governor.

inated by the major parties since 1900 have a collective record of office-holding that includes service as governors (thirteen), senators (nine), members of the House of Representatives (nine), vice-presidents (eight), judges (three), and cabinet members (two).[17] These men have moved through a maze of political jobs in order to reach the ultimate goal, and in eighty-four years only two members of that charmed circle—business executive Wendell L. Willkie and General Eisenhower—had never held civil public office before running for president.

Celebrity Politicians

To draw career histories of presidential nominees, thus illustrating the extent to which they have come from the ranks of professional politicians, is not to imply that the only way to reach the White House is to climb a political ladder, step by step, starting perhaps in the state legislature and gradually rising to a governorship or a seat in the Senate before attempting the final ascent. While the ladder metaphor reflects the most common pattern, lateral entry into a governor's chair or Congress is not uncommon. Ronald Reagan was not the first person to transfer fame or wealth earned outside politics into success as an officeseeker.

With the decline of parties, it would be expected that more persons could reach elected office without serving an apprenticeship, and this has happened.[18] It should be remembered, however, that Americans have always had what Robert Dahl calls "our belief in the supposed superiority of the amateur," a belief, he contends, that "we hold to only in politics and in the athletic activities of a small number of private colleges and universi-

17. The governors were William McKinley, Theodore Roosevelt, Woodrow Wilson, Charles Evans Hughes, James Cox, Calvin Coolidge, Alfred E. Smith, Franklin D. Roosevelt, Alfred Landon, Thomas E. Dewey, Adlai E. Stevenson, Jimmy Carter, and Ronald Reagan. The senators were Warren G. Harding, Harry S. Truman, John F. Kennedy, Richard M. Nixon, Lyndon B. Johnson, Barry Goldwater, Hubert H. Humphrey, George McGovern, and Walter Mondale. Members of the House of Representatives were William Jennings Bryan, McKinley, Cox, John W. Davis, Nixon, Kennedy, Johnson, McGovern, and Gerald R. Ford. T. Roosevelt, Coolidge, Truman, Nixon, Johnson, Humphrey, Ford, and Mondale were vice-presidents; Alton B. Parker, William Howard Taft, and Hughes were judges; and Taft and Herbert Hoover were cabinet members.
18. See Dennis M. Simon and David T. Canon, "Actors, Athletes, and Astronauts: Amateurism and Changing Career Paths in the United States Senate," paper delivered at the 1984 annual meeting of the Midwest Political Science Association.

ties whose alumni permit them the luxury of bad football teams."[19] Twentieth century Americans may attribute special leadership qualities to astronauts, but nineteenth century Americans attributed similar qualities to explorers. Recall that John C. Frémont, "the Pathfinder of the Rockies," was the first Republican presidential nominee in 1856. A journalist-celebrity, Horace Greeley, was the Democratic choice for president in 1872. Those advantaged by birth, whether an Adams, Harrison, or Kennedy, have had a leg up since colonial times.[20] Nor did the cleric-turned-politician begin with Pat Robertson and Jesse Jackson. The Muhlenberg family of Pennsylvania, for example, sent three ordained ministers to the U.S. Congress. In contrast, the businessman-celebrity has fared poorly at the presidential level, despite Calvin Coolidge's axiom that the business of America is business.

With the passage of time, what changes, of course, is which groups of celebrities turn to politics. The sports celebrity, such as Jack Kemp, is a recent political phenomenon. At least the only nineteenth century athlete-politico that comes to mind, also an upstate New York congressman, was John Morrissey, who had been world heavyweight boxing champion.

My point is that while contenders for presidential nominations may have to appeal to different selectors as the selection process changes, the winners to date in the TV-and-primaries era—Carter and Reagan—are not unprecedented in what they offer the voters. Whether today's nominees get there by climbing a political ladder or by lateral entry, they still would be recognizable to Lord Bryce. The system in Bryce's time promoted those experienced in coalition building; today's system promotes expert persuaders. Both are qualities considered presidentially important. The finite differences between politicians running for president under the old system and politicians chosen by newer rules are mainly of interest to those of us who make a living sniffing such fine distinctions.

The idea of a political career ladder based on ambition was masterfully presented in 1966 by Joseph A. Schlesinger. "Ambition lies at the heart of politics," he wrote. "Politics thrive on the hope of preferment and the drive for office."[21] Other political scientists then used Schlesinger's theory

19. "Foreword" to Joseph A. Schlesinger, *How They Became Governor* (Michigan State University, 1957).

20. There have been some 700 families in which two or more members have served in the U.S. Congress. See Stephen Hess, *America's Political Dynasties* (Doubleday, 1966), p. 1.

21. Joseph A. Schlesinger, *Ambition and Politics: Political Careers in the United States* (Rand McNally, 1966), p. 1.

to show how elimination occurs as politicians attempt to move up the rungs.[22] The final ambition, of course, is the presidency, which rises so high above the other steps as to constitute a separate ladder. The dramatic distance between the presidency and the other levels of public employment has consequences for what Schlesinger calls progressive ambition ("The politician aspires to attain an office more important than the one he now seeks or is holding").[23] While no person becomes vice-president without being willing to become president, what of the others whose jobs make them eligible to be mentioned as prospective presidential candidates? Ordinary ambition can carry a supplicant to the level of U.S. senator or governor, but then, because of the wide gap that must be bridged, another dynamic takes over. President Eisenhower once mused that the only thing successful politicians have in common is that they all married above themselves. But the only common denominator I have observed for those who would be president is the depth of their ambition. What distinguishes the group of candidates seeking their parties' 1988 presidential nomination from other high officeholders of their generation? Not their intelligence, accomplishments, style, or the reality of their prospects. What distinguishes them is *presidential ambition,* the ultimate in progressive ambition.

In applying the concept of progressive ambition to the presidency, scholars assume almost all U.S. senators would accept the highest office if it were offered to them without cost or risk. It cannot be. Costs of running for president can be very great. In some cases the candidate must give up a Senate seat, as Barry Goldwater did in 1964. In all cases there are physical

---

22. See Kenneth Prewitt and William Nowlin, "Political Ambitions and the Behavior of Incumbent Politicians," *Western Political Quarterly,* vol. 22 (June 1969), pp. 248–308; Michael L. Mezey, "Ambition Theory and the Office of Congressman," *Journal of Politics,* vol. 32 (August 1970), pp. 563–79; Jeff Fishel, "Ambition and the Political Vocation: Congressional Challengers in American Politics," *Journal of Politics,* vol. 33 (February 1971), pp. 25–56; Gordon S. Black, "A Theory of Political Ambition: Career Choices and the Role of Structural Incentives," *American Political Science Review,* vol. 66 (March 1972), pp. 144–59; Paul L. Hain, "Age, Ambitions, and Political Careers: The Middle-Age Crisis," *Western Political Quarterly,* vol. 27 (June 1974), pp. 265–74; David W. Rohde, "Risk-Bearing and Progressive Ambition: The Case of Members of the United States House of Representatives," *American Journal of Political Science,* vol. 23 (February 1979), pp. 1–26; Paul Brace, "Progressive Ambition in the House: A Probabilistic Approach," *Journal of Politics,* vol. 46 (May 1984), pp. 556–71; and Paul R. Abramson, John H. Aldrich, and David W. Rohde, "Progressive Ambition among United States Senators: 1972–1988," *Journal of Politics,* vol. 49 (February 1987), pp. 3–35.

23. Schlesinger, *Ambition and Politics,* p. 10.

costs. When Senator Dale Bumpers declined to become a candidate for the 1988 Democratic nomination, he publicly questioned whether he had the stamina for the "18 months of 18-hour days" that presidential campaigns can require.[24] There are, of course, financial costs. Donald Rumsfeld said he was not prepared to go deeply into debt in order to seek the 1988 Republican nomination. Potential candidates must also consider the almost total loss of privacy. As TV reporter Sam Donaldson said he told Jimmy Carter, "We're going to cover you one way or the other." Donaldson then noted, "Presidents must understand they live in a glass house when they move to the White House."[25] What are the effects that running for president can have on a candidate's family? Whether to expose spouse, children, even siblings, to this ordeal could be considered the test of what divides those with presidential ambition from others who are simply eligible to be contenders. Meg Greenfield wrote, "People who have made a serious run for the office or been around those that do will tell you that until you have experienced a presidential candidacy close up, nothing prepares you for the total onslaught on your life and that of your family that comes with the campaign."[26] Mario Cuomo seemed to have all the political attributes necessary to run for president in 1988. He was reelected governor of New York in 1986 by the biggest gubernatorial landslide in his state's history and had more than $3 million left over from that campaign. But he was not prepared to subject his family to "the total onslaught" and announced that he would not seek the Democratic nomination.[27]

The Motor of Ambition

In their imaginative attempt to factor risk-taking potential into the equation, Paul R. Abramson, John H. Aldrich, and David W. Rohde have

24. See Paul Taylor, "Bumpers Decides Against Presidential Bid," *Washington Post*, March 21, 1987.

25. Sam Donaldson, *Hold On, Mr. President!* (Random House, 1987), p. 16.

26. Meg Greenfield, "The Bradley-Nunn Problem," *Washington Post*, November 11, 1986.

27. Commenting on his 1986 campaign, Cuomo said, "What it makes you think about is look, is this really an ego exercise by you? Look at what it's done to your kids. What about [daughter] Madeline? Three times she's stopped for a red light. Then she's in the newspapers. Somebody refers to her as a bleached blonde. I mean, I could strangle the guy." Quoted in Paul Taylor, "Cuomo Sends the Word That He's Weighing Entering the Fray," *Washington Post*, January 25, 1987; also see Michael Oreskes, "Cuomo Leaves the Ring," *Washington Journalism Review* (April 1987), p. 17.

shown that Democratic senators who are proven risk-takers have been "a good deal more likely to run for president [since 1972] than those who were not."[28] Yet as they state in their analysis of the 1984 election, seventeen Democratic senators were "well situated" to run for president and thirteen of them chose not to make the race.[29] (The percentage of Republican senators who would not have run for president if Reagan had retired would have been even higher.)

This finding is in keeping with my survey of Senate news coverage in 1983, which showed that ten senators received 50 percent—and thirty-five senators received 5 percent—of the national media attention.[30] Some of the underexposed senators were too old or too new to be of interest to the national press corps. Their time had passed or will come. But most of the senators who are rarely, if ever, on network TV do not wish to be president. Quentin Burdick, one of seventeen senators never seen on the networks' 1,095 nightly news programs during 1983, told a Washington reporter, "I'm very conscious about what they're saying in North Dakota, but not outside the state. I'm not running for president." His press secretary added, "To him if it doesn't happen in North Dakota, it doesn't happen."[31] In any event, Burdick's age—he will be eighty in 1988—now bars him from a run for the presidency. Yet many other senators without such liabilities will never offer themselves as candidates for the top office. The Senate is their ceiling of progressive ambition. In some cases they may have judged that they are not qualified for the higher office. But mainly their reasons are deeply personal, beyond scholars' ability to measure. Strangely, perhaps, the ego strength that one might associate with a Senate leadership position seems not to correlate with presidential ambition, which strikes some leaders (Lyndon Johnson, Robert Dole) and not others (Mike Mansfield, Hugh Scott).

How best to describe presidential ambition (apparently so much more intense than senatorial ambition)? William Howard Taft may have come close in a story he told about a friend's "little daughter Mary":

28. Abramson, Aldrich, and Rohde, "Progressive Ambition," p. 13.

29. See Paul R. Abramson, John H. Aldrich, and David W. Rohde, *Change and Continuity in the 1984 Elections* (CQ Press, 1986), p. 16.

30. Stephen Hess, *The Ultimate Insiders: U.S. Senators in the National Media* (Brookings, 1986), pp. 11, 16.

31. Bill Blocher, "Study of U.S. Senators Is Worthless," *Williston* (N. Dak.) *Herald*, May 13, 1986; and Steve Adams, "Study Calls Burdick 'Underachiever,'" *Minot* (N. Dak.) *Daily News*, May 10, 1986.

As he came walking home after a business day, she ran out from the house to greet him, all aglow with the importance of what she wished to tell him. She said, "Papa, I am the best scholar in the class." The father's heart throbbed with pleasure as he inquired, "Why, Mary, you surprise me. When did the teacher tell you? This afternoon?" "Oh, no," Mary's reply was, "the teacher didn't tell me—I just noticed it myself."[32]

Taft's gentle tale was his way of chiding Teddy Roosevelt for placing himself in a class with Lincoln (and Taft in a class with James Buchanan). But it was TR's concept of the presidency as a stewardship that separates the modern era from the nineteenth century. "My view," he wrote, "was that every executive officer [read president] . . . was a steward of the people bound actively and affirmatively to do all he could for the people, and not to content himself with the negative merit of keeping his talents undamaged in a napkin."[33] Indeed, given the Rooseveltian way of doing the president's business, Bryce's 1910 edition deleted a paragraph designed to remind Britons that the U.S. president "ought not to address meetings, except on ornamental and (usually) non-political occasions, that he cannot submit bills nor otherwise influence the action of the legislature."[34]

It may well be, of course, that in those days when presidents "ought not to address meetings," presidential ambition was less the motor force that governed the number and kind of contenders. After all, William Howard Taft did not have presidential ambition in 1908 (TR had it for him). Deeply deadlocked nineteenth century conventions sometimes produced surprised winners, notably Horatio Seymour, the Democrats' choice in 1868, who was so opposed to becoming the nominee that the convention quickly adjourned before he could refuse the honor.[35] Today, however,

32. William Howard Taft, *Our Chief Magistrate and His Powers* (Columbia University Press, 1925), p. 144.
33. *The Autobiography of Theodore Roosevelt,* Wayne Andrews, ed. (Octagon, 1975), p. 197.
34. Bryce, vol. 1, p. 76.
35. See Malcolm Moos and Stephen Hess, *Hats in the Ring: The Making of Presidential Candidates* (Random House, 1960), p. 28. It is true, of course, that the old system produced more deadlocked conventions, but dark horse nominees were a decided mixed bag in terms of quality and should not be romanticized by political scientists and journalists who miss not having an opportunity to watch a convention of politicians trying to dig itself out of a hole. A checklist of dark horse nominees (who were behind on the first ballot and won after more

before submitting oneself to the obligations of being "the leader of the free world," one might apply the litmus test of ambition stated by John F. Kennedy, who told 1960 audiences:

> I want to be a President who acts as well as reacts—who originates programs as well as study groups—who masters complex problems as well as one-page memorandums. I want to be a President who is a Chief Executive in every sense of the word—who responds to a problem, not by hoping his subordinates will act, but by directing them to act—a President who is willing to take the responsibility for getting things done, and take the blame if they are not done right. [36]

One recognizes the hyperbole of the moment. Still, something more distinguishes Kennedy's statement from the garden-variety ambition of most politicians (perhaps *chutzpa,* the Yiddish word that Leo Rosten translates as "presumption-plus-arrogance such as no other word, and no other language, can do justice to").[37] Or as Alexander Haig urged the voters of New Hampshire on the day in 1987 that he announced his candidacy, "Inside this exterior, militant, turf-conscious, excessively ambitious demeanor is a heart as big as all outdoors."[38] If this looks like a strictly contemporary phenomenon, however, consider William Jennings Bryan, thirty-six years old, a former two-term member of the House of Representatives from Nebraska, most recently defeated for the U.S. Senate, who won the 1896 Democratic presidential nomination. Or Thomas E. Dewey, thirty-eight, New York City district attorney, defeated Republican candidate for governor of New York, who almost captured his party's presidential nomination in 1940. Yes, the serious candidates are a self-anointed breed whose ambition sets the contours of presidential selection.

Note, however, that not all presidential contenders really expect to get

---

than four ballots): James K. Polk (1844), Franklin Pierce (1852), Winfield Scott (1852), Horatio Seymour (1868), Rutherford B. Hayes (1876), James A. Garfield (1880), Benjamin Harrison (1888), William Jennings Bryan (1896), Woodrow Wilson (1912), James Cox (1920), Warren G. Harding (1920), John W. Davis (1924), and Wendell Willkie (1940).

36. Quoted in James MacGregor Burns, *Leadership* (Harper and Row, 1978), p. 394.

37. Leo Rosten, *The Joys of Yiddish* (Pocket Books, 1970), p. 93. Overriding ambition should not be thought of as limited to politicians, of course; it was even stressed as a characteristic of the great theologian Reinhold Niebuhr in a sympathetic essay by Wilson Carey McWilliams, "A Glorious Discontent," *Freedom at Issue,* no. 92–93 (November–December 1986), p. 21.

38. Quoted in David Shribman, "Haig Embarks On 1988 Quest for Presidency," *Wall Street Journal,* March 25, 1987.

the nod. Some candidates are in the race primarily to further policy goals or to focus attention on the needs of certain groups or to advance themselves in other pursuits. Archconservative Patrick Buchanan, for example, gave thought to running for the 1988 Republican nomination because "there is no better forum to advance the ideas you believe in and to give them elevation."[39] It is only the serious candidate to whom we attribute the italicized form of presidential ambition.

William Herndon said of his law partner, Abraham Lincoln, "His ambition was a little engine that knew no rest."[40] Alexander and Juliette George wrote of the "insatiable" and "compulsive" ambition that seemed to govern Woodrow Wilson's career.[41] Yet psychological insights cannot predict when an ambition will turn presidential. Franklin Roosevelt was said to have viewed the presidency as "his birthright."[42] But Jimmy Carter claims that he did not see himself as belonging in the White House until 1971 and 1972, when he met "other presidential hopefuls, and I lost my feeling of awe about presidents."[43] Nor does presidential ambition describe a set of personality traits, given candidates as diverse as Eugene McCarthy and Lyndon Johnson.

A Question of Timing

Presidential ambition sets off a sort of biological timeclock. The Constitution requires that a president must be at least thirty-five years of age. Realistically candidates do not run much before their mid-forties or after their mid-sixties. Given that elections come at four-year intervals, this allows five shots at the office. At least one chance must be deducted, though, because incumbents are almost always renominated. A Republican who reached the age of presidential ascent after the 1952 election, for example, would have had to stand aside in 1956 and 1972 while Presidents Eisenhower and Nixon ran for second terms. Thus presidential opportu-

39. Quoted in John B. Judis, "White House Vigilante," *New Republic* (January 26, 1987), p. 17.

40. William H. Herndon and Jesse W. Weik, *Herndon's Life of Lincoln: The History and Personal Recollections of Abraham Lincoln* (New York: Albert and Charles Boni, 1930), p. 304.

41. Alexander L. George and Juliette L. George, *Woodrow Wilson and Colonel House: A Personality Study* (John Day, 1956), p. 320.

42. Richard E. Neustadt, *Presidential Power* (Wiley, 1960), p. 180.

43. Jimmy Carter, *Why Not the Best?* (Broadman, 1975), p. 137.

nity is more like a four-per-lifetime proposition. Yet the odds are even longer in that three unsuccessful races for the nomination turn a candidate into a laugh line for late-night TV comedians. Indeed, that three sitting presidents were seriously challenged for renomination in 1968, 1976, and 1980 can be partly explained by how narrow the window of opportunity is for those with presidential ambition.

In short, contenders have remarkably little maneuvering room, and much of their strategic planning is held hostage to fortuity. Take the case of Richard Nixon, who reached the White House in 1969 via this Rube Goldberg "stratagem": (a) run for president in 1960 against John Kennedy and lose by a hair; (b) seek a way to sit out the 1964 race so you can run in 1968 when Kennedy's second term ends; (c) decide to run for governor of California in 1962 so you can promise you will serve a four-year term; (d) lose the gubernatorial race, move to New York, and retire from office-seeking; (e) watch the Republican party self-destruct in the 1964 election and the Democratic party self-destruct over the Vietnam War; (f) return from exile to be elected president in 1968.[44]

Unlike the lower rungs on the political ladder, where aspirants for an office have more time to wait for their most opportune moment (and may even be rewarded for being the good soldier, putting party above self), a person on the presidential track has little incentive to wait. To do so means that professional staff, volunteers, financial backers, and sympathetic political leaders will drift into other camps. A rule of thumb might be that each serious contender gets three chances and one bye. Robert Taft, for instance, sought the Republican nomination in 1940, 1948, and 1952, but passed in 1944. William Jennings Bryan was the Democratic nominee in 1896, 1900, and 1908, passed in 1904, and became increasingly implausible after his third defeat. Nor are there Damon-and-Pythias relationships in a hardball world. If a bunch of greats happen along in the same era, some will be pushed out of the way on the road to the conventions. Thus are all persons with presidential ambition generationally trapped. Years from now we will be able to identify the politicians for whom 1988 was the year of the bye.

This formulation does not assume that all persons with presidential ambition will run for president, merely that persons without presidential ambition will not run for president and all persons who run for president

44. See Jules Witcover, *The Resurrection of Richard Nixon* (Putnam, 1970), especially pp. 25–35.

have presidential ambition. Likewise, all professional politicians do not run for president, but all serious candidates for president are professional politicians—at least until the nation produces Ike-like heroes again. It is this combination of ambition and political professionalism that limits the field in any given election year. For example, Lowell Weicker, the liberal Republican senator, said he has presidential ambition but will not run for president in 1988. As a professional politician he knows he "would stand no chance whatsoever in a Republican convention for getting the nomination."[45]

Opportunities for Fine-Tuning

In man's eternal search for the structural fix—Charles Krauthammer's felicitous phrase—there are modest ways to expand the pool of presidential contenders in a particular presidential generation, such as by repealing the Twenty-second Amendment, revising gubernatorial election schedules, and revoking the constitutional ban against naturalized citizens serving as president. But under the Twenty-second Amendment, added to the Constitution in 1951, only three persons have been prevented from running for president, Dwight Eisenhower in 1960, Richard Nixon in 1976, and Ronald Reagan in 1988, and none of them would have sought the office again anyway.[46] An additional governor or two might be encouraged to seek the presidency if they did not have to give up their state job to make the race, but there are now only twelve states in which presidential and gubernatorial elections fall in the same year.[47] And while naturalized

45. Quoted in Richard E. Cohen, "Weicker's Wing," *National Journal*, vol. 19 (January 10, 1987), p. 108.

46. The history of amending the Constitution has usually had the effect of expanding the rights of citizens (the Bill of Rights, the Reconstruction amendments following the Civil War, direct election of U.S. senators, female suffrage, the presidential vote for the District of Columbia, abolition of the poll tax, and the eighteen-year-old vote). But the Twenty-second Amendment denies citizens the right to elect the same president more than twice consecutively. This is an idea that is bad in principle yet works well in practice, presidents usually being of an age where eight years is a sufficient drain on their energies. Nevertheless, it should be up to the voters to decide. For arguments favoring retention, see Thomas E. Cronin, "Two Cheers for the 22nd Amendment," *Christian Science Monitor*, February 23, 1987.

47. The states that presently hold elections for governor and president in the same year are Delaware, Indiana, Missouri, Montana, North Carolina, North Dakota, Utah, Washington, West Virginia, New Hampshire, Rhode Island, and Vermont (the last four having two-year terms for governor).

citizens (discriminated against under Article II, section 4) deserve to be treated equally with the native-born, removal of this impediment would not result in a massive incursion of presidential hopefuls.[48] Another means of encouraging more candidacies, some contend, would be to lower the cost of running for president. Contemplating the next nomination fight, Edward J. Rollins, who headed President Reagan's 1984 campaign, said, "Anyone who isn't able to raise between $6 million and $8 million in 1987 is not going to be a player."[49] While this is a great deal of money in terms of personal wealth, in commercial terms it means that the race for a presidential nomination has about the same price tag as a small fleet of New York City taxicabs (at $100,000 per medallion) or a midwestern newspaper of 10,000 to 12,000 circulation.

If fine-tuners wish to alter the type of persons who seek the presidency, the best place to tinker is the vice-presidential selection process. For who gets the nod for vice-president is the single most important predictor of future nominees for president. (Of the men who have been major party candidates for president since 1900, 30 percent previously had been vice-presidents or vice-presidential candidates, 50 percent since 1960.) It is a sensible precedent that presidential nominees are allowed their choice for running mate. The worst mistake a convention could make would be to pick a vice-presidential candidate who did not get along, personally or philosophically, with the president-to-be. The choice is usually a governor, senator, or House member—that is, another professional politician. The presidential candidate thinks that a running mate can add electoral weight to the ticket; in fact, John Kennedy may be the only president who owes his election to his choice for vice-president in that Lyndon Johnson was the reason the Democrats carried Texas in 1960. When voters must decide who will be the next president, the candidate for vice-president has proven to be a very modest influence. This suggests that presidential conventions can afford to be a lot more daring if they desire to bring new

48. Among the prominent naturalized citizens are foreign policy experts Henry Kissinger and Zbigniew Brzezinski, industrialists An Wang and Gerald Tsai, journalists James Reston and Max Frankel, university president Hanna H. Gray, scientist Albert Sabin, scholar Kenneth Clark, Vermont Governor Madeleine Kunin, U.S. Senator Rudy Boschwitz, and U.S. Representatives Mervyn M. Dymally, Samuel Gejdenson, Ernest L. Konnyu, Thomas P. Lantos, and Ted Weiss. Persons born abroad whose parents are U.S. citizens are thought to be eligible to serve as president, although this has not been decided in the courts. See Edwin S. Corwin, *The Constitution and What It Means Today*, 14th ed. (Princeton University Press, 1978), pp. 154–55.

49. Phil Gailey, "Babbitt of Arizona First Democrat To Form Key Presidential Group," *New York Times*, January 8, 1987.

blood into the political system,[50] that is, if Americans prefer to have their leaders come from the ranks of auto executives, consumer advocates, college administrators, TV anchors, and movie stars.[51]

The fascination with process that has governed the energies of political science and political journalism has made academics increasingly useful to politicians and other practitioners, while, at the same time, journalists such as David S. Broder have added a new richness to the public understanding of politics. The matter of process has consequences for the presidential selection system, and the rapidity of change since 1968 has seemingly created a series of near-laboratory experiments. By changing the composition of the convention can we increase a party's chances of electoral success? In what proportions should parties use delegate slots to reward the faithful or encourage converts? Will an altered convention produce a different sort of platform? Which changes fuel ideology and which changes tamp it? Will presidents differently chosen become beholden to different groups and individuals? What changes increase voter participation? Has a decade of changes invigorated the parties or made them even less important in our society? All questions worth asking—and answering.

And yet in the paramount purpose of the process—choosing the major party nominees to be president of the United States—changes in the system since Lord Bryce's time do not limit the field or alter the character of the winners. While there are a few contenders who would not have previously emerged, such as Jesse Jackson and Pat Robertson, they have not yet been successful. There may also have been marginal or regional contenders of the past, such as Richard Russell of Georgia in 1952, who would not have entered the race today. But in broad outline, then and now, and with rare exception, serious contenders for the nomination are professional politicians, people of extraordinary ambition who cannot be discouraged by

50. One suggestion calls for presidential candidates coming to the convention with a list of acceptable running mates in a sealed envelope (rather like the Academy Awards); the winner's list is then opened and the delegates must choose one of the names on it. See Warren Weaver, Jr., "Change Proposed for Picking G.O.P. Running Mate," *New York Times,* January 18, 1980; also see Stephen Hess, "How We Might Have Avoided Spiro Agnew," *Baltimore Sun,* February 15, 1980.

51. For a "CBS News Special" (September 21, 1986), Walter Cronkite asked 1,000 Americans, randomly selected from *Who's Who,* to list people who might make good presidents "other than the usually mentioned possibilities." There were 400 replies: 61 percent chose the usually mentioned politicians; of the others, Lee Iacocca received the most votes (11.75 percent), followed by Walter Cronkite (2.25 percent), with seven university presidents also mentioned.

changes in the rules of the game. This ambition determines the number who seek the presidency at any one time, taking into account the modest room for strategic maneuver. No doubt a particular contender will be more advantaged by one change in the process than will another, just as different contenders will be differently affected by the rate of employment and the rate of inflation. But those possessed by presidential ambition will participate regardless of whether selection occurs through a national primary, a series of regional primaries, a combination of state primaries and caucuses, or any permutation of the above.

Any democratic system is likely to produce the same range of contenders; in this regard, process does not determine outcome. A change in process may have some effect on which contender wins a specific nomination, and some presidential attributes are tested by the process. But regrettably for voters, journalists, and social scientists, the process will neither predict nor determine the chances of the winners turning out to be great presidents.

PART TWO

Voter Participation

CHAPTER FIVE

The Turnout Problem

WALTER DEAN BURNHAM

ELECTIONS American style are peculiar in many respects. One of their chief peculiarities today is that so few eligible citizens vote in them. For example, in 1984 there were roughly 167.7 million citizens of voting age, of whom 92.7 million voted for president, while 75 million (44.8 percent) did not.[1] In 1986, with 171.9 million citizens potentially eligible to vote, 64.6 million cast ballots for the highest offices in their states, and 61.3 million voted for members of Congress—turnout rates of 37.6 percent and 35.7 percent. Thus well over three-fifths of potentially eligible Americans failed to vote in 1986. This produced the third lowest midterm election

---

1. Most accounts give the total voting-age population as the denominator, although the census gives the noncitizen component and no state in the union has permitted aliens to vote since the election of 1920. Total voting-age population in the 1980s is about 104 percent of the citizen voting-age population, and the noncitizen trend has clearly been rising over the past twenty years. Using the citizen base, rather than the total, marginally increases the turnout estimate (in 1980, from 53 percent to 55.2 percent). In addition, the total participation rate (including "blank, void, and scattering," as New York calls it) is marginally higher than the vote cast for the highest office, that is, president, or in off-years governor or U.S. senator. In the 1980 Massachusetts election, for example, the total vote for all presidential candidates was 2,524,298, but an additional 42,509 blank votes were cast for this office, making a total participation of 2,566,807. The presidential vote cast was thus 98.3 percent of all ballots cast. Something like this is very probably the national average, and would mean that, while the turnout for president was 55.2 percent of potential voters in 1980, the whole vote cast would produce a participation rate of 56.1 percent. Even today, the conduct and reporting of elections is very largely the responsibility of each of the fifty states, and these differ considerably in both areas. Most of them do not report on the "blanks and voids," and therefore virtually all American election reporting gives only the valid vote. Comparatively, most continental European countries report both the total of all votes cast and the total of valid votes cast. The relationship between the two, except in countries that have compulsory voting, tends to be similar to the Massachusetts example.

turnout in a century and a half (only 1926 and 1942 showed lower figures). Excluding the southern quarter of the country, with its unique regional political history, the 1986 participation rate fell to the lowest level recorded for an off-year election since 1798.

Today, I would estimate that about 38 percent of American citizens are "core" or regular voters for major national and state offices; another 17 percent or so are marginals who come to the polls only when stimulated by the dramas of presidential campaign politics; and 45 percent are more or less habitual nonvoters. This level of nonvoting is characteristically, almost uniquely, American. Voting participation in other advanced capitalist democracies—the curious anomaly of the Swiss Confederation apart—is much higher than it is here. An off-year congressional election is not, of course, the equivalent of a parliamentary election elsewhere. Still, it is striking that the participation rate in the German Bundestag election of February 1987 was nearly 50 percentage points higher than the American congressional turnout rate in November 1986.[2]

Once upon a time, in the lost Atlantis of nineteenth century politics, American participation rates in both presidential and midterm elections were very close to current participation rates abroad. The characteristic American participation rate is a singular property of politics in this century.[3] Outside the special southern region, voter turnout in the United States has declined heavily and nearly continuously since 1960, despite educational and structural changes that in themselves should have led to an increase. This decline is skewed very heavily across class lines—the skew becoming more extreme the lower the overall rate falls. The partisan implications of this change are not symmetrical, but are much more concentrated on the Democratic than the Republican side.

One would have thought that political science's research mainstream would long ago have considered turnout issues to represent a real "problem," as many activists and opinion leaders outside academe do. To be sure, "mass apathy" in America presents a certain public relations problem: it doesn't look good, especially in a comparative context. But is

2. There was much unhappiness in ruling Christian Democratic party circles following the February 1987 election because many believed that the party's unexpectedly disappointing showing was partly caused by a slump in the participation rate—from nearly 90 percent in 1983 to about 85 percent in 1987.

3. The evidence on this is by now overwhelming. For the most complete analysis, see Paul Kleppner, *Who Voted?: The Dynamics of Electoral Turnout, 1870–1980* (Praeger, 1982).

turnout really a "problem" in any more fundamental sense? The answer to this question must depend upon the perspectives of the person analyzing the question. In the days of the Cold War synthesis, it was fashionable to dismiss the issue (when nonsouthern turnouts were considerably higher than now) as being the fruit of a "politics of happiness" and beneficent low pressure.[4] For many obvious reasons, such views are less in vogue today.

In what follows, I will be concerned to evaluate the social "incidence" of nonvoting, concentrating (to what many would regard as an excessive degree) on the class dimensions of voting and nonvoting in American elections. Now it is no new doctrine that social class is subjectively a feeble behavioral anchor in a society that is immensely complex in demography, cultural subtraditions, and locally dominant economic sectors. The United States, after all, is noteworthy for having a dominant, single "liberal tradition" in its political culture, and, very much related to this, for lacking any significant organized socialist or laborite alternative in its electoral market.[5] Nevertheless, from a systemic perspective social class differentials loom rather larger, especially where participation is concerned. For the old saw remains profoundly true: if you don't vote, you don't count. [Consider, for example, formal education, which is so significant as a political sorting-out variable. Viewed at the individual level, there is little reason to challenge the usual view that this is a more powerful discriminator than occupation, income, or other measures of social differentials.[6] Yet the first thing that would occur to one from a

4. This was very often associated with the presentation of German elections in the 1930–33 crisis period as a "horrible example" of voter mobilization. See, for example, Seymour Martin Lipset, *Political Man: The Social Bases of Politics* (Doubleday, 1960), especially pp. 140–52. It has become clear in recent years that such analyses, in addition to failing to incorporate the nearly half-century of electoral material that preceded the Weimar era, fundamentally misspecified the relative importance of the mobilization of former non-voters to the Nazi upsurge. The best technical discussion of the issues is Adam Przeworski, "Institutionalization of Voting Patterns, or Is Mobilization the Source of Decay?" *American Political Science Review*, vol. 69 (March 1975), pp. 49–67. See also Thomas Childers, *The Nazi Voter: The Social Foundations of Facism in Germany* (University of North Carolina Press, 1983).

5. It is now a generation since Louis Hartz published his seminal work, *The Liberal Tradition in America: An Interpretation of American Political Thought since the Revolution* (Harcourt Brace, 1955); but time has not diminished its importance. For a more empirical but very convergent study, see Donald J. Devine, *The Political Culture of the United States: The Influence of Member Values on Regime Maintenance* (Little, Brown, 1972).

6. Raymond E. Wolfinger and Steven J. Rosenstone, *Who Votes?* (Yale University Press, 1980), pp. 13–36.

structural or systemic perspective is that access to higher education is expensive and therefore tends to be pretty strictly rationed in economic and social terms. It is one of a variety of interrelated functional measures that discriminate quite effectively between the have-mores and have-lesses in a stratified class system.⌋

Competing Perspectives

At the level of explaining individual voting behavior, two sets of perspectives seem to dominate the field today. They are often thought incompatible or incommensurable with each other, but perhaps are not as much so as was once supposed. These are the perspectives derived from survey research on the one hand and post-Downsian rational-actor models on the other.

The survey research approach has found that if respondents strongly identify with a party and are otherwise cognitively "plugged into" the larger world of politics, there is high probability that they will vote. Another particularly strong predictor of participation seems to be the respondents' sense of external political efficacy—that is, their perception that purposive action directed at the political system (such as voting) would or would not produce positive results.[7] Respondents who agree with such statements as "Sometimes I don't think that government officials care what people like me think," or "Parties are only interested in your vote, not in delivering what they promise to you" are more likely at any income, occupation, or education level to abstain than their counterparts who disagree with these statements. Recently, Arthur Hadley has identified another element in the puzzle: do the respondents believe that in their own personal life, purposive actions will succeed in producing desired results, or do they think that life is dominated by chance?[8] According to

7. See the discussion in Sidney Verba and Norman H. Nie, *Participation in America: Political Democracy and Social Equality* (Harper and Row, 1972), especially pp. 125–37. This rich work represents the very best of the survey research tradition. However, it has become clearer since 1972 that there are significant differences between two types of political efficacy indices as constructed from sets of questions: *internal* ("Sometimes government and politics are so complicated . . .") and *external* ("Officials don't care what people like me think . . ."). The former taps a sense of personal inadequacy; the latter, a sense of system unresponsiveness.

8. Arthur T. Hadley, *The Empty Polling Booth* (Prentice-Hall, 1978).

Hadley, response to this question powerfully discriminates between voters and nonvoters who are at the same socioeconomic or demographic level.

Overall, a survey research perspective suggests that affective relationships to the larger political world interact with other predictors to shape the respondent's decision to vote or abstain. As American surveys have regularly documented, turnout levels also fall—quite precipitously these days—with education levels, and these remain among all the socioeconomic indicators the best predictors of voting and nonvoting.[9] Although there are many nuances that this brief survey cannot capture, a person of low formal education is relatively likely to have weak party identification and a very low cognitive capacity—little information and little sign of ability or willingness to respond to political stimuli on any significant level of issue conceptualization, much less ideology.

All this is well enough known. Equally so is the fact that in other advanced capitalist democracies things work very differently. For example, in Italy in the late 1960s, "mass" respondents viewed the party landscape in ways very similar to the perspectives of party activists and elites.[10] They were in the same story, as they notoriously often are not in the United States.[11] It seems too that in the European context, party identification works differently, so that when an individual decides to shift voting from one party to another, identification tends to change as well.[12] Party identification thus seems to be much more instrumentally viewed by the individual and much less a matter of general affect and family-transmitted social identity than is the case in the United States. Finally, in countries like Italy or Sweden, turnouts basically do not vary along lines of formal education. With a general participation rate in the high 80s or

9. See the classic survey study, Angus Campbell and others, *The American Voter* (Wiley, 1960), especially pp. 475–81. Compare also Philip E. Converse's analysis, "The Nature of Belief Systems in Mass Publics," in David E. Apter, ed., *Ideology and Discontent* (Free Press, 1964).

10. Samuel H. Barnes, *Representation in Italy: Institutionalized Tradition and Electoral Choice* (University of Chicago Press, 1977), especially pp. 97–115. For some similar findings about Spain's "new democracy," see Juan J. Linz, "The New Spanish Party System," in Richard Rose, ed., *Electoral Participation: A Comparative Analysis* (Beverly Hills: Sage, 1980), pp. 101–89.

11. The classic expression of this is Donald E. Stokes, "Spatial Models of Party Competition," in Angus Campbell and others, *Elections and the Political Order* (Wiley, 1966), pp. 161–79.

12. See David Butler and Donald E. Stokes, *Political Change in Britain* (London: Macmillan, 1969), pp. 23–43.

more, this would have to be so in any case. This suggests that a population with a mean formal-education level of six to nine years gets politically educated and involved through means other than the schools. The key intervening factor is clearly the party system, including the capacity of the parties (along with other organizations) to act as political educators and mobilizers.

The second major "school" was essentially founded by Anthony Downs and to a degree by V. O. Key, Jr.[13] It has now ramified and expanded through the literature on "retrospective voting," which has considerable overlap with public-choice theory.[14] The assumptions of this school are essentially those of neoclassical capitalist economics as translated into the realm of politics. They are in a sense the polar opposite of survey research perspectives rooted in the discipline of social psychology. The individual is viewed in this model as a social atom or monad, whose basic motivation is rational utility maximization.

This reductionist view has obvious shortcomings, but it has analytic power too. It focuses analytic attention squarely on the organization of the electoral market by political entrepreneurs and on the individual's capacity to arrive at a rational judgment as to how maximum utilities are to be achieved through voting. Under conditions of imperfect information, it is parties, party ideologies, images, and promises that provide the necessary nexus for such calculations. As Downs suggests, elites in a two-party system have considerable electoral incentive to converge toward each other, blurring their appeals, and, in doing so, making it harder for individuals to calculate utility differentials between them. In a multiparty system, on the other hand, politicians' incentives are served best by getting out every last voter they can find in their specialized clientele, rather than by attempting to woo "swing voters" at the center—for there is no center, at least of the convergent two-party type.[15] This should produce

13. Anthony Downs, *An Economic Theory of Democracy* (Harper, 1957); and V. O. Key, Jr., *The Responsible Electorate* (Harvard University Press, 1966).

14. The most comprehensive and elegant statement thus far is Morris P. Fiorina, *Retrospective Voting in American National Elections* (Yale University Press, 1981).

15. One can easily imagine a *U*-shaped distribution in a two-party system that would produce similar incentives for competitive mobilization rather than outreach to a (largely nonexistent) "swing vote." The Civil War party system seems to have produced a number of such cases—perhaps most notably in Indiana. See Melvyn Hammarberg, *The Indiana Voter: The Historical Dynamics of Party Allegiance during the 1870s* (University of Chicago Press, 1977), especially pp. 27–35; and also V. O. Key, Jr., and Frank Munger, "Social Determinism and Electoral Decision: The Case of Indiana," in Frank Munger and Douglas

maximum clarity on issues for voters during the election period and thus, one would anticipate, extremely high normal turnouts—as indeed one usually finds in such electoral systems. On the other hand, the coalition governments that often result from bargaining after the election will deliver far less to any given voting group than "its" party originally promised.

More recently, studies based on survey materials have argued for the presence of a strong component of retrospective voting, that is, voting based on positive or negative judgments about the records of the two parties. This approach was pioneered by V. O. Key, Jr., who argued that there was a sharp analytic difference between weak party identifiers and people who switch their vote from election to election. In recent years the discussion has been extended further, notably by Morris Fiorina, who demonstrates the existence of a powerful element of retrospective judgment in voting, but stresses that for such judgments to be rational sharply identified and responsible parties are necessary:

> What is the future of party identification in a system where each officeholder bears responsibility only for his individual actions, where the actions themselves are differentiated by office? There is none. No party will receive the credits or demerits in the individual's calculus, because the parties become too inchoate to be the focus of evaluations and because the nominal members of either become unable to govern successfully.[16]

Neither Key nor Fiorina discusses changes in voting and abstention in this context; but the argument is certainly implicit, and is made explicitly and extensively in Downs's analyses of the causes and effects of rational abstention.[17] Ultimately, all abstention in this model arises when the citi-

---

Price, eds., *Readings in Political Parties and Pressure Groups* (Crowell, 1964), pp. 366–84. Politics in this state between 1868 and 1900 or so had striking structural similarities to certain properties of contemporary multiparty systems. Electoral swings were usually tiny from year to year, and the state typically had presidential year turnouts well above 90 percent of the eligible electorate. Campaign styles sometimes in vogue at that time can be appreciated by a well-known comment by Republican Governor (and later U.S. Senator) Oliver P. Morton: "The Democratic party is the common sewer and loathsome receptacle of mankind. While it may be true that not every Democrat is a traitor, every traitor is a Democrat."

16. Fiorina, *Retrospective Voting*, pp. 210–11.
17. Downs, *Economic Theory of Democracy*, pp. 260–76.

zen can discern no utility difference at all among the rival candidates or parties. The larger the abstention rate, the greater the number of citizens whose search for utilities has been baffled or thwarted by the organization of the electoral market. Thus under this model turnout is closely and sensitively related to the nature and capacities of parties and other entrepreneurial organizers of electoral politics. The kind of situation described by Fiorina—the breakup of electoral coalitions along office-specific lines and the rise of personalistic incentives to replace team incentives—should therefore be systemically associated with a persistent rise of the "party of nonvoters." As I will show in detail below, this is exactly what has occurred over the past generation.

To summarize, there is accumulating evidence that American citizens respond to politics both affectively and instrumentally—that is, both through social-psychological dispositions and through efforts at rational pursuit of personal objectives through voting. Politicians well understand that the public is a "rational god of vengeance and reward" and do what they can to make major election years times of peace and prosperity.[18]

The political information on which voters base their instrumental decisions is, however, significantly limited and shaped by a number of factors. These include, at the least, the comparatively defective mobilizing and educating capacities of today's American major parties (especially the Democrats); certain important and recent transformations of the electoral market and its organization; and the relative absence in American culture of socially solidaristic traditions of the kind that commonly exist in other countries. In a class society with no true Left, the extent to which relevant political information is present or missing is very strongly arrayed along class lines.[19] In this kind of context, one should anticipate that people who believe their lives are dominated by chance and most people who have a low sense of external political efficacy will be concentrated toward the bottom of the class structure. Absence of a genuine Left also leads to

18. Edward R. Tufte, *Political Control of the Economy* (Princeton University Press, 1978). The "political business cycle" literature has grown to vast proportions since Tufte wrote. See, for example, David R. Cameron, "The Politics and Economics of the Business Cycle," in Thomas Ferguson and Joel D. Rogers, eds., *The Political Economy: Readings in the Politics and Economics of American Public Policy* (Armonk, N.Y.: M. E. Sharpe, 1984), pp. 237–62.

19. Philip E. Converse, "The Nature of Belief Systems in Mass Publics," in David E. Apter, ed., *Ideology and Discontent* (Free Press, 1964).

political parties that lack the educative and mobilizing functions found in the major parties of other advanced capitalist democracies. This deficiency generally makes the individual's calculation of utilities more difficult than in other systems. The lower the social class, one should anticipate, the greater this difficulty will be.

Dynamically, then, the more electoral politics offers a choice between contending collective wills and engages the public in collective decisions of both psychological and instrumental importance to many individuals, the higher the turnout rate will be, and the less class skew there will be in participation. When these conditions are approximated today, as in Sweden, Italy, and other countries, this is true. Most accounts of critical realignment in American political history also stress that one of the leading criteria of realignment is a major expansion of participation among the electorate. It is at such times that polarization on some collective issue of fundamental importance occurs and potential voters have the greatest incentives to come to the polls and participate in the collective decision.[20]

Effect of Electoral Rules on Turnout

Before filling in the details of this picture, it will be well to consider a related subject that has received an enormous amount of attention: the influence of the rules of the electoral game on participation. No one can doubt that rules of the game have major effects on electoral behavior (including abstention as a form of behavior). These effects are broadly of two types.

One flows from the rules through which votes are translated into political power. Very broadly, these rules can be divided into the system of election by simple plurality from single-member constituencies on the one

---

20. Two general accounts of realignment and party-system dynamics are Walter Dean Burnham, *Critical Elections and the Mainsprings of American Politics* (Norton, 1970); and James A. Sundquist, *Dynamics of the Party System: Alignment and Realignment of Political Parties in the United States,* rev. ed. (Brookings, 1983). With the exception of the New Deal realignment sequence, literature that specifically and empirically explores turnout dynamics in these crises is much less abundant than it should be. See Kristi Andersen, "Generation, Partisan Shift and Realignment: A Glance Back to the New Deal," in Norman Nie, Sidney Verba, and John R. Petrocik, *The Changing American Voter,* 2d ed. (Harvard University Press, 1979), pp. 74–95.

hand and various proportional-representation systems on the other.[21] There is a generally marked relationship between systems and turnouts outside the United States. On average, systems with proportional-representation elements have contemporary participation rates that fluctuate around 85 percent on average, while the mean turnout for single-member constituency systems is about 10 to 15 percentage points lower (see table 5-1).

If one considers that proportional-representation systems by definition come close to eliminating "wasted votes" and are also associated with multiple parties that optimize voters' utility calculations, this differential should not be surprising. Great Britain has a classic "first-past-the-post" electoral regime. Although it now has three major partisan contenders, the third force, the Alliance, lacks a solid geographical base and therefore gets practically no seats for the nearly one-quarter of the popular vote it wins at the polls. Thus in 1983 it required about 33,000 votes to elect a Conservative, 40,000 to elect a Labourite, and 338,000 to elect an Alliance member of Parliament. The turnout in that election was 72.7 percent of the potential electorate; it surely would have been considerably higher (and the Alliance vote higher too, in all probability) if the election rules had been governed by proportional representation.

The United States, of course, has single-member constituencies. The "wasted vote" constraint is heavily reinforced at the national level by multiple-member, at-large slates of presidential electors elected by simple plurality. Moreover, unlike the situation in Britain, Canada, or elsewhere, many legislative seats are often unopposed by a second major-party candidate—some 72 of the 435 U.S. House seats in 1986, for example, and considerably more than an absolute majority of seats in both houses of the current Massachusetts legislature. Obviously, this negatively affects turnout. But there is something else too. Former House Speaker Thomas P. O'Neill commented not long ago that in any other country the Democrats would be four or five parties and the Republicans two or three. The fact that the vastly complex United States offers only two significant parties no doubt also increases the number of potential voters who can find no useful

21. A short but classic study is Douglas Rae, *The Political Consequences of Electoral Laws* (Yale University Press, 1967). The late Stein Rokkan produced a multitude of first-rate work on this topic and its relationship to the historical mobilization of social and geographical peripheries into the active electorate. See in particular his *Citizens, Elections, and Parties: Approaches to the Comparative Study of the Processes of Development* (David McKay, 1970), pp. 145–247.

Table 5-1. *Voter Participation Rates in Selected Countries, by Type of Electoral System*
Percent

Electoral system and country	Period	Valid voting rate[a]
Compulsory voting		
Belgium	1971–85	85.9
Luxembourg	1968–79	83.7
Italy[b]	1972–83	87.9
Mean	. . .	85.8
Proportional representation or election by district with runoff		
Austria[c]	1971–83	91.5
Denmark	1971–84	86.3
Finland	1970–83	78.3
France		
Parliament	1973–86	76.4
President	1974–81	84.8
West Germany	1972–83	89.1
Greece	1974–85	78.9
Iceland	1971–83	88.4
Ireland	1973–82	74.5
Israel	1973–84	77.8
Netherlands	1971–86	84.2
Norway	1973–85	82.2
Portugal	1975–85	80.7
Spain	1977–86	72.6
Sweden	1970–85	90.0
Switzerland	1971–83	51.0
Mean	. . .	82.8[d]
Election by district, plurality on one ballot		
Canada	1972–84	72.6
Japan	1972–83	70.3
United Kingdom	1970–87	74.6
Mean	. . .	72.5
United States		
Presidential	1972–84	55.5
Off-year	1974–86	39.4

Sources: Inter-Parliamentary Union, *Chronicle of Parliamentary Elections and Developments*, vols. 10–20 (Geneva: International Centre for Parliamentary Documentation, 1975–86), and other sources in the public domain.

a. Because only the valid vote is universally reported in the United States, that is the figure given here for all countries.

b. Voting is not compulsory, but nonvoting is noted on individuals' documents.

c. Voting is compulsory in several states making up about one-fourth of the country's electorate.

d. Excluding the anomalous case of Switzerland.

ɛ for their purposes between parties.[22] Still, even though much ɔe said in the abstract for introducing proportional representation ɔongressional elections, no such thing is likely to happen soon.

The second broad effect of rules comes through those that control access by citizens to the ballot box, in particular, the uniquely American requirement of personal registration as preliminary to voting. The literature on this and related issues is truly enormous and can hardly be touched upon here. It is enough to note that first-rate empirical work has demonstrated that personal registration systematically reduces turnout. All other things being equal, the participation rate would go up about 10 percent if an enrollment system were adopted where the state rather than the individual bore the responsibility, as in Canada or Britain.[23] It is also known that much depends on what kind of registration system is employed. Some, such as the periodic reregistration requirement used in New York City from 1911 to 1957, or cutting off registration on January 31 of the election year as Texas attempted in the 1960s, are much more burdensome on voters than others.[24]

Historically, American elections were by today's standards extremely informal affairs. In most of the nineteenth century parties printed ballots, and access to the ballot box was legally unconstrained. But reform flowed as society became more complex and anonymous, and as issues of fraud became important to a changing middle-class culture. Thus, with adoption of the Australian ballot in the early 1890s, parties lost their monopoly over

22. But specific historical context seems to be, if not all the story, then most of it. Although the basic electoral system in the United States has been one of its most stable political characteristics, presidential-year turnouts outside the South regularly exceeded 80 percent of the estimated potential electorate from 1876 through 1900 (see table 5-3).

23. Wolfinger and Rosenstone, *Who Votes?* pp. 61–88, provide an extensive discussion of the effect of registration laws on turnout. Their estimate is that if all states had registration laws as permissive as the most permissive states, turnout in 1972 would have been 9.1 percent higher than it actually was. I concluded in a 1978 study that the depressant impact of personal registration on turnout lay between 8 and 10 percent in 1960–76. See Walter Dean Burnham, "The Appearance and Disappearance of the American Voter," in Burnham, *The Current Crisis in American Politics* (Oxford University Press, 1982), pp. 139–40.

24. The classic statement of this point is Stanley Kelley, Jr., Richard E. Ayres, and William G. Bowen, "Registration and Voting: Putting First Things First," *American Political Science Review*, vol. 61 (June 1967), pp. 359–79. The 1966 Texas statute, properly labeled by critics as the old poll-tax law with the poll tax left out, occasioned litigation: *Beare* v. *Smith*, 32 F. Supp. 1100 (S.D. Tex. 1971). The case is discussed in Walter Dean Burnham, "A Political Scientist and Voting-Rights Litigation: The Case of the 1966 Texas Registration Statute," *Washington University Law Quarterly* (1971), pp. 335–58.

the printing and distribution of ballots. Personal registration statutes came into vogue during the Progressive era a decade or so later. Voter lists were needed, especially in large anonymous urban environments, and personal registration was one way of getting them. Personal registration as an institution continues to be supported by public opinion for two reasons: adoption of state enrollment seems to be regarded as somehow "un-American" (though Canadians live with it well enough); and sensitivity to the potential for fraud—for example, in schemes that permit registration on the day of election—remains quite high.

All rules of the game have explicit or implicit political purposes and assumptions. As more is known about the effect of personal-registration statutes on shaping who votes and who does not, its differential class effects become more evident and its defense becomes more explicitly— though even today, not very openly stated—a class-linked political choice. Much rhetoric discusses the citizen's "right to vote." But in fact, there always have been a substantial number of Americans who have believed that voting is not a right but a privilege for which individuals must demonstrate their worthiness.[25]

It has been evident for some time that conservatives are less disposed than liberals to making it easier for people to register, though this is by no means a clear-cut partisan issue. Reformers, recognizing that personal registration retains commanding support in American culture, have exercised much ingenuity in finding ways to reduce the effects of this socially differential legal burden on the franchise. Since 1960 there has been substantial relaxation of registration and residence requirements.[26] At the

---

25. In the *Beare* opinion, Judge Singleton summarized the position advanced by Texas's attorney general: "One such interest suggested by the state as compelling . . . is the purity of the ballot. In other words, the state contends that those who overcome the annual hurdle of registering at a time remote to the fall elections will more likely be better informed and have greater capabilities of making an intelligent choice than those who do not care enough to register." (321 F. Supp. at 1106.) This is, in a word, the old *melior pars* argument common to conservative thought in the seventeenth and eighteenth centuries. Elsewhere, such arguments and perspectives simply do not exist and have not for the past fifty to a hundred years. Here they persist, and the result is a remarkably opaque but very persistent struggle over the franchise—perhaps what one could expect from a political system in some ways so archaic and undeveloped that Samuel P. Huntington has aptly labeled it a "Tudor polity." Samuel P. Huntington, *Political Order in Changing Societies* (Yale University Press, 1968), chap. 2.

26. The Civil Rights Act of 1965 lowered the minimum residence requirement for voting in presidential elections to thirty days, recognizing that this is a country whose population is very physically mobile. A number of states (for example, Minnesota and

same time, there has been among the American electorate a vast upgrading of levels of formal education—a factor usually held to be closely and positively related to participation. In 1964, 19.5 percent of the electorate had at least some college-level education; twenty years later, this figure had risen to 35.0 percent.[27] Conventional wisdom of either the Downsian or survey research schools would predict that the American participation rate should have accordingly increased, not only in the southern quarter of the country, which was specially affected by the Voting Rights Act of 1965 (discussed in chapter 6), but also in the nonsouthern parts as well. If the marginal costs of voting have been reduced, the marginal propensity to vote should go up, all other things being equal. By the same token, a better-educated electorate should vote more, if the significance of the formal-education variable has been properly specified. Obviously, all other things have not been equal. Turnout rates outside the South declined in presidential years from 72.8 percent of eligibles in 1960 to 57.8 percent in 1984 (a loss of more than one-fifth of the 1960 base) and in off-years from 56.8 percent in 1962 to 39.0 percent in 1986 (a loss of nearly one-third of the 1962 base).

It is easy to speak in terms of percentages (though far less easy to derive them). One should not lose sight of the fact that in a country with a large population these percentages convert into millions of individuals. There is no better way of getting some sense of the absolute magnitude of the "hole" that exists in today's American electorate than by looking at the raw numbers of what voting would be under various assumptions (see table 5-2). Such measures are obviously crude and subject to various estimation errors, but they give a rough statement of what American turnouts are today and what they might be (or might have been) under other empirical conditions. Long ago, using more sophisticated techniques, I concluded that no more than one-third of the nonsouthern turnout

---

Maine) have adopted election-day registration, which practically abolishes the requirement and, for that matter, the electoral list. Others have drastically simplified the procedures, for example, by adopting drivers' license or postcard registration. As of this writing, a detailed analysis of reforms and their estimated consequences for the turnout rate is being generated by the Committee for the Study of the American Electorate. This document will provide a full survey of the diverse legal terrain affecting access to the ballot box in the fifty states.

27. These figures are derived from U.S. Bureau of the Census, *Current Population Reports,* series P-20, no. 143, "Voter Participation in the National Election: November 1964" (Government Printing Office, 1965); and no. 405, "Voting and Registration in the Election of November 1984" (GPO, 1986).

Table 5-2. *Actual Voter Turnout and Hypothetical Additions to the Voting Population, under Various Assumptions, Total United States and Outside the South, 1984 and 1986*
Voters in millions

Assumption	Turnout rate[a]	Voters	Nonvoters	Additional voters under assumption
Total United States				
1984				
Actual turnout	55.2	92.7	75.1	. . .
Actual turnout plus 10 percent for easier registration	65.2	109.4	58.4	16.7
Turnout if same rate as 1896	82.6	138.6	29.2	45.9
Turnout if same rate as 1960	62.5	104.8	62.9	12.2
Turnout if same rate as 1960 plus 5 percent for more education and easier registration	67.5	113.2	54.5	20.6
1986				
Actual turnout	37.6	64.7	107.2	. . .
Actual turnout plus 10 percent for easier registration	47.6	81.8	90.0	17.1
Turnout if same rate as 1894	68.8	118.2	53.6	53.6
Turnout if same rate as 1962	49.2	84.6	87.3	19.9
Turnout if same rate as 1962 plus 5 percent for more education and easier registration	54.2	93.1	78.7	28.5
Outside the South				
1984				
Actual turnout	57.8	69.7	50.9	. . .
Actual turnout plus 10 percent for easier registration	67.8	81.6	38.8	12.1
Turnout if same rate as 1896	86.2	103.9	16.6	34.3
Turnout if same rate as 1960	72.8	87.8	32.8	18.1
Turnout if same rate as 1960 plus 5 percent for more education and easier registration	77.8	93.8	26.8	24.1
1986				
Actual turnout	39.0	48.1	75.4	. . .
Actual turnout plus 10 percent for easier registration	49.0	60.5	63.0	12.4
Turnout if same rate as 1894	74.0	91.4	32.1	43.3
Turnout if same rate as 1962	56.8	70.2	53.4	22.0
Turnout if same rate as 1962 plus 5 percent for more education and easier registration	61.8	76.4	47.2	28.2

Source: Underlying data in tables 5-1 and 5-3, as projected onto potential U.S. citizen electorate in 1984 and 1986.
a. Estimates of potential electorate for these calculations are based on citizen voting-age population, not total, since aliens are not permitted to register or vote in the United States.

decline between 1900 and 1930 could be accounted for by changes in the
rules of the game.[28] Much the same figure is suggested by this array.

Turnout before 1960

The broad contours of voting participation in American elections across
the country's history are now pretty well known. As my focus here is on
contemporary American elections, my remarks on pre-1960 history will be
of a very summary kind.

Table 5-3 presents the entire array of election turnouts for the country
outside the South, the South, and the country as a whole from 1788 to the
present. In the first decade of the republic under the present Constitution,
participation by adult males, almost always white, ranged as a rule between one-fifth and one-quarter of the potential electorate. In an age
characterized by a "deferential-participant political culture" and a complete absence of political parties, this was what one might expect.[29]

Presidential elections were not democratized until the arrival of Andrew
Jackson on the scene in 1828. As late as 1824, no fewer than six of the
twenty-four states in the Union still chose their presidential electors
through the state legislatures. Even where electors were chosen by popular
vote, turnout was always less than for major state offices in the same
period.[30] Participation in elections for other offices during the 1800–26

28. Walter Dean Burnham, "Theory and Voting Research: Some Reflections on Converse's 'Change in the American Electorate,'" *American Political Science Review*, vol. 68
(September 1974), pp. 1002–23. See also Kleppner, *Who Voted?* p. 62, where he concludes,
"Personal-registration requirements accounted for between 30 and 40 percent of the turnout
decrement in the counties in which they were in force." The other two-thirds, obviously,
finds a much more directly political explanation.

29. Ronald P. Formisano, "Deferential-Participant Politics: The Early Republic's Political Culture, 1789–1840," *American Political Science Review*, vol. 68 (June 1974), pp.
473–87. See also his "Federalists and Republicans: Parties, Yes—System, No" in Paul
Kleppner and others, *The Evolution of American Electoral Systems* (Greenwood, 1981), pp.
113–46.

30. In many respects, the first presidential election that the Inter-University Consortium
for Political and Social Research archive and most others report, 1824, belongs to the
preceding political order and not to the Jacksonian period that followed. Not only did six
states lack popular choice for presidential electors, but the election involved four individuals
(J. Q. Adams, Jackson, Crawford, and Clay) who all at the time claimed allegiance to the
same "party." It is thus hardly surprising that the turnout rate for this election in the states
where there was popular election was only 26.7 percent, considerably below the 1812
figure.

Table 5-3. *Voter Turnout Rates, by Region and Total United States,*
1789-1986
Percent

Year	Outside the South	South	Total United States	Year[a]	Outside the South	South	Total United States
Presidential election years				Off-years			
1789	11.0	13.5	11.4	1790	n.a.	n.a.	21.1
1792	n.a.	n.a.	2.6	1794	n.a.	n.a.	27.7
1796	n.a.	n.a.	20.4	1798	34.5	35.8	34.6
1800	39.2	28.0	31.4	1802	43.7	57.2	44.2
1804	28.7	11.9	25.3	1806	47.7	37.9	47.3
1808	43.0	17.8	36.9	1810	48.6	49.0	48.6
1812	47.1	17.8	41.6	1814	50.1	75.7	51.5
1816	26.8	8.3	20.5	1818	41.4	77.7	44.5
1820	12.0	3.8	9.8	1822	46.4	56.2	47.2
1824	26.5	27.4	26.7	1826	42.4	67.8	45.7
1828	62.8	42.6	57.3	1830	53.7	72.3	57.5
1832	64.2	30.1	56.7	1834	63.3	61.7	63.0
1836	58.5	49.2	56.5	1838	69.5	62.5	67.9
1840	81.6	75.4	80.3	1842	63.7	64.6	63.9
1844	80.3	74.2	79.0	1846	59.7	58.3	59.4
1848	74.0	68.2	72.8	1850	61.4	58.9	60.9
1852	72.1	59.5	69.5	1854	64.2	75.8	66.5
1856	82.3	67.9	79.4	1858	69.3	66.9	68.9
1860	83.1	76.5	81.8	1862	63.0	n.a.	63.0
1864	76.3	n.a.	76.3	1866	71.7	51.5	71.1
1868	82.8	71.6	80.9	1870	67.3	68.7	67.7
1872	73.7	67.0	72.1	1874	66.1	64.1	65.6
1876	85.0	75.1	82.6	1878	70.4	50.3	65.6
1880	85.5	65.1	80.6	1882	70.0	57.5	67.0
1884	83.1	63.3	78.3	1886	70.5	52.3	66.2
1888	85.5	64.2	80.5	1890	70.3	50.1	65.7
1892	80.7	59.4	75.9	1894	74.0	51.2	68.8
1896	86.2	57.6	79.7	1898	68.5	40.2	62.0
1900	82.6	43.5	73.7	1902	66.2	26.8	57.2
1904	76.5	29.0	65.5	1906	62.9	22.0	53.6
1908	76.1	30.7	65.7	1910	62.6	24.1	53.8
1912	67.7	27.8	59.0	1914	61.4	21.3	52.9
1916	69.1	31.7	61.8	1918	48.4	15.9	42.2
1920[b]	57.3	21.7	49.3	1922[b]	44.7	13.5	37.7
1924	57.5	19.0	48.9	1926	42.5	9.7	35.2

Table 5-3 *(continued)*
Percent

Year	Outside the South	South	Total United States	Year[a]	Outside the South	South	Total United States
	Presidential election years				Off-years		
1928	66.7	22.5	56.9	1930	46.7	13.4	39.4
1932	66.2	24.5	57.0	1934	56.3	13.6	46.8
1936	71.4	25.0	61.0	1938	59.3	11.8	48.7
1940	72.9	26.5	62.5	1942	43.7	8.4	35.7
1944	65.1	24.5	55.9	1946	48.6	10.9	40.0
1948	61.8	25.0	53.4	1950	54.0	13.3	44.6
1952	71.4	38.4	63.8	1954	53.0	16.8	44.6
1956	69.2	36.6	61.6	1958	55.0	16.1	45.9
1960	72.8	41.4	65.4	1962	56.8	24.9	49.2
1964	68.6	46.4	63.3	1966	55.5	33.5	49.3
1968	65.7	51.8	62.3	1970	52.4	36.0	48.4
1972[c]	61.1	45.1	57.1	1974[c]	43.8	27.3	39.5
1976	57.9	47.5	55.2	1978	42.0	30.6	39.0
1980	56.6	48.1	54.3	1982	44.9	33.0	41.6
1984	57.8	48.7	55.2	1986	39.0	34.2	37.6

Sources: These estimates are based on underlying population and election data of varying quality and completeness. The population-denominator files represent the best estimates available. I have not found returns for any office in some states between 1789 and about 1820, but such cases form only a minority of the whole country. Federal census material is problematic as a source before 1860 and very much so before 1840. It can often by supplemented, however, by better state-level information, such as state censuses like New York's or lists of taxables (males twenty and over) in Pennsylvania from 1790 to 1841. While I attempt a little more precision than this, it is roughly correct to estimate for the 1790–1830 period that adult white males constitute about one-fifth of the entire population at any given time. From 1870 on, the definition of eligibles, in addition to race and gender (where relevant by state before 1920), excludes aliens in those states where they were (or became) ineligible to vote. From 1924 on, this ban extended to the entire country. Since the alien component of the voting-age population was particularly large in many states between 1890 and 1930, a reasonably accurate picture of the potentially eligible electorate requires excluding it. The estimates used here converge pretty closely for the very early period with the work of Robert J. Dinkin; see his *Voting in Provincial America* (Greenwood, 1977), and *Voting in Revolutionary America* (Greenwood, 1982). A more general treatment of the issues in constructing these estimates is Walter Dean Burnham, "Those High Nineteenth-Century American Voting Turnouts: Fact or Fiction?" *Journal of Interdisciplinary History*, vol. 16 (Spring 1986), pp. 613–44.

n.a. Not available.

a. Before 1880 congressional elections were spread out across almost an entire year, rather than being held on the same day. I have calculated each state's potential electorate in a given year during the period from 1789 until 1880 and then aggregated it to a regional or national total.

b. General women's suffrage was introduced in 1920.

c. The vote was extended to eighteen-year-olds in 1971.

period, on the other hand, expanded substantially to almost one-half of the potential. In this period—marked, in Ronald Formisano's phrase, by parties but *not* by a party system—there was considerable difference between the scale of voter participation in states with established "standing orders," as in New England, and that in the robustly democratic states of the "new frontier" like Kentucky, Tennessee, and Georgia.

The period 1828–40 was marked by the creation of the institutional vehicles through which de Tocqueville's "democracy in America" was given political expression. The entrepreneurial, mobilizing, and entertainment functions of parties and election campaigns in this era—indeed from then on throughout the nineteenth century—form a commonplace theme for historians' writings. Participation surged forward in two stages. The first, from 1828 through 1836, brought national presidential turnouts of about 57 percent. The second, culminating in the 1840 "Tippecanoe and Tyler Too" election, saw the creation of the Whig party and the full nationalization of party competition. The off-year congressional election of 1838–39 showed a national turnout rate of about 68 percent (10 points higher than in any of the three preceding presidential contests and fully 30 points higher than in 1986). In 1840 the turnout rate surged to one of its all-time highs, 80.3 percent in the country, and 81.6 percent in the nonsouthern states.

Important but marginal ups and downs occurred thereafter. The most significant of these grew out of the Civil War crisis and its aftermath. The period 1860–96 witnessed, by common consent, the historic apex of political parties, especially the Republicans, as articulators of collective will, mobilizers of voters, and, particularly during the crisis proper, effective organizers of governmental power and performance. This achievement was supported by a political culture that was intensely and enthusiastically partisan. One should hardly be surprised that the mean nonsouthern presidential turnout between 1856 and 1896 was 82.2 percent, with an all-time high of 86.2 percent reached in the critical election of 1896; or that the mean 1858–94 off-year turnout rate outside the former Confederate states was 69.3 percent.

The South presents a strikingly different picture. Before secession in 1860–61, the South's electorate was only somewhat less participant than that outside this region. Until the political crisis of the 1850s, it had competitive party politics. Secession brought a new government that was nonpartisan by design. Eric McKitrick some years ago analyzed the consequences of this arrangement in a seminal comparative study of Union and Confederate politics in wartime.[31] His main conclusion was that lack of parties in the Confederacy, by releasing Madisonian "ambition pitted against ambition," made a significant contribution to its eventual destruction.

Two points related to McKitrick's essay can be mentioned. First, voting

31. Eric L. McKitrick, "Party Politics and the Union and Confederate War Efforts," in William N. Chambers and Walter Dean Burnham, eds., *The American Party Systems: Stages of Political Development,* 2d ed. (Oxford University Press, 1975), pp. 117–51.

participation collapsed in the Confederacy's nonpartisan elections, especially in voting for Congress, eventually reaching levels not far removed from those of the country as a whole in the 1790s or in Southern primaries in the 1920s.[32] Second, it is of course through the political revolution of the 1860s and southern white reaction to it that the South's long-term deviation from the rest of the country across the next century became firmly established. With the semiviolent termination of Reconstruction, southern turnouts fell sharply in two distinct steps. The first of these, during the "redemption era," partially crippled the southern Republicans, partially disfranchised blacks, and produced a mean regional participation rate of 61.9 percent in presidential elections (1880–96) and 52.3 percent in off-year elections (1878–94). Thereafter, in the wake of the Populist uprising, the "Great Disfranchisements," aimed at blacks but including many whites as well, were carried out. By the early twentieth century, the presidential-year and off-year averages had fallen to 29.8 percent (1904–16) and 22.0 percent (1902–18). They were to fall still further following the enfranchisement of women, hitting all-time presidential-year and off-year lows of 19.0 percent (1924) and 8.4 percent (1942). Particularly in off-year elections, the region's participation rate was not thereafter to climb much from these abysmal depths until the 1960s.

The vast voter demobilization that developed in the long generation after 1896 in the nonsouthern parts of the country has been discussed in detail elsewhere.[33] All that can be affirmed here—in the wake of extensive controversy—is that the high nineteenth century turnouts were real, and not artifacts of either overwhelming census error or universal ballot box stuffing.[34] By the same token, the demobilizations of the early twentieth century were also real and increasingly class-skewed.[35]

32. A discussion of these Confederate data is to be found in Walter Dean Burnham, "Elections as Democratic Institutions," in Kay L. Schlozman, ed., *Elections in America* (Allen and Unwin, 1987), pp. 37–43.

33. See Kleppner, *Who Voted?* For an earlier discussion, see Walter Dean Burnham, "The Changing Shape of the American Political Universe," *American Political Science Review*, vol. 59 (March 1965), pp. 7–28. Kleppner has just published his comprehensive treatment of the "system of 1896": *Continuity and Change in Electoral Politics, 1893–1928* (Greenwood, 1987).

34. See Burnham, "Theory and Voting Research," and the attendant discussion. A more recent and explicit explanation of the considerations that entered into my estimates is Walter Dean Burnham, "Those High Nineteenth-Century American Voting Turnouts: Fact or Fiction?" *Journal of Interdisciplinary History*, vol. 16 (Spring 1986), pp. 613–44.

35. Sources previously cited strongly imply this, and some parts of the pattern are visible in figures 1 and 2 below. A qualitative discussion of this era, heavily based on

Specific technical and historical explanations for this major increase in the nonvoting pool are many and varied. Several factors were clearly at work to produce it. For one thing, the extreme sectionalism produced by the "colony-metropole" cleavages under the "system of 1896" meant that very large parts of the North and West saw less and less genuine party competition in general elections. For another, the cumulative effects of the direct primary reinforced the practical local electoral monopoly of the majority party in many areas.[36] And, it is quite clear, a very large sea change in the political culture occurred around the turn of the century: the collapse of intense partisanship, its replacement by widespread hostility to political parties and political machines, and a parallel shift of campaign styles from the typical militia-drill model of the nineteenth century to the advertising-oriented techniques of the twentieth.[37] The new campaign style was already strongly if marginally evident in the 1904 presidential election. In 1916 Woodrow Wilson's personalistic "he-kept-us-out-of-war" campaign made extensive use of professional advertising techniques. By then, the shift to personality politics had been consummated as far as available mass-media technology and residual cultural lag would allow. Today's politics of the "permanent campaign" thus has much deeper historical roots than is often supposed. It is almost correct to say that since 1916 only the technological resources have undergone basic change.

By the same token, the nineteenth century "state of courts and parties" was already supplemented and increasingly supplanted by a more positive, bureaucratic, and "nonpartisan" state during the first two decades of this century.[38] The transformations here reflect the emergence of a culture oriented toward high mass consumption, which required the development of advertising and survey research of consumer preferences. At the same time, both culture and specific political action during the First World War

---

archival research, suggests some parallels and causes of this demobilization. See Michael E. McGerr, *The Decline of Popular Politics: The American North, 1865–1928* (Oxford University Press, 1986).

36. See chap. 11. The classic discussion of these and other effects of direct primaries (and other state laws) on the integrity of party structure and function is V. O. Key, Jr., *American State Politics* (Knopf, 1956).

37. See the discussion of the transition to "advertised politics" in McGerr, *Decline of Popular Politics,* chap. 6.

38. See Stephen Skowroneck, *Building A New American State: The Expansion of National Administrative Capacities, 1877–1920* (New York and Cambridge: Cambridge University Press, 1982).

contributed to the destruction of a socialist third-party alternative that even in its 1912 heyday was probably not as promising or powerful as it seemed to some at the time.

The "system of 1896" reached the logical culmination of its development in the "normalcy era" of 1920–28. Aided by the enfranchisement of women and their relative lack of incorporation into the active electorate before the New Deal realignment, nationwide presidential-year and off-year turnouts during this decade reached their lowest points in a century or more (48.9 percent of estimated citizen electorate in 1924, 35.2 percent in 1926). Perpetuation of a partisan cleavage that was largely rooted in a "horizontal" polarization between the manufacturing and farming economies, coupled with the absence of a genuine industrial-era Left, provided little incentive for the urban manual-labor workforce to participate in elections.[39] Evidence drawn from analysis of turnout reinforces the view that the ascendancy of corporate capitalism and its preferred political vehicle, the Republican party, was based in very large part upon this socially selective voter demobilization. To a remarkable extent, politics in the 1920s had turned into a politics of oligarchy dressed up in the rhetoric and processes of democracy.[40]

The counterpart to this striking state of political affairs in the 1920s, after the collapse of the capitalist free-market economy, was the New Deal realignment of the 1930s. Nonsouthern turnouts swelled very heavily during the transition, as is so often the case with true electoral realignment. This involved a massive reincorporation—overwhelmingly on the Democratic side—of voters, largely concentrated toward the bottom of the class structure, who had been in the ranks of the "party of nonvoters" in the 1920s. A recent account correctly stresses the vital significance of this

39. See Herbert L. A. Tingsten, *Political Behavior: Studies in Election Statistics* (London: P. S. King, 1937), pp. 156–58. In his analysis of the small city of Delaware, Ohio, in 1924, Tingsten found significantly lower participation rates among industrial workers and by similar socioeconomic differences.

40. This was an issue of direct concern to reformist political scientists of an earlier generation such as Charles E. Merriam and Harold F. Gosnell (see their *Non-Voting, Causes and Methods of Control* [University of Chicago Press, 1924]). See also E. E. Schattschneider, *The Semisovereign People: A Realist's View of Democracy in America* (Holt, Rinehart and Winston, 1960); and his analysis, "United States: The Functional Approach to Party Government," in Sigmund Neumann, ed., *Modern Political Parties* (University of Chicago Press, 1956), pp. 194–215. In the South of this period and for long after, the term *oligarchy* is the only accurate characterization. See V. O. Key, Jr., *Southern Politics in State and Nation* (Knopf, 1949).

conversion of former abstainers into mostly Democratic voters to the building of the New Deal coalition and the political overthrow of the old regime.[41]

Politics in the 1920s, as earlier, had little or no visible sign of class polarization independent of other factors (for example, religion in the 1928 election). By 1940 social-class position had become a powerful explanatory variable. Indeed, the 1940 election looms in retrospect as the most class-polarized election in American political history thus far.[42] By this criterion, one would anticipate finding that the story is more complicated on several fronts than most discussions have indicated. These complications can be seen adequately only by measuring change across the range of alternatives (that is, nonvoting, Democratic, Republican, and other-party shares of the potential electorate). For example, while writers from Samuel Lubell onward have noted the "Al Smith surge" in urban-proletarian (largely Catholic) environments in 1928, most have missed the point that in non-Catholic environments there was at least as large a "Hoover surge." During the 1930s there was a very strong mobilizing surge toward the Democrats among working-class voters, but there was also a noteworthy pro-Republican mobilizing surge, missed by most analysts, within the upper reaches of the social structure.

Two exercises in regression estimation capture some elements of the dynamic picture of voter participation from the early twentieth century through 1960. One is taken from the ward divisions in the city of Pittsburgh and the other from the forty-six cities and towns of eastern Massachusetts that had a population of at least 10,000 in 1940 (see figures 5-1 and 5-2).

---

41. Kristi Andersen, *The Creation of a Democratic Majority: 1928–1936* (University of Chicago Press, 1979). The problem with Andersen's analysis is that it is based upon assumptions that are partially false because they are anachronistic. The "Hoover surge" of 1928 that was so conspicuous in Protestant areas should have made it clear that in pre-New Deal conditions mobilizations among these "potential Democrats" could have led as easily to Republican as to Democratic voting among the new entrants.

42. See the first modern survey of American voters, Paul Lazersfeld and others, *The People's Choice: How the Voter Makes Up His Mind in a Presidential Campaign* (New York: Duell Sloan Pearce, 1944). For further evidence on this point, see Robert R. Alford, *Party and Society: The Anglo-American Democracies* (Rand McNally, 1963), p. 152. It is now commonly understood that the success of the prescientific *Literary Digest* poll from 1908 through 1932 rested on the absence of any autonomous class cleavage in electoral politics, just as the poll's disastrous failure in 1936 reflected the emergence of this fatally decisive variable.

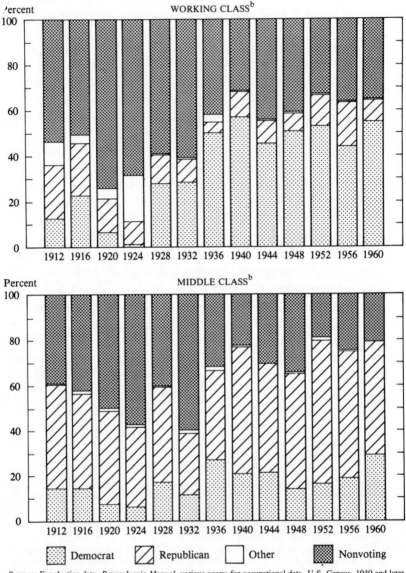

ıre 5-1. *Estimates of Percentage of Potential Electorate Voting and*
ıt Voting, by Class, in Pittsburgh, 1912–60[a]

Percent   WORKING CLASS[b]

Percent   MIDDLE CLASS[b]

   Democrat   Republican   Other   Nonvoting

Sources: For election data, *Pennsylvania Manual*, various years; for occupational data, U.S. Census, 1940 and later years. From 1912 to 1940, the units are twenty-nine election wards; from 1940 to 1960, thirty-two wards. Ward boundaries have remained essentially unchanged, except for additions, since 1912; and each ward contains one or more census tracts that do not cut across ward boundaries. In 1912 the Republican and Progressive shares are summed as Republican.

a. The procedures used are those of simple bivariate regression estimation. The dependent variable is the nonvoting, Democratic, Republican, or other share of the potential electorate. The regression used is based on a linear model of the form $Y = a + bX + e$, where Y is the value of the dependent variable, a is the intercept (the point at which the line derived from the equation crosses the vertical axis), bX is the slope, and e is the error term.

b. As defined by occupational data in the census for 1940 and later years.

Figure 5-2. *Estimates of Percentage of Potential Electorate Voting and Not Voting, by Class, in Boston Area, 1912–60[a]*

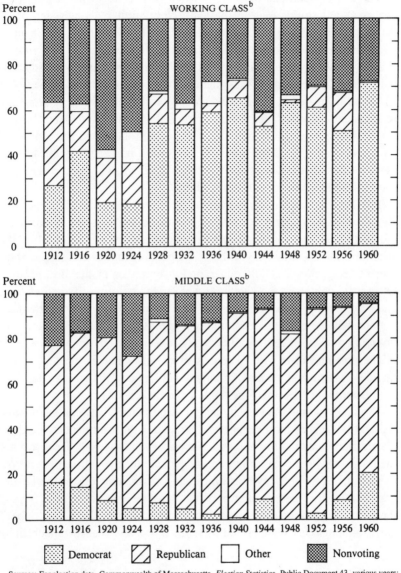

Sources: For election data, Commonwealth of Massachusetts, *Election Statistics*, Public Document 43, various years; for occupational data, U.S. Census, 1940 and later years. The units are forty-six towns comprising all cities in Massachusetts with a 1940 population of 100,000 and above and all towns and cities in the Boston metropolitan area with a 1940 population of 10,000 and above. In 1912 the Republican and Progressive shares are summed as Republican.

a. See figure 1 for explanation of procedures.

b. As defined by occupational data in census for 1940 and later years.

These "sociopolitical maps" from two very different northeastern urban areas tell stories that are basically very similar, though significant details such as response to the stimulus of the Hoover-Smith campaign of 1928 differ quite a bit. In both cases, abstention before the realignment "surge" (1928 in Boston, as late as 1936 in Pittsburgh) is always substantially larger at the working-class than at the middle-class end of the social spectrum.[43] In both cases, there are bilateral mobilizations during the realignment sequence: abstention drops at both ends of the social spectrum, while a powerful Democratic surge occurs at one end and a substantial Republican surge at the other. (In the Boston area, the Republican 91.1 percent of estimated potential vote in hypothetical solid middle-class settings in 1940 represents an all-time high).

But it is also noteworthy that while the class differential in turnout was significantly and enduringly reduced with realignment, it was by no means eliminated. In fact, with competitive mobilizations at each end of the spectrum, the absolute size of the participation gap between top and bottom scarcely closed at all, either in Pittsburgh or in the Boston area. Obviously, politics in the two areas was organized very differently before and after the New Deal realignment. This seems not to matter much at the bottom, where both sets of estimates suggest that the working-class nonvoting floor even in 1940 or 1960 was between one-quarter and one-third of the potential electorate. There is more difference at the top, where middle-class areas show a minimum nonvoting floor of a bit over one-fifth in Pittsburgh, but less than one-tenth in the Boston area.

Even considering the vast numerical disproportion between the relative top and bottom of the occupational structure, the continuation of these class differentials in nonvoting across and beyond the New Deal realignment was nowhere near enough to compensate for the political overthrow created in 1928–40 by mobilizations and conversions toward the Democrats in the lower reaches of society. On the other hand, even in its heyday the party of Franklin Roosevelt was by no means a "Left" or "labor" party, although it was supported by both. It was and is a liberal substitute

43. Predominantly for ethnocultural reasons—the intense antagonism between a largely proletarian Irish Catholic community and a largely middle-class Yankee-Protestant counterpart—partisan competition in the Boston metropolitan area (and Massachusetts as a whole) remained much more robust there than in overwhelmingly Republican Pittsburgh (and Pennsylvania) during the tenure of the "system of 1896." Working-class participation rates tended over time, even in the trough of the 1920s, to be considerably higher in Eastern Massachusetts than in Pittsburgh.

in a polity that does not admit alternatives of that sort. Persistence of the class gap in participation may provide a new reinforcement for this argument.

Selective Demobilization: The Contemporary Situation

American politics since 1960 has gone through changes that, cumulatively, are of almost revolutionary dimensions. These changes extend to all levels of action, from the policy initiatives of the 1980s to the altered foundations of electoral politics. To a striking extent, one can see contemporary parallels to the political situation of the 1920s: conservative and probusiness hegemony; a Democratic opposition, representing the interests of many peripheries against a center and lacking common energizing perspectives and mobilizing capacities; and low, declining, and very skewed voting participation.

At the level of electoral entrepreneurship, the most decisive transformation has been the partial displacement of the parties as organizers of politics by the technologies, operatives, and candidates of what Sidney Blumenthal calls "the permanent campaign."[44] Blumenthal believes that the decisive moment of transition to the new order can be dated to 1968–72, and that this change is momentous enough to be described as a critical realignment in its own right, leading to the current "sixth electoral era." My own view is that he is almost certainly right in this intuitive judgment. The concept of the "permanent campaign" means partial or total dissolution of many of the features of party that are linked to the cognitive reactions of voters: collective identity, a kind of historical memory transmitted through party identification, and long-term collective commitments that permit relatively easy individual calculation of utilities at election time. What is substituted is personalism and a variety of imagistic appeals. "Party" coalitions tend increasingly to break down across the lines of constitutional separation between the executive and legislative branches. This in turn leads to intractable problems of accountability and governability, as a whole chorus of writers has complained.[45]

Inchoate politics, fragmented electoral choices, and personalistic cam-

---

44. Sidney Blumenthal, *The Permanent Campaign*, rev. ed. (Simon and Schuster, 1983).
45. Most recently James L. Sundquist in chap. 9 of this volume.

paign images lead naturally to growth in the number of citizens who have a low sense of their external political efficacy; more citizens who find it difficult or impossible to make a utility calculation different from zero (or perhaps make one at all); and general erosion of the strength of party identification.[46] As politicians' incentives at elections shift more and more to considerations of "every person for himself," the notion of collective will tends to disappear; and so, in a highly selective way, does the active electorate.

Or, more precisely, one should say that "collective will" disappears not across the board, but in a differential way. Long ago, Maurice Duverger argued, "Parties are always more developed on the Left than on the Right, because they are always more necessary on the Left than on the Right."[47] This perfectly valid remark reflects realities of differentials in power and political consciousness in any class society between the better-educated, better-off owning classes on one side and the less-educated, propertyless, and poorer classes beneath them on the other. In modern American political conditions, the electoral vehicle for some of the interests of the latter has been the Democratic party, just as the electoral vehicle for the former has been the Republican. While no one doubts that the Republican party suffers from some internal divisions and even occasional bouts of selective abstention among its supporters (as notably in the 1974 congressional election), the GOP remains much closer to being a true political party in the comparative sense than do today's Democrats. As the Democrats fall apart, and attempt continually to find a way to shift their appeals "upscale" in the information society's evolving structure of classes and strata, it should be no surprise that the post-1960 turnout decline has been concentrated among those who had already participated least in the 1940–60

46. For a current survey-based analysis that stresses this point, see Martin P. Wattenberg, *The Decline of American Political Parties, 1952–1984* (Harvard University Press, 1985). The basic cognitive transformation has been away from a combined positive-negative response (that is, people who like Democrats tend to dislike Republicans and vice versa) to an affective neutral-neutral position. The latter implies that the parties are becoming more and more irrelevant at the level of popular politics. It is of course an open question as to whether the major changes in politics associated with the Reagan years have brought, or may bring, a reversal in these trends. At the moment, the more cautious view seems to be that they have considerably flattened out since 1980.

47. Maurice Duverger, *Political Parties: Their Organization and Activity in the Modern State,* trans. Barbara and Robert North, 2d ed. rev. (Wiley, 1959), p. 426. Except in the United States, of course, where parties are more developed on the Right than on the Left.

period. Predominantly, these are people who, if they had any reason to vote at all, would vote mostly Democratic.

This assertion can be very straightforwardly documented, for the Census Bureau has provided since 1964 survey information that, because of the very large base of respondents, is the most accurate available.[48] Snapshots taken toward the beginning of this series and in 1980 suggest the direction of change in the electorate as measured by distribution among occupational categories of males in the labor force, the most stable longterm indicator of social stratification (see table 5-4).

The *rate* of decline in participation revealed here is strongly differentiated along class lines. But the *fact* of decline is general. This means that increased nonvoting has also produced larger numbers of middle-class nonvoters, even at the highest reaches of the reported occupational structure. It is not just working-class voters who, at the margins, seem to lack motivation to vote under the conditions created by the institutions and operations of the "permanent campaign." If one thinks about possibilities for party rebuilding or reforming the rules of the game in a society dominated by the middle classes, it is almost certainly going to be middle-class segments who are dissatisfied with the existing order who will lead the way if anyone does.

Yet granted all this, the overwhelming pattern that comes from these data is one of demobilization that, while general, is also strikingly selective. Relative to the mid-1960s (when decline had already begun), the attrition rate among various working-class categories is more than three times as high as in the professional and technical category and well over twice as high as for the middle classes as a whole, a relationship that is common both to presidential and off-year turnout dynamics.

The more recent surveys give considerably more information than the earlier ones. For example, they tell not only who votes but who registers, and among nonvoters the reasons they give for not voting or registering. Responses reflecting indifference to or dislike of politics as the chief reason for nonparticipation also climb systematically in both relative and

48. This has become part of the bureau's Current Population Surveys (Series P-20) with biennial reports of varying comprehensiveness. The most complete and informative was produced for the 1972 election. The 1984 report's comprehensiveness is considerably below that of 1980s, probably reflecting the Reagan administration's choices regarding the availability to the public of officially gathered information at reasonable cost, or sometimes at all. (One example is the unfortunate discontinuation in 1981–82 of Census Bureau election-year estimates of voting age population by congressional district.)

Table 5-4. *Voter Turnout Rates in Presidential and Off-Year Elections,
by Occupation, Male Labor Force, 1964–80*

Occupational category	Turnout rate, presidential years		Percent decline, 1964–80	Turnout rate, off-years		Percent decline, 1966–78
	1964	1980[a]	1964–80	1966	1978[b]	1966–78
Middle-class and white collar	**83.2**	**73.0**	**12.3**	**68.7**	**58.9**	**14.3**
Professional and technical	84.7[c]	77.0	9.1	70.1	62.7	10.6
Managers (excluding farm)	82.8[c]	72.6	12.3	68.9	57.9	16.0
Farm owners and managers	84.7[c]	76.1	10.2	71.0	64.4	9.3
Sales and clerical	81.3[c]	67.8	16.6	66.3	54.3	18.1
Service occupations	**72.8**	**53.0**	**27.2**	**57.9**	**43.6**	**24.7**
Manual (excluding service)	**66.1**	**48.0**	**27.4**	**50.6**	**35.1**	**30.6**
Craft and skilled workers	72.2[c]	53.6	25.8	56.7	40.6	28.4
Semiskilled operatives	63.5[c]	44.7	29.6	48.3	32.1	33.5
Laborers (excluding farm)	57.7[c]	41.4	28.2	41.1	28.1	31.6
Farm laborers	44.6[c]	35.0	21.5	32.7	24.4	25.4
Unemployed	**56.9**	**38.1**	**33.0**	**42.7**	**25.9**	**39.3**
Total	73.0	58.1	20.4	58.9	45.2	23.3

Sources: U.S. Bureau of the Census, *Current Population Reports*, series P-20, no. 143, "Voter Participation in the National Election: November 1964" (Government Printing Office, 1965); no. 174, "Voting and Registration in the Election of November 1966" (GPO, 1968); no. 344, "Voting and Registration in the Election of November 1978" (GPO, 1979); and no. 370, "Voting and Registration in the Election of November 1980" (GPO, 1982).

a. The Census Bureau occupational classification scheme changed between the 1980 and 1982 reports on registration and voter participation. Particularly in view of the very small increase in presidential turnout between 1980 and 1984, it seemed best to use the 1980 data in order to maintain full time-series compatibility.

b. I chose to use data for 1978 rather than 1982 because the latter year showed the only substantial turnout increase in the entire series to date, while in 1986 participation levels fell even below those of 1978. Since 1986 data are as yet unavailable, 1978 data appeared to be the closest approximation to the current situation.

c. The 1964 survey, the first in the census series, gives occupation only by extremely broad categories (white-collar, manual, etc.). The 1980 survey gives the fuller picture. These turnouts by category are "retrodicted" estimates based on weighted figures derived from the immediate post-1964 surveys.

absolute terms as one moves down the occupational structure. Many other attributes related to turnout and abstention are also now evident. Blacks typically vote less than whites, though if one allows for the great differences between black and white occupational structure, a large part of the difference disappears; and there are notable occasions (such as the 1983 and 1987 Chicago mayoral elections) in which black voting rates are at least the equal of white participation. Hispanics, on the other hand, are in a class by themselves, having much the lowest participation rate of any major "nonclass" group in the population.

Some analyses of the 1984 election pointed to the considerable differences in support for Ronald Reagan in terms not merely of social class but also of other measures of distance from or proximity to the various "cores" of American society. People with strong religious (especially Protestant and most especially evangelical) ties were much more solidly behind the president than those with weaker ties. Members of working nuclear families were more supportive than those living alone (as single heads of households, divorced, widowed) or in a collection of unrelated individuals sharing the same dwelling. By the same token, perhaps, recent census surveys show a huge participation differential along such lines as nuclear family versus other living arrangements and between homeowners and renters.[49] One senses the empirical existence of a kind of Norman Rockwell picture as part of a general cultural ideal—a picture of a republic of property owners. The closer one is to this image—as well as to owner-ship of some of the productive assets of the political economy—the more likely one is to vote and participate in other ways, and the more likely that vote is to be Republican.

Viewing either the long run of American political evolution or the record of the most recent elections, one finds ample evidence for the existence of a center of the society and political economy competing with a periphery. More accurately, this could be said to include a number of "centers" and "peripheries" that over time seem to have an increasing tendency to converge around one or another of competing poles. For a considerable period after the smashup of the old laissez-faire political economy in 1929, the "periphery party," the Democrats, welded together a new majority coalition whose energizing center was not Wall Street or Main Street, but Washington, D.C. But its position as a combined Left and center in a political system that has no genuine Left but does have a genuine Right implied, as it still implies, that if anything should ever happen to dissolve this federal glue, the peripheries that the party largely represents will become dissociated and go their several ways. Such a case, which has of course duly materialized, is not far removed from a 1980s version of the Democrats' "politics of provincialism" of sixty and more years ago.[50] It is for some such reason that there was and is a systematic

49. In 1984, for example, the survey reports a turnout rate of 71.8 percent among homeowners (73 percent of the sample), compared with 43.7 percent among renters, a participation gap of nearly 30 points. For whites only, the rates are 72.5 percent and 42.8 respectively—an even larger gap than for the population as a whole.

50. David Burner, *The Politics of Provincialism: The Democratic Party in Transition, 1918–1932* (Knopf, 1968).

relationship at the margins between the party of nonvoters and the active Democratic electoral clientele. As the Democratic party dissociates and loses its common organizing institutions and principles, therefore, the ranks of the party of nonvoters are mightily swelled. So it was in the 1920s, so it is now. When the level of nonparticipation recorded in these two similar decades is reached, one could almost assert that so far as issues of social class are concerned, there are more significant differences between nonvoters and the active electorate than between voting Democrats and voting Republicans. One certainly can assert that the shift toward voting abstention since 1960 is by far the largest mass movement of our time, and that it is related, not coincidentally, to the rise of Ronald Reagan and his "new direction in American politics."

For understandable reasons, the census surveys do not report the partisan preferences of their respondents. It is thus necessary to turn again to some aggregate evidence that supports this partisan part of the discussion. Once again I will use the eastern Massachusetts conurbation, the only area for which at present I have data to spin out a forty-year time series. There are some noteworthy local peculiarities about the Bay State that have prompted President Reagan to call it the "people's republic of Massachusetts," despite the fact that he carried the state in both of his elections. In particular, there is vastly more support for the Democrats among the Boston area's upper strata than in most of the country, just as there was for John Anderson (for similar locally relevant reasons) in 1980. In this particular segment of the population, there is no doubt at all that Barry Goldwater's nomination and campaign in 1964 produced a genuine "critical realignment." The ascendancy of "upscale Democrats" in key leadership positions, and the extraordinary collapse of the Republican party at the state and local levels, are equally reflective of this phenomenon of a "middle class leading the way." To repeat, this is a specific local peculiarity. Nevertheless, the profiles of the top and bottom of the class structure (as based on simple regression estimation) are striking (see figure 5-3).

One could almost say these figures portray electoral change in two different countries. While there has been some increase in working-class Republican support from the trace levels of the 1960s, the key change has been that turnout and the Democratic share of the potential working-class electorate have collapsed together.[51] In fact, if these estimates remotely

51. As has also happened in New York State and especially in New York City. There are assembly districts in the city where fewer than one-fifth of the potential electorate voted in

Figure 5-3. *Estimates of Percentage of Potential Electorate Voting and Not Voting, by Class, in Boston Area, 1964–84*[a]

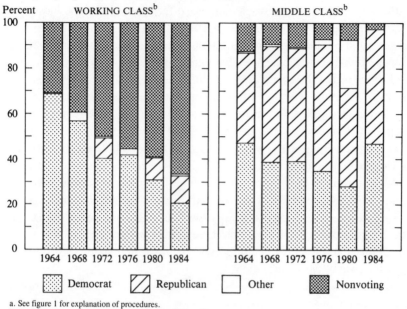

a. See figure 1 for explanation of procedures.
b. As defined by occupational data in census for 1964 and later years.

correspond to reality, the abstention rate of two-thirds of working-class eligibles in 1984 considerably exceeds even those recorded in the 1920 and 1924 elections; it is by far the largest of all time. Assuming that Democratic party elites have realigned their interests and appeals toward high-tech and "yuppie" concerns (as clearly has happened under the leadership of Governor Michael Dukakis) and that the state Republican party has now been taken over by the Right, this enormous demobilization would make considerable sense from either of the analytic points of view here presented, especially from the utility-maximizing perspective. If poor

---

the 1984 presidential election. For the state as a whole, the turnout rate for governor in 1986 was 33.4 percent of the potential electorate—the lowest since the election of 1820 (32.7 percent). Indeed, before constitutional reform in 1821, New York allowed only freeholders with property worth $100 to vote, thus disfranchising about three-fifths of the adult white male population. During this period, there were six gubernatorial elections (1801–1816) that, despite this property qualification, showed higher voter participation than in 1986.

or working-class voters feel abandoned by the Democrats, most would (as usual) have little incentive to vote for Republicans, since the latter have little but the politics of resentment to offer them. It might indeed be difficult for such people to feel connected, affectively or instrumentally, to choices and candidates hugely different from those presented in the age of James Michael Curley, Leverett Saltonstall, and John F. Kennedy.

For the top of the social array, on the other hand, there is a profoundly different ordering. The pool of nonvoters in this environment is minuscule and has in fact declined over the years; at the top, fully nine-tenths or more of potential voters come to the polls. What they do when they get there differs extremely from the working-class profile; and in Massachusetts this is closely tied, even now, to major differences on matters of culture and history as well as economics between Irish Catholics and Yankee Protestants. The Yankees have remained participants but are strikingly politically divided—a division that clearly owes its origin and persistence to the local impact of the GOP's national realignment to the right in 1964 and to the choices and policies identified with national and state political elites over the twenty years since then.

In most environments, of course, no such division has occurred—just as there is today probably no state in the union in which the Republican party is organizationally or electorally in such bad shape as in Massachusetts. The evidence elsewhere is not only for a very wide class gap in participation, but also for Republican dominance toward the top, particularly in presidential elections, that almost reaches levels common before 1964 in Massachusetts. One very simple bivariate analysis is illustrative: turnout and partisanship in the 1980 election among the seventy-two cities that make up most of Los Angeles County, California, using median family income as the independent variable. Since blacks and Hispanics constitute so large a share of the county's electorate, estimates are presented for cities whose 1980 population was at least two-thirds white and non-Hispanic, as well as all the cities (see table 5-5).

Two features of this array should be noted: the powerful relationship between affluence and turnout, and the enormous bilateral asymmetry in the parties' mobilizing capacity at the highest and lowest points in the affluence continuum. The Democrat (Carter) was unable to win as much as one-fifth of the potential electorate in any category, and his share of eligibles dropped quite little from the poor to the rich ends of the spectrum. Republican (Reagan) support vaulted forward from very little at the bottom to three-quarters or more of the potential electorate at the top.

Table 5-5. *Estimates of Turnout and Presidential Vote, at Selected Levels in Median Family Income and by Race, Los Angeles County, 1980*
Percent

Selected level in median family income (dollars)[a]	*All cities in county (N = 72)*				*Cities with population 66.7 percent or more white, non-Hispanic (N = 35)*			
	Nonvoting	*Carter*	*Reagan*	*Other*[b]	*Nonvoting*	*Carter*	*Reagan*	*Other*[b]
0	84.3	19.7	−4.5[c]	0.5	69.0	17.9	9.5	3.6
3,100	79.6	19.4	0.1	1.1	65.8	17.7	12.7	3.9
15,000	61.8	18.0	17.0	1.1	53.1	16.6	25.3	5.0
40,000	24.4	15.2	53.1	3.2	26.5	14.5	51.7	7.3
56,200	0.1	13.3	76.4	7.7	9.3	13.1	68.8[d]	8.8

Sources: Election data, Secretary of State of California, Supplement to Statement of Vote (1980 and 1984 elections); demographic data, data from American Civil Liberties Union of Southern California and 1980 U.S. Census.

a. The selected median family income values correspond to points in the distribution where positive values of 0.1 or more in the estimated share of the electorate are recorded in at least one cell in one of the two arrays.

b. Mostly for John Anderson.

c. As not infrequently happens with linear regression estimation, "impossible" values (negative votes) can be produced, as here. The convention in such cases is to set the value at zero.

d. As is well known from the survey literature, Reagan did not do less well among upper-status whites than among upper-status blacks. Linear regression is very sensitive to extreme values in either of the two variables. Removal of most blacks and Hispanics has the effect, therefore, of reducing the steepness of the slope that defines the relationship, but only, as is clear, by a very limited amount.

Major racial diversity is vastly more significant in Los Angeles County, with its large black and third world population, than in largely white Pittsburgh (as of 1960) and the even whiter Boston metropolitan area. The very crude "control" I have used—separately evaluating relationships in the cities that are predominantly white and non-Hispanic—is clear enough evidence that the relationship between nonvoting and poverty remains very strong even with minorities largely disregarded. Equally noteworthy is the considerable relative strength of Republican support not just at the top, but very far down toward the bottom of the income scale. Reagan in 1980 began moving into a lead when the median family income was no more than about $7,500. Of course, if the 57 percent abstention rate at that level were reduced to 25 percent and three-quarters of this difference voted Democratic, the results would probably look much more like 1940 or 1960 than 1980 or 1984.

A Political State of Nature

When nonvoting is examined across time, space, and political context, it emerges as an important indicator of the relative health of democracy in any political system based upon elections and the consent of the governed. In performing this examination, it is hardly possible to do full justice to the subject without some attempt to specify the relationship between turnout and partisanship.

In every political system that leaves it up to the individual to decide whether or not to vote, there is an irreducible minimum of adult citizens who are apolitical or disaffected or for other reasons abstain. But in most other democratic-capitalist polities, this minimum is relatively small. The body of nonvoters in these polities seems on the whole not to reflect systematic biases along sociological lines of obvious political importance, and tends to be highly stable, or at least has been so in the generation since the end of the Second World War.

In the United States, by contrast, there is overwhelming evidence of systematic participation biases along sociological lines of political importance. For my purposes here I have concentrated on only one but perhaps the most important of these, social class. Participation in the United States is also highly volatile by comparative standards. Since 1960, for example, about one-quarter of the active electorate as then defined has shifted into the party of nonvoters. There is a persistent, very strong, historical, and cross-sectional relationship at the margins between the Democratic voting streams and the party of nonvoters—a very dynamic relationship that has little counterpart on the Republican side. Marked social-structure bias in turnout and nonvoting is thus paralleled in politics by a no less striking asymmetry in the mobilizing capacities of the two rival parties. The two are indissolubly linked, appear to arise from the same systemic causes, and are becoming ever more manifest.

It is very hard to avoid the conclusion that the profound reorganization of the entrepreneurial foundations of the American electoral market in recent years is a vital causal agent in this swelling tide of nonvoting. The rise of the permanent campaign creates a network of conditions that could be predicted to contribute to the disconnection of voters—especially, but by no means exclusively, lower-status voters. Put another way, the relative disappearance of partisan teams in campaigns and their replacement by personalistic and imagistic appeals to voters creates conditions that make individual utility calculations difficult, if not impossible. If people are left to their own devices in a society with marked inequalities on all relevant dimensions of political consciousness, education, and information, some people will remain far better positioned to make accurate utility calculations than others. As the vast literature on the development of parties attests, it was the whole purpose of party-as-team and party-in-the-electorate to reduce this particular inequality as much as possible through organization, political education, and mass mobilization. The partial dissolution of those linkages in the permanent-campaign era inevitably means that this gradient will grow ever steeper until the situation approximates a political "state of nature"—a state that it was the entire purpose of party builders to end.

I sometimes think that, given the specific conditions and constraints surrounding democracy in America, a general political situation approximating that of the 1920s or the 1980s represents a kind of end point toward which we have been evolving. Such a view might be challenged as carrying determinism and pessimism to excess. Whether it does or not, the ultimate key to the problem of mass abstention clearly lies in the broader problem of American electoral politics and its modern party system. New challenges may arise that create a new basis for serious contests among collective wills and for collective decisionmaking on some very powerful issue. If so, politicians will likely rediscover the need and thus the personal incentives for collective action. But this would require the elimination or at least the radical transformation of the existing permanent campaign structure. Obviously this would be a task of the most awesome magnitude. Yet there seems little reason to suppose that the general decomposition of the American political regime, of which growing voter abstention is only one of the more important components, can be arrested—much less reversed—unless that task is undertaken and successfully carried out.

CHAPTER SIX

Is the Electoral Process Stacked against Minorities?

EDDIE N. WILLIAMS AND MILTON D. MORRIS

EVEN AS the start of another presidential election campaign approaches, one can still hear echoes from the last election, in which questions about access by minorities to the electoral process figured prominently. Presidential candidate Jesse Jackson frequently claimed to be speaking on behalf of those, mostly minorities, who were "locked out" of the electoral process. He complained vigorously about party rules that worked to the disadvantage of candidates who, like himself, were outsiders to the party's leadership structure. Jackson also campaigned against burdensome registration procedures and electoral arrangements, such as the run-off or "second primary," that he believed discriminated against minority candidates.

Complaints about inequities in minority access to the electoral process continue to come from the grassroots as well. For example, U.S. Representative Don Edwards, chairman of the Subcommittee on Civil and Constitutional Rights of the House Judiciary Committee, reported that the more than 120 witnesses who testified at hearings around the country in 1981 "presented compelling evidence that discrimination [in voting] against racial and language minorities still persisted and was widespread."[1] Organizations like the Lawyers' Committee for Civil Rights and the NAACP Legal Defense Fund still claim a full agenda of voting

---

1. Don Edwards, "The Voting Rights Act of 1965, as Amended," in Lorn S. Foster, ed., *The Voting Rights Act: Consequences and Implications* (Praeger, 1985), p. 7.

rights cases. These developments suggest that minorities have not yet achieved equal access to the electoral process.

But there is also compelling evidence of dramatic progress by minorities toward full electoral participation. In spite of Jackson's complaints, his campaign for the Democratic party's presidential nomination in 1984 demonstrated this progress within the Democratic party. He amassed far more delegates and occupied a more prominent role in the party's national convention than any previous minority candidate in either party. Several other developments also reflect progress in this area, among them a substantial reduction in the gap between black and white voting levels, increased minority participation in party affairs, and rapid growth in the number of minority elected officeholders over the past two decades.

Ascertaining the extent and character of remaining impediments to minority electoral participation is essential, even critical, to an appraisal of the electoral process and to any effort to improve it. Historically, the single most important and persistent problem of the American electoral process has been that of inequitable limitations on access. In sharp contrast to the democratic values associated with the Constitution and espoused by American society, the electoral process long excluded large segments of society or severely limited their influence as participants. Women, the poor, youth, and blacks were either excluded or severely disadvantaged. Their participation came about in recent years as a result of lengthy, vigorous struggle. Constitutional amendments extending the franchise to women, eliminating the poll tax, and reducing the minimum voting age to eighteen removed most barriers to these groups except blacks.

The experience of blacks in seeking access to the electoral process has been unique. The Fourteenth and Fifteenth Amendments to the Constitution presumably bestowed full civil and political rights on them a century ago. Yet, for a majority of blacks, access to the electoral process has been won only after nearly 100 years of struggle in the courts and in Congress and through mass protests. Comparing the experience of blacks with other ethnic groups, Charles V. Hamilton notes that blacks have

> had to devote a substantial amount of time and energy simply to estab-
> lishing their claim to political citizenship. While the earlier ethnic
> groups could launch careers as precinct captains and political bargain-
> ers, blacks had to spend time as plaintiffs and protesters.[2]

2. Charles V. Hamilton, "Political Access, Minority Participation, and the New Nor-

Blacks faced special barriers imposed by numerous state and local laws and regulations, party rules, and unofficial but effective violence by whites. Their efforts to overcome these barriers and to eliminate other inequities in participation have profoundly altered the electoral process and ensured more equitable participation by other disadvantaged groups as well. In considering the extent to which the electoral process remains stacked against minorities, we concentrate on the experience of blacks since that experience is more extensively documented. However, we use the term *minorities* to include blacks and historically disadvantaged Hispanics. We define the electoral process to include all aspects of nominating and electing candidates to public office, voting, party organization and rules, and the structure of elections.

Minorities have made considerable progress in eliminating barriers to their electoral participation, with beneficial effects on the entire electoral process. That progress, however, has not occurred evenly across all parts of the process, and substantial barriers remain. These barriers include tedious registration requirements that impede minority voting, various districting arrangements that dilute the vote of those who overcome the registration hurdle, and the attitudes of white voters toward blacks. Continued voting rights activism and the growing power of the minority electorate are likely to ensure gradual eradication of most remaining barriers. However, even with the removal of these barriers, the system will still remain stacked against minorities to some extent.

Electoral Participation

In November 1986 attorney Mike Espy won election to Congress from Mississippi's Second Congressional District, thereby becoming the first black to represent Mississippi in Congress in this century. That event more than any other in recent years underscores the extent to which barriers to black electoral participation have been disappearing. About 45 percent of the eligible black voters of this impoverished Mississippi delta district turned out, and about 93 percent of them voted for Espy.[3] Espy's victory came more than two decades after the Voting Rights Act of 1965 elimi-

malcy," in Leslie W. Dunbar, ed., *Minority Report: What Has Happened to Blacks, Hispanics, American Indians, and Other Minorities in the Eighties* (Pantheon Books, 1984), p. 11.

3. Voter Education Project, "Analysis of the 2nd District Congressional Election" (Atlanta: Voter Education Project, 1987).

nated the most formidable obstacles to voting, after a federal court order ended a blatant racial gerrymander and allowed creation of the majority-black congressional district in which Espy was elected, and after years of vigorous efforts by civil rights and other private organizations to surmount major obstacles to registration of blacks in the district. The history of black exclusion from the electoral process in Mississippi and most of the South has been told often and need not be repeated here.[4] However, that history and the struggle of southern blacks for full electoral participation have been critical factors in blacks' voting behavior and in recent reforms of the electoral system for minorities.

The wide gap between the voting rates of black and white citizens, in large part caused by the exclusion of many blacks from the electoral process, has narrowed dramatically in recent years as enforcement of the Voting Rights Act of 1965 enabled southern blacks to vote. In the 1964 presidential election the gap in black-white voting rates was approximately 12 percentage points, but by 1984 it had closed to a mere 5.6 percentage points (table 6-1). The trend has been the same in off-year congressional elections: the gap went from 15.3 percentage points in 1966 to 6.9 in 1982. In a society where voting patterns change slowly and in a period when the trend in turnout has been mostly downward, this narrowing of the voting gap is strong evidence of disappearing barriers to voting by minorities. Indeed, table 6-1 shows that the gains by blacks have been greatest in the South, where the gap in presidential elections narrowed from 15.5 to 4.9 percentage points. Since 1974 absolute turnout has increased among blacks and Hispanics, although less so among Hispanics.

Another indicator of progress is rapid growth in the number of blacks and Hispanics elected to public office over the past two decades. For blacks, the number of elected officials grew from fewer than 103 in 1964 to 6,384 in 1986. Between 1973 and 1985 the number of Hispanic public officials more than doubled, from about 1,280 to 3,147.[5] For both groups,

4. Jack Bass and Walter De Vries, *The Transformation of Southern Politics* (Basic Books, 1976).

5. U.S. Bureau of the Census, *Current Population Reports, Special Studies*, series P-23, no. 80, "Social and Economic Status of the Black Population in the United States: An Historical View 1790-1978" (Government Printing Office, 1979), p. 156; Joint Center for Political Studies, *Black Elected Officials: A National Roster 1986* (Washington, D.C.: JCPS, 1986); National Association of Latino Elected and Appointed Officials, *1985 National Roster of Hispanic Elected Officials* (Washington, D.C.: NALEO Education Fund, 1985); and Frank Lemus, *National Roster of Spanish Surnamed Elected Officials* (Los Angeles: Aztlan, 1973).

Table 6-1. *Voter Turnout for Presidential and Congressional Elections, by Region and Race, 1964–84*[a]

Percent

Region and race	Presidential elections						Congressional elections				
	1964	1968	1972	1976	1980	1984	1966	1970	1974	1978	1982
United States											
White	70.1	69.1	64.5	60.9	60.9	61.4	57.0	56.0	46.3	47.3	49.9
Black	58.5	57.6	52.1	48.7	50.5	55.8	41.7	43.5	33.8	37.2	43.0
Spanish origin	n.a.	n.a.	37.5	31.8	29.9	32.9	n.a.	n.a.	22.9	23.5	25.3
Black-white difference	12.2	11.5	12.4	12.2	10.4	5.6	15.3	12.5	12.5	10.1	6.9
North and West											
White	74.7	71.8	67.5	62.6	62.4	63.0	61.7	59.8	50.0	50.0	53.1
Black	72.0	64.8	56.7	52.2	52.8	58.9	52.1	51.4	37.9	41.3	48.5
Difference	2.7	7.0	10.8	10.4	9.6	4.1	9.6	8.4	12.1	8.7	4.6
South											
White	59.6	61.9	57.0	57.1	57.4	58.1	45.1	46.4	37.4	41.1	42.9
Black	44.0	51.6	47.8	45.7	48.2	53.2	32.9	36.8	30.0	33.5	38.3
Difference	15.5	10.3	9.2	11.4	9.2	4.9	12.2	9.6	7.4	7.6	4.6

Source: U.S. Bureau of the Census, *Current Population Reports*, series P-20, no. 405, "Voting and Registration in the Election of November 1984" (Government Printing Office, 1986).

n.a. Not available.

a. In the postelection surveys, samples of the population are asked whether they voted in the last election. Thus the percentages reflect those who *reported* voting; these percentages are usually higher than the percentages of people who actually voted.

this increase in the number of elected officials is an important measure of their voting strength.

Today minorities are not systematically denied the right to vote anywhere in the United States. Informal obstacles such as intimidation and bureaucratic obstructions continue to discourage voting in some localities in the South, but even these seem to be disappearing. The principal impediments to voting that blacks and other minorities now face are burdensome registration requirements. Some of these registration requirements were enacted for racial purposes; others were not, but nevertheless disproportionately disadvantage minorities.

The Registration Barrier

The rules governing registration and voting vary somewhat from state to state, but in most places those rules are not designed to simplify participation. On the contrary, registration requirements are typically burdensome enough to discourage voting by all but the highly motivated. According to G. Bingham Powell, "registration laws make voting more difficult in the United States than in almost any other democracy." Powell calculates that the resulting reduction in turnout might be as much as 13 percent. The burdensome requirements have the greatest vote-inhibiting effect, Powell notes, among lower socioeconomic groups, within which minorities are disproportionately represented.[6] Other social scientists also have shown that cumbersome registration requirements significantly reduce voting levels.[7]

In addition to the general inhibiting effects of registration requirements on voting, such requirements often have been used deliberately to discourage minority voting. Historians Jack Bass and Morgan Kousser have documented how several southern states for more than a century used discriminatory registration procedures to disfranchise blacks.[8] In 1882 South

6. G. Bingham Powell, Jr., "American Voter Turnout in Comparative Perspective," *American Political Science Review,* vol. 80 (March 1986), pp. 20-21, 36.

7. Steven J. Rosenstone and Raymond Wolfinger, "The Effect of Registration Laws on Voter Turnout," *American Political Science Review,* vol. 72 (March 1978), pp. 22-45. See also Walter Dean Burnham's calculations in chap. 5 of this book.

8. Jack Bass, "Election Laws and their Manipulation to Exclude Minority Voters," in *The Right to Vote: A Rockefeller Foundation Conference* (Rockefeller Foundation, 1981), pp. 1-32; and J. Morgan Kousser, "The Undermining of the First Reconstruction: Lessons for the Second," in Chandler Davidson, ed., *Minority Vote Dilution* (Washington, D.C.: Howard University Press, 1984), pp. 27-46.

Carolina enacted registration laws that gave voting registrars considerable discretion in enrolling qualified voters, a discretion zealously used to prevent blacks from registering. Other southern states followed in using registration as a means of disfranchising blacks. Even now, after the removal of blatantly discriminatory registration procedures, minorities and other low-income voters continue to face hardships in registering to vote. In many southern localities, individuals must travel several miles to the county seat to register at registration offices that are open only on weekdays during working hours. Furthermore, some of these localities purge the voter rolls frequently, making it necessary for many citizens to reregister at relatively frequent intervals. Partly because of these continued obstacles, considerable private resources have had to be spent on costly, labor-intensive campaigns to get otherwise eligible minorities registered to vote.

Many voting rights advocates now seek to achieve "equal ballot access" for minorities by making registration much easier. Some are using lawsuits to challenge registration arrangements that primarily obstruct minorities in the South. Others want to simplify registration requirements for everyone nationally by persuading state and local officials to institute registration by mail, registration in government offices extensively used by the public, or registration at the time of voting. Another strategy rapidly gaining support is to seek congressional legislation mandating simplified registration procedures for all federal elections.

The Language Barrier

Hispanics and other minorities whose native language is not English face a language barrier in electoral participation. According to William Diaz, approximately 75 percent of the Hispanic population speaks Spanish at home,[9] and a significant percentage of Hispanic citizens are not proficient in English. The general lack of election material and ballots in Spanish handicaps these voters. Puerto Rican voters in New York City obtained some relief from the courts in 1985 through a lawsuit, *Campaign for a Progressive Bronx* v. *Black*. The Hispanic voter plaintiffs sought to have the city undertake a voter education campaign in Spanish and to provide Spanish-speaking inspectors and interpreters at polling places where Hispanics were expected to vote. Plaintiffs and the city reached agreement out of court to meet the special needs of Spanish-speaking

9. William Diaz, *Hispanics: Challenges and Opportunities* (Ford Foundation, 1984), p. 40.

voters.[10] However, such help for Hispanic voters remains far from commonplace.

Recent court decisions and state and local government actions suggest that these registration and language barriers to minority voting, the lingering fragments of a once formidable array of obstacles, will soon disappear. American society is moving substantially closer to the universally accessible ballot our democratic values dictate.

Structural Discrimination

Although most traditional barriers to voting by minorities have been overcome, at-large or multimember districts and racial gerrymanders are still widely used to reduce the impact of minorities' votes in electing candidates of their choice. These electoral arrangements, along with a pattern of racial bloc voting, have made it extremely difficult in some places for a minority group to elect a member of that group or a candidate favored by that group to office. They therefore constitute some of the more effective ways to stack the electoral system against minorities.

Districting to prevent the election of minority group candidates is a longstanding tradition. As early as 1868 Atlanta adopted a system of at-large election largely to prevent blacks from winning public office. Local governments throughout the South soon followed, even though blacks already had been effectively denied the franchise. Between 1901 and 1920 a number of other governments in the South and elsewhere adopted at-large electoral arrangements as part of reforms to improve the quality of government. According to Edward Banfield and James Q. Wilson, as of 1960 about 60 percent of all local governments representing populations of more than 10,000 elected their councils at large or from multimember districts.[11] Even though the primary purpose of these arrangements was not to dilute minority voting strength, they clearly had that effect. Analysts have long observed that at-large electoral arrangements tend to exclude or reduce minority representation.[12] Several recent empirical studies have

10. Lawyers' Committee for Civil Rights under Law, Voting Rights Project, "Narrative Report, 1986" (LCCRL, December 1986), pp. 46–47.
11. Edward C. Banfield and James Q. Wilson, *City Politics* (Harvard University Press, 1963), p. 88.
12. Gunnar Myrdal, *An American Dilemma* (Harper and Row, 1944), pp. 493–94, 501; and Robert E. Lane, *Political Life: Why People Get Involved in Politics* (Free Press, 1959), pp. 270–71.

documented the correlation between at-large and multimember electoral structures and the underrepresentation of minorities on city councils.[13] They also show that minority representation improves after a locality switches from at-large to single-member districts. As is shown in table 6-2, black membership in southern legislatures increased significantly between 1971 and 1981, a period when these states were eliminating multimember districts.

The continuing discrepancy between the proportion of blacks and Hispanics in the population and the proportion of black and Hispanic elected officials indicates that such vote-dilution strategies are still taking a toll on minority political representation. Blacks make up slightly more than 11.5 percent of the U.S. population, but less than 1.5 percent of the elected officials. Similarly, Hispanics comprise about 7 percent of the population, but just about 0.6 percent of the elected officials.[14]

The racial gerrymander, through which minority voters are either spread out across several districts or compacted into the fewest possible to limit their effect on electoral outcomes, has been a longstanding and highly effective companion vote-dilution strategy to at-large elections.[15] Mississippi created its famous congressional "shoestring" district of 1876–82, which was 500 miles long and 40 miles wide, to prevent the reelection of John R. Lynch, a black Mississippi congressman. And after passage of the Voting Rights Act of 1965, the same state gerrymandered its traditional delta congressional district out of existence. Several other states have created equally novel electoral district boundaries to limit the influence of minority voters.[16]

Vote dilution through racial gerrymandering and multimember districts has been ruled unconstitutional by the Supreme Court. In 1960 the court outlawed the racial gerrymander in *Gomillion* v. *Lightfoot*. Thirteen years later, in *White* v. *Regester*, it held that an at-large electoral arrangement

13. This literature is reviewed in Chandler Davidson and George Korbel, "At-Large Elections and Minority Group Representation: A Reexamination of Historical and Contemporary Evidence," in Davidson, ed., *Minority Vote Dilution*, pp. 65–81.

14. JCPS, *Black Elected Officials*, pp. 11, 12; U.S. Bureau of the Census, *Current Population Reports*, series P-20, no. 403, "Persons of Spanish Origin in the United States: March 1985" (Advance Report) (GPO, 1985); Bureau of the Census, *1977 Census of Governments*, vol. 1, no. 2, "Popularly Elected Officials" (GPO, 1979), p. 9; and NALEO, *1985 National Roster.*

15. Frank Parker, "Racial Gerrymandering and Legislative Reapportionment," in Davidson, ed., *Minority Vote Dilution*, pp. 85–117.

16. Bass and De Vries, *Transformation of Southern Politics.*

Table 6-2. *Black Membership in Selected Southern Legislatures, 1971, 1976, and 1981*

State	Black percentage of 1980 population	Black membership in legislature (percentage in parentheses)					
		1971		1976		1981	
		House	Senate	House	Senate	House	Senate
Alabama	24.5	2	0	13	2	13	3
	...	(1.9)	(0)	(12.4)	(5.7)	(12.4)	(8.6)
Georgia[a]	26.2	13	2	20	2	21	2
	...	(7.2)	(3.6)	(11.1)	(3.6)	(11.7)	(3.6)
Louisiana	29.6	1	0	9	1	10	2
	...	(1.0)	(0)	(8.6)	(2.6)	(9.5)	(5.9)
Mississippi	35.1	1	0	4	0	15	2
	...	(0.8)	(0)	(3.3)	(0)	(12.3)	(3.8)
South Carolina[b]	31.0	3	0	13	0	15	0
	...	(2.4)	(0)	(10.5)	(0)	(12.1)	(0)
Texas	12.5	2	1	9	0	13	0
	...	(1.3)	(3.2)	(6.0)	(0)	(8.7)	(0)

Source: Frank R. Parker, "Racial Gerrymandering and Legislative Reapportionment," in Chandler Davidson, ed., *Minority Vote Dilution* (Washington, D.C.: Howard University Press, 1984), p. 88.

a. The attorney general's 1972 objections to Georgia's legislative reapportionment plan for the state House of Representatives attacked discriminatory multimember districts in areas that then had black population concentrations. Multimember districts in then predominantly white areas, where they had no discriminatory impact, were to be retained. Some of these multimember districts, nondiscriminatory in 1972, may now be discriminatory as a result of population changes.

b. Multimember districts were eliminated in the state House of Representatives only; multimember state Senate districts were retained.

was unconstitutional on the ground that it diluted black and Hispanic votes.[17]

The Court has long struggled over the evidentiary standard to be employed in determining when a multimember district is unconstitutional. In *Mobile* v. *Bolden,* the Court overturned the finding of a lower court that the city of Mobile's at-large election system unconstitutionally diluted black votes, ruling that the plaintiffs had not established the city's intent to discriminate.[18] This "intent" test, as opposed to an "effects" or "results" test used by the lower courts, posed an almost insurmountable obstacle to further legal challenges to vote-diluting electoral arrangements. The Court's decision prompted considerable attention to the evidentiary issue and resulted in an amendment to section 2 of the Voting Rights Act by

17. *Gomillion* v. *Lightfoot,* 364 U.S. 339 (1960); and *White* v. *Regester,* 412 U.S. 755 (1973).

18. *City of Mobile* v. *Bolden,* 446 U.S. 55 (1980).

Congress in 1982, undoing the Supreme Court's *Mobile* ruling by instituting the effects or results test.

In *Thornburg* v. *Gingles* the Supreme Court had its first clear opportunity to revisit the vote-dilution issue using the new standard established by the Voting Rights Act amendments.[19] At issue was a challenge to a system composed of six multimember and one single-member districts in North Carolina that, blacks alleged, deprived them of a fair opportunity to elect a candidate of their choice. In upholding the lower court's decision outlawing these electoral arrangements, the Supreme Court used the effects test to pave the way for challenges to similar electoral arrangements throughout the country.

The shift in emphasis from combating traditional forms of vote denial to vote dilution has at least two important implications. First, it raises new and more complex issues with respect to representation and consequently imposes new evidentiary demands. What minorities are now seeking is not merely the right to cast a ballot, but the right to cast a "meaningful" ballot. The courts have accepted the argument that the dilution of a group's voting strength through structural electoral arrangements is unconstitutional whether intended or not. The evidence required for a showing of dilution is primarily the minority group's experience in electing its members to legislative bodies in the context of a history of racially polarized voting. However, both the criteria and the concept of bloc voting remain controversial and will almost certainly be elaborated further.

Second, the focus on the right to a meaningful ballot expands the challenge beyond state and local legislative elections in the South. In one of the first vote-dilution challenges outside the South, the Federal District Court for Central Illinois found that the city of Springfield's commission form of government, with its at-large election system and history of racially polarized voting, denied blacks a reasonable opportunity to elect candidates of their choice. The court ordered the city to replace the at-large commission with a council elected by wards.[20] Already other cities in the Midwest with similar government structures and voting histories have been challenged in the courts.

If at-large elections for legislative bodies discriminate against minorities, might not the same be said of at-large elections for state court judges? Here, too, minorities are underrepresented. As of 1985 blacks in the

19. *Thornburg* v. *Gingles*, 92 L.Ed. 2d 25, 475 U.S. 106 2752 (1986).
20. *McNeil* v. *City of Springfield*, Memorandum Op. 86-2365 (C.D. Ill. January 12, 1987).

United States held only 3.8 percent of the 12,093 state court judgeships and Hispanics 1.2 percent.[21] Since a high proportion of these judges are elected, this issue is one of the most recent extensions of the vote-dilution principle. In two recent cases challenging Mississippi's at-large election of judges, *Martin* v. *Allain* and *Kirksey* v. *Allain,* the court outlawed this mode of selecting judges on the ground that it violated section 2 of the Voting Rights Act.[22] This decision paves the way for similar challenges elsewhere.

For blacks and other minorities the continuing challenges to election structures and procedures that curtail their influence have prompted new consideration of what constitutes equal participation and how it is achieved. Although definitive answers are not yet available, understanding of the electoral process and the status of minorities in it is being considerably enhanced by the search.

Party Reform and Minority Participation

Despite frequent assertions by some analysts about the weakening of political parties, they remain central to the electoral process. They organize and structure competition for public office, mobilize support for specific candidates, facilitate the development and presentation of issues before the electorate, and manage the recruitment of candidates for elective office. Consequently, the rules and structures of the political parties determine to a great extent the openness of the electoral process.

The two major political parties have been important arenas in the struggle by minorities, women, and others for increased access to the electoral process. Historically, the parties reflected and accommodated the prejudices of the larger society and erected their own barriers to participation by minorities. In the South, for example, the long dominant Democratic party was an integral part of a racially exclusive electoral process. Some blacks in the South managed to obtain the franchise, but the Democratic party used mechanisms like the "white primary" to exclude them from the only meaningful exercise of the vote—the primary election. Furthermore, can-

21. Fund for Modern Courts, *The Success of Women and Minorities in Achieving Judicial Office: The Selection Process* (New York: Fund for Modern Courts, 1985), p. 15.

22. *Martin* v. *Allain, Kirksey* v. *Allain,* Civil No. J84-0708[B] (S.D. Miss. April 1, 1987).

didate-slating arrangements were adopted that virtually eliminated minorities' chances of winning nomination for public office.[23]

Elimination of barriers to minority participation in the political parties has occurred slowly. The Democratic party changed gradually in response to court decisions outlawing some discriminatory practices, vigorous protests by blacks locally and at the national conventions, and the growing size and strategic importance of minorities in the electorate. Massive protests at the 1964 and 1968 Democratic national conventions, much of it aimed at racially discriminatory practices, precipitated an era of reforms that profoundly altered the party system and greatly increased minority participation within it.

While blacks had been demanding greater inclusion in Democratic party affairs before 1964 and forced the issue on the Democratic national convention in 1964, the party reforms began in earnest with the McGovern-Fraser Commission between 1969 and 1972 and continued through 1980. Race, long a central issue in the affairs of the Democratic party, was one of the principal issues driving the decade of reform. Eliminating discrimination against blacks and other minorities became inseparable from broader demands for wider participation and greater democracy in party affairs. The reform movement produced two types of changes that directly benefited minorities: greater use of primaries in selecting delegates to the national conventions; and adoption of the "proportionality principle" in the composition of state delegations and to a lesser extent in party committees.[24] The switch to primaries instead of caucuses as the means of selecting delegates enabled more of the party's rank-and-file supporters to participate directly in choosing convention delegates. It also made it easier for outsiders to the party's leadership to compete for the party's presidential nomination.

Adoption of the proportionality principle required state party organizations to ensure the selection of delegations that reflected as nearly as possible the racial, ethnic, and gender composition of the party's voters. This policy sharply increased the number and proportion of black convention delegates. Between 1964, the last convention under the old order, and 1984, the proportion of black delegates to the Democratic party's national convention grew from 2.8 percent to 17.7 percent (table 6-3).

Few similar changes have occurred in the Republican party. The Demo-

23. Chandler Davidson and Luis Ricardo Fraga, "Nonpartisan Slating Groups in an At-Large Setting," in Davidson, ed., *Minority Vote Dilution*, pp. 119–43.

24. Byron E. Shafer, *Quiet Revolution* (Russell Sage Foundation, 1983).

Table 6-3. *Black Delegates to Democratic and Republican National Conventions, 1912–84*

Year	Total number of delegates		Number of black delegates		Black delegates as percent of total		Number of black alternates	
	Demo-cratic	Repub-lican	Demo-cratic	Repub-lican	Demo-cratic	Repub-lican	Demo-cratic	Repub-lican
1912	n.a.	1,078	n.a.	65	n.a.	6.0	n.a.	n.a.
1916	n.a.	985	n.a.	35	n.a.	3.5	n.a.	n.a.
1920	n.a.	984	n.a.	29	n.a.	2.9	n.a.	n.a.
1924	n.a.	1,109	n.a.	39	n.a.	3.5	n.a.	1
1928	n.a.	1,098	n.a.	49	n.a.	4.4	n.a.	55
1932	1,154	1,154	0	26	0	2.2	10	27
1936	1,204	1,003	12	45	0.1	4.5	18	34
1940	1,094	1,000	7	32	0.6	3.2	18	53
1944	1,176	1,057	11	18	0.9	1.7	13	27
1948	1,234	1,094	17	41	1.3	3.7	n.a.	34
1952	1,230	1,206	33	29	2.6	2.4	n.a.	34
1956	1,372	1,323	24	36	1.7	2.7	21	41
1960	1,521	1,331	46	22	3.0	1.6	37	28
1964	2,316	1,308	65	14	2.8	1.0	55	29
1968	3,084	1,333	209	26	6.7	1.9	173	52
1972	3,103	1,348	452	56	14.6	4.2	n.a.	84
1976	3,048	2,259	323	76	10.6	3.4	170	74
1980	3,331	1,993	481	55	14.4	2.7	297	66
1984	3,933	2,235	697	69	17.7	3.1	225	88

Sources: Joint Center for Political Studies, *Blacks and the 1984 Democratic National Convention* (Washington, D.C.: JCPS, 1984), p. 70; JCPS, *Blacks and the 1984 Republican National Convention* (Washington, D.C.: JCPS, 1984), p. 19; *Negro Year Book, 1931–32*.
n.a. Not available.

cratic party's shift to greater use of primaries in delegate selection prompted a similar alteration by the Republicans, but they changed little else. This comparative lack of movement reflects, most of all, the minuscule presence of minorities in the Republican party and a resulting lack of powerful internal pressures for change. It also reflects a strategic shift in the base of support for both parties. The reforms carried out by the Democratic party, especially those making it more open to minorities as well as its strong pro–civil rights posture, reduced the party's support among southern whites, a constituency Republicans have courted assiduously since 1964.[25] The Democratic party has consolidated the massive black

25. James L. Sundquist, *Dynamics of the Party System: Alignment and Realignment of Political Parties in the United States,* rev. ed. (Brookings, 1983), pp. 374–75.

support it achieved in the presidential contest between Lyndon Johnson and Barry Goldwater in 1964, and it now draws about 25 percent of its total electoral support from this group.[26] During this same period, the Republicans have improved their position among southern whites. One result of these changes is a significantly more competitive party system.[27]

Currently, there are no major obstacles to minority participation in party affairs. A number of concerns remain, but most involve the precise mechanisms through which minority influence will be brought to bear on party decisionmaking, the extent to which the remaining caucus systems reduce minority influence, and the manner in which delegates are allocated among candidates in primary contests.

Remaining Barriers

Today minority voters are a large and rapidly growing segment of the American electorate. Blacks and Hispanics together comprise about 28 million voters, roughly 17 percent of the electorate. Registration and voting levels for blacks have risen rapidly since 1974 to nearly equal that of whites, and the traditionally very low registration rates of Hispanics have begun to rise. These minority groups will occupy an increasingly influential role in a more open electoral system.

In spite of the remarkable progress made by minorities in recent years in gaining access to the political system, some significant barriers remain. Future reforms should address these three important questions: (1) What steps are needed to eliminate remaining barriers to minority participation? (2) To what extent will persisting white-for-white voting preferences continue to inhibit the access of blacks to elective office? (3) How will further success in removing barriers affect the electoral process?

A Focus for Reform

The experience of the past two decades provides grounds for optimism about the prospects for increasing minority access to the electoral process. That experience underscores the flexibility of the electoral system and the

26. Robert Axelrod, "Presidential Election Coalitions in 1984," *American Political Science Review*, vol. 80 (March 1986), pp. 281–84.

27. Joseph A. Schlesinger, "The New American Political Party," *American Political Science Review*, vol. 79 (December 1985), p. 1166.

efficacy of certain strategies for inducing change. Yet the system has also demonstrated the capacity to resist demands for reform. Many of the recent gains are relatively tenuous and could be undone by a slightly altered judicial climate or even changes in the electoral strategies of the parties.

Reforms in the electoral process have strong implications for the relative status of minority groups in the society. Both blacks and whites have long perceived access to the electoral process by blacks as a means of ensuring sweeping changes in the structure of race relations. For southern whites, disfranchisement of blacks was the key to continued racial segregation and white domination. For blacks, the franchise was the key to equality. Events of the past two decades partly confirm these views as the structure of segregation quickly crumbled before ballot-wielding blacks. Given the link between the ballot and such profound social changes, it is hardly surprising that the white majority still seeks to maintain some vestiges of past political dominance, albeit through more subtle structural means.

Another factor that tends to preserve barriers to minority participation is society's strong bias toward the status quo. Removing some barriers to minorities has meant replacing or modifying familiar structures and processes. Even without strong discriminatory motives, many in the political system are likely to seek to preserve traditional party nominating procedures, at-large elections, existing registration laws, and other familiar electoral arrangements.

Still another factor that could sustain barriers to minority participation, paradoxically, is party competition. Arguably, race has been the most powerful single issue in American politics. The two major parties and several of the minor ones often defined themselves or were defined in relation to that issue. Thus, for nearly a century after the Civil War the Republican party was to some extent defined by its position on emancipation, reconstruction, and basic civil rights for blacks. During this time it functioned almost exclusively in the North, while the Democratic party by espousing white supremacy endeared itself to southern whites. In the late 1930s a shift in partisanship among blacks began that had its origins in social welfare policies rather than in race-related issues. By 1964 the shift became virtually complete as more than 94 percent of black voters supported the Democratic presidential ticket.[28] Conservatives within the Re-

28. George H. Gallup, *The Gallup Poll: Public Opinion 1935–1971*, vol. 3 (Random House, 1972), p. 1901.

publican party, led by Barry Goldwater, opposed civil rights legislation and won the hearts of southern whites, while the Democrats embraced civil rights and lost substantial white support in the South, picking up massive black support instead.[29]

The struggle for greater access by minorities in party affairs will continue to be influenced by the competitive needs of the parties in the electorate. Already there are signs that the Democratic party is becoming increasingly uncomfortable about its strong identification with blacks and might be seeking to reduce that identification as it tries to woo southern white voters again.[30]

These factors notwithstanding, the strong momentum of the struggle for full access will almost certainly result in the elimination of most remaining barriers to minority participation in the electoral process. For the immediate future, reform should focus on three areas. First, action is needed to make registration simpler and easier. A growing number of state and local governments are adopting some form of simplified registration. This trend should accelerate. Second, at-large and multimember districts, particularly where these have discriminatory effects, must give way to single-member districts. Finally, although the gerrymander is probably immortal, its use to dilute minority voting must be further minimized.

Racial Attitudes

The gains made through the courts and through pressure on the political parties go a long way toward ensuring full and effective minority political participation. That goal cannot be realized, however, until white voters are willing to accept minorities as legitimate, competent participants in all phases of the political process, and especially as candidates for elective office. Progress in this regard has been slow. Because white voters remain very reluctant to vote for black candidates, most minorities elected to public office are elected by minority group voters. There are notable exceptions to this rule, such as Los Angeles Mayor Tom Bradley, Denver Mayor Federico Peña, Representatives Allan Wheat of Missouri and Ronald Dellums of California, and Virginia Lieutenant Governor L. Douglas Wilder. But such cases in which a high proportion of the white electorate supports a minority candidate remain very few. Even the elec-

29. Sundquist, *Dynamics of the Party System*, pp. 357–63.
30. Thomas Ferguson and Joel Rogers, *Right Turn: The Decline of the Democrats and the Future of American Politics* (Hill and Wang, 1986), pp. 5–11.

tion of blacks as big city mayors, although widely applauded as evidence of the progress of blacks in the electoral process, has been notable for the small proportion of white voters who supported the black candidate.

There is very little reliable data on white attitudes toward black candidates for public office, but what are available suggest that racial attitudes remain a formidable barrier to black electoral participation in spite of some improvement. Since 1958, surveys by the Gallup Organization have asked whites: "If your party nominated a generally well qualified man for President, would you vote for him if he happened to be a black?" Affirmative responses to this question have grown from 37 percent in 1958 to 81 percent in 1983.[31] While the 75 percent affirmative response suggests great progress, the fact remains that 25 percent of the electorate still would probably not vote for a black candidate on purely racial grounds. Furthermore, even the apparent growth in the proportion of whites willing to vote for a black candidate for president might be misleading. Exit polls by the National Broadcasting Company during the 1986 gubernatorial elections in California and Michigan found that only 52 percent of California voters and 40 percent of Michigan voters thought their state was ready to elect a black as governor. And although whites rated Jesse Jackson highly on a number of attributes for the presidency in 1984, only 4 percent thought he should be his party's nominee.[32] In an electoral arena as intensely competitive as ours, these attitudes constitute truly formidable obstacles to blacks and, by inference, to Hispanics. The removal of structural and procedural barriers to participation will improve the level of minority participation in the electoral process, but change in prejudicial attitudes also is essential. Unfortunately, the pace of such change suggests that an electoral arena unencumbered by racial and ethnic prejudice is a long way off.

Implications for the Electoral Process

Inadequate access to electoral participation for some voters has flawed American politics and prompted a vigorous struggle to achieve a more open, democratic system. That struggle has influenced the electoral process in at least two important ways. First, it has helped bring into being genuinely universal adult suffrage by eradicating or reducing obstacles to the poor as well as to minorities. Second, it has expanded the concept of

31. Howard Schuman and others, *Racial Attitudes in America: Trends and Interpretations* (Harvard University Press, 1985), p. 194.
32. Gallup Poll data provided to Joint Center for Political Studies.

PART THREE

Sources of Corruption

CHAPTER SEVEN

Real and Imagined Corruption
in Campaign Financing

LARRY SABATO

—SENATOR Lloyd Bentsen, Democrat of Texas, shortly after becoming chairman of the Senate Finance Committee in January 1987, offered about 200 Washington lobbyists and political action committee (PAC) directors the opportunity to have breakfast with him once a month in exchange for a $10,000 contribution to his reelection campaign. Following press disclosure of his "Chairman's Council" and a torrent of adverse publicity, Bentsen dissolved his club and returned all the money.[1] At least five other senators with similar fund-raising organizations, including Majority Leader Robert Byrd, refused to follow suit and continued peddling access to well-heeled groups and individuals.[2]

—In the seven 1986 U.S. Senate races where a Democratic challenger defeated a Republican incumbent, there were 150 instances in which a PAC gave to the GOP candidate before the election and then made a contribution to the victorious Democrat after the votes were counted.[3]

—As of December 31, 1986, the thirty-three U.S. senators whose terms will expire in 1988 had already accumulated $12.2 million among them,

1. See Thomas B. Edsall, "Breakfast with the Senate Finance Chairman—for $10,000," *Washington Post*, February 3, 1987; and Edsall, "Bentsen Decides to Disband His $10,000 Breakfast Club," *Washington Post*, February 7, 1987.
2. See Thomas B. Edsall, "Big Checks Opening Doors on Capitol Hill," *Washington Post*, February 6, 1987; Edsall, "Document File," *Washington Post*, February 27, 1987; and "Quaffin' With Quentin," *Washington Post*, March 4, 1987.
3. Common Cause press release, "If At First You Don't Succeed, Give, Give Again," March 20, 1987.

and another thirty-three who are not up for reelection until 1990 had
acquired nearly $7 million four years before their next campaign.[4] Shortly
after the 1986 congressional elections—a time when a campaign kitty is
most likely to be depleted—fifty-one House members reported having
more than $250,000 in the bank for future campaigns. Twenty of these
congressmen had war chests of $400,000, and nine exceeded $500,000.[5]

The disturbing statistics and the horror stories about campaign finance
seem to flow like a swollen river, week after week, year in and year out.
Outrage extends across the ideological spectrum: the liberal interest group
Common Cause has called the system "scandalous," while conservative
former senator Barry Goldwater has bluntly declared, "PAC money is
destroying the election process."[6] In recent congressional campaigns,
PACs have been portrayed as the chief corrupting evil in American
politics. Candidates from Maine to California have scored points by
forswearing the acceptance of PAC gifts earlier and more fervently than
their opponents. In Massachusetts in 1984, for example, all the major
contenders for the U.S. Senate in both parties refused to take PAC money,
and one House candidate badgered his Democratic primary foe to sign a
statement pledging to resign his seat in Congress should he "ever
knowingly accept and keep a campaign contribution from a political action
committee."[7] Despite its aggressiveness in attracting PAC money, the
Democratic party included in its 1984 national platform a call for banning
PAC funds from all federal elections, and newspapers such as the *Boston
Globe* have crusaded against PACs.[8]

PAC bashing is undeniably a popular campaign sport, but the "big PAC
attack" is an opiate that pleasantly obscures more vital concerns and
problems in campaign finance. PAC excesses are merely a symptom of
other serious maladies related to political money, and the near-obsessive
focus by public interest groups and the news media on the purported evils
of PACs has diverted attention from these more fundamental matters. I

4. Jeremy Gaunt, "Senators Amass Funds for Future Campaigns," *Campaign Practices Reports,* vol. 14 (February 9, 1987), pp. 1–3.
5. Thomas B. Edsall, "How Congress Spells 'Safety': M-O-N-E-Y," *Washington
Post,* January 28, 1987.
6. Common Cause direct-mail package to members, January 1987.
7. Steve Lilienthal, "Massachusetts 5: Seizing an Issue," *Political Report,* vol. 7
(August 24, 1984), p. 2.
8. "Democratic Convention Report: Party Approves Anti-PAC Platform," *Campaign
Practices Reports,* vol. 11 (July 30, 1984), pp. 1–3; and "Running from the PACs," *New
Republic,* vol. 190 (May 28, 1984), p. 9.

will first briefly sketch the dimensions of the PAC controversy and review the charges most frequently made against PACs. Then I will review and evaluate a number of reforms in campaign financing, proposing an agenda for change that targets real, not imagined, corruption.[9]

The Age of PACs

While many PACs of all political persuasions existed before the 1970s, it was during the 1970s—the decade of campaign reform—that the modern PAC era began. Spawned by the Watergate-inspired revisions of the campaign finance laws, PACs grew in number from 113 in 1972 to 4,157 by the end of 1986, and their contributions to congressional candidates multiplied from $8.5 million in 1972 to $130.3 million by 1986.[10] This rapid rise of PACs inevitably proved controversial, yet many of the charges made against them are exaggerated and dubious. It is said that PACs are disturbingly novel and have flooded the political system with money, mainly from business. While the widespread use of the PAC structure is new, special-interest money of all types has always found its way into politics, and before the 1970s it did so in less traceable and far more disturbing and unsavory ways.

In absolute terms PACs contribute a massive sum to candidates, but it is not clear that there is proportionately more interest group money in the system than before. As Michael Malbin has argued, the truth will never be known because the earlier record is so incomplete.[11] The proportion of House and Senate campaign funds provided by PACs has certainly increased since the early 1970s, but individuals, most of whom are unaffiliated with PACs, still supply over three-fifths of all the money raised by House candidates and three-quarters of the campaign budgets of Senate contenders. Although the importance of PAC spending has grown, PACs clearly remain secondary to individuals as a source of election funding.

Apart from the argument over the relative weight of PAC funds, critics claim that PACs are making it more expensive to run for office. There is some validity to this assertion. Money provided to one side funds the

9. Some of this material is drawn from the author's *PAC Power: Inside the World of Political Action Committees*, rev. ed. (Norton, 1985).

10. Data from Federal Election Commission.

11. Michael J. Malbin, "The Problem of PAC-Journalism," *Public Opinion*, vol. 5 (December–January 1983), pp. 15–16, 59.

purchase of campaign tools that the other side must then match in order to stay competitive. In the aggregate, American campaign expenditures seem huge. Congressional candidates in the 1986 election spent a total of about $450 million, for instance.[12] Will Rogers's remark has never been more true: "Politics has got so expensive that it takes lots of money to even get beat with."

Yet these days it is enormously expensive to communicate, whether the message is political or commercial. Television time, polling costs, consultants' fees, direct-mail investment, and other standard campaign expenditures have been soaring in price, over and above inflation.[13] PACs have been fueling the use of new campaign techniques, but a reasonable case can be made that such expenses are necessary and that more and better communication is required between candidates and an electorate that often appears woefully uninformed about politics. PACs therefore may be making a positive contribution by providing the means to increase the flow of information during elections (though one can legitimately question whether thirty-second TV spots can enlighten anyone).

PACs are also accused of favoring incumbents, and except for the ideological ones, PACs do display a clear preference for incumbents. But the same bias is apparent in contributions from individuals. Facing all contributors is a rational, perhaps decisive, economic question: why waste money on nonincumbents if incumbents almost always win? On the other hand, the best challengers—those perceived as having fair to good chances of winning—are generously funded by PACs. Well-targeted PAC challenger money clearly helped the Republicans win a majority in the U.S. Senate in 1980, for instance, and in turn aided the Democrats in their 1986 Senate takeover. It is true that PACs limit the number of strong challengers by giving so much early money to incumbents and thus helping to deter potential opponents. But the money that PACs channel to competitive challengers late in the election season may then increase the turnover of officeholders on election day. PAC money also certainly increases the level of competitiveness in congressional races without an incumbent candidate.

Another line of attack on PACs is more justified. The undemocratic character of the process by which some PACs choose which candidates to support completely severs the connecting link between contributor and

---

12. Data from Federal Election Commission.
13. See Larry Sabato, *The Rise of Political Consultants* (Basic Books, 1981); see also "Campaign Spending Report: Where the Money Goes," *National Journal*, vol. 15 (April 16, 1983), pp. 780–81.

candidate. As political scientist David Adamany has noted, this unhealthy condition is most apparent in many of the ideological nonconnected PACs, whose free-style organization and lack of a parent body make them accountable to no one and responsive mainly to their own whims.[14]

Leaders of ideological PACs insist that their committees are democratic in the sense that their contributors will stop giving if dissatisfied with the PACs' candidate choices. But these PACs, like most independent committees, raise money by direct mail. Except for perhaps an occasional news article, the average donor's only source of information about the PAC's activities is its own direct mail, which, not surprisingly, tends to be upbeat and selective in reporting the committee's work. Moreover, as political scientist Frank Sorauf has stressed, since direct mail can succeed with a response rate of only 2–5 percent and prospecting for new donors is continuous, decisions by even a large number of givers to drop out will have little effect on PAC fund-raising.[15]

Ideological PACs are not alone in following undemocratic practices. When the AFL-CIO overwhelmingly endorsed Democrat Walter Mondale for president in 1983, making available to him the invaluable resources of most labor PACs, a CBS/*New York Times* poll showed that among the union members they interviewed, less than a quarter reported having had their presidential preferences solicited in any fashion.[16] If a democratic sampling had been taken, the AFL-CIO might not have been so pro-Mondale. The CBS/*Times* poll indicated that not only was Mondale not favored by a majority of the union respondents, he was in a dead heat with Senator John Glenn for a plurality edge. Nor can many corporate PACs be considered showcases of democracy. In a few the chief executive officers completely rule the roost, and in many the CEOs have inordinate influence.

Does PAC Money Buy Congressional Votes?

The most serious charge leveled at PACs is that they succeed in buying the votes of legislators on issues important to each committee's constituency. That many PACs are shopping for congressional votes seems hardly

14. David Adamany, "The New Faces of American Politics," *Annals of the American Academy of Political and Social Sciences,* vol. 486 (July 1986), pp. 31–32.

15. Frank J. Sorauf, "Accountability in Political Action Committees: Who's in Charge?" paper prepared for the 1982 annual meeting of the American Political Science Association, pp. 21–22.

16. The random-sample telephone poll of 1,587 adults was taken in September 1983, at about the time of the AFL-CIO endorsement.

worth arguing. That PAC money buys access to congressmen is similarly disputed by few. But the "vote-buying" allegation is generally not supported by a careful examination of the facts.[17] PAC contributions do make a difference, at least on some occasions, in securing access and influencing the course of events on the House and Senate floors. But those occasions are not nearly as frequent as anti-PAC spokesmen often suggest.

PACs affect legislative proceedings to a decisive degree only when certain conditions prevail. First, the less visible the issue, the more likely that PAC funds can influence congressional votes. A corollary of this rule might be that PAC money has more effect on the early stages of the legislative process, such as agenda setting and votes in subcommittee meetings, than on later and more public floor deliberations. Press, public, and even "watchdog" groups are not nearly as attentive to initial legislative proceedings.

Second, PAC contributions are more likely to influence the legislature when the matter at hand is specialized and narrow or unopposed by other organized interests. PAC gifts are less likely to be decisive on broad national issues such as American policy in El Salvador or the adoption of an MX missile system. Additionally, PAC influence in Congress is greater when large PACs or groups of them are allied. In recent years business and labor, despite their natural enmity, have lobbied together on a number of issues including defense spending, trade policy, environmental regulation, maritime legislation, trucking legislation, and nuclear power.[18] The combination is a weighty one, checked in many instances only by a tendency for business and labor in one industry (say, the railroads) to combine and oppose their cooperating counterparts in another industry (perhaps the truckers and Teamsters).

It is worth stressing, however, that most congressmen are not unduly influenced by PAC money on most votes. The special conditions I have outlined simply do not apply to most legislative issues. Other considerations—foremost among them a congressman's party affiliation, ideology, and constituents' needs and desires—are the overriding factors in determining a legislator's votes. Much has been made of the passage of large

17. For an extended discussion of this subject, see Sabato, *PAC Power,* pp. 122–59, 222–28.

18. See, for example, Edwin M. Epstein, "An Irony of Electoral Reform," *Regulation,* vol. 3 (May–June 1979), pp. 35–44; and Christopher Madison, "Federal Subsidy Programs under Attack by Unlikely Marriage of Left and Right," *National Journal,* vol. 15 (December 31, 1983), pp. 2682–84.

tax cuts for oil and business interests in the 1981 omnibus tax package. Journalist Elizabeth Drew said there was a "bidding war" to trade campaign contributions for tax breaks benefiting the independent oil producers.[19] Ralph Nader's Public Citizen group charged that the $280,000 in corporate PAC money accepted by members of the House Ways and Means Committee had helped to produce a bill that "contained everything business ever dared to ask for, and more."[20] Yet, as Robert Samuelson has convincingly argued, the "bidding war" between Democrats and Republicans was waged not for PAC money but for control of a House of Representatives sharply divided between Reaganite Republicans and liberal Democrats, with conservative "boll weevil" Democrats from the southern oil states as the crucial swing votes.[21] The Ways and Means Committee actions cited by Nader were also more correctly explained in partisan terms. After all, if these special interests were so influential in the writing of the 1981 omnibus tax package, how could they fail so completely to derail the much more important (and, for them, threatening) tax reform legislation of 1986?

The answer goes beyond the tug of party ties, of course. If party loyalty can have a stronger pull than PAC contributions, then surely the views of a congressman's constituents usually take precedence over those of PACs. PAC gifts are merely a means to an end: reelection. If accepting money will cause a candidate embarassment, then even a maximum donation is likely to be rejected. If an incumbent is faced with a choice of either voting for a PAC-backed bill that is very unpopular in his district or forgoing donations from the PAC or even a whole industry, the odds are that he will side with his constituency and vote against the PAC's interest. The flip side of this proposition makes sense as well: if a PAC's parent organization has many members or a major financial stake in the congressman's home district, he is much more likely to vote the PAC's way—not so much because he receives PAC money but because the group accounts for an important part of his electorate. Does Senator David Durenberger of Minnesota vote for dairy price supports because he received 11 percent of his PAC contributions from agriculture, or because the farm population of his state is relatively large and politically active? Do congressmen generally

19. Elizabeth Drew, "Politics and Money, Part I," *New Yorker* (December 6, 1982), pp. 38–45.

20. Herbert E. Alexander, *Financing the 1980 Election* (D.C. Heath, 1983), p. 379.

21. Robert J. Samuelson, "The Campaign Reform Failure," *New Republic* (September 5, 1983), pp. 32–33.

vote the National Rifle Association's preferences because of the money the
NRA's PAC distributes or because the NRA, unlike gun-control advocates,
has repeatedly demonstrated the ability to produce a sizable number of
votes in many legislative districts?

If PACs have appeared more influential than they actually are, perhaps
it is partly because many people's views of congressmen have been tainted
by scandals such as Abscam. The spectacle of a congressman exclaiming
on candid camera, "I've got larceny in my blood!" leaves a powerful
impression. It is both disturbing and amusing that the National Republican
Congressional Committee felt obliged to warn PAC-soliciting Republican
candidates; "Don't *ever* suggest to the PAC that it is 'buying' your vote
should you get elected."[22] Yet all knowledgeable Capitol Hill observers
agree that there are few truly corrupt congressmen. Simple correlations
notwithstanding, when legislators vote for a PAC-supported bill, it is
usually because they have been convinced of the merits of the case by
arguments or pressure from their party leaders, peers, or constituents
rather than by money from the PAC.

When the PAC phenomenon is viewed in the broad perspective, and
when the complex nature of the congressional and electoral process is fully
considered, what matters most to congressmen as they vote is merit, as
defined by the specifics of each case, general ideological beliefs, party
loyalty, and the interests of district constituents. It is ludicrously naive to
contend that PAC money never influences congressmen's decisions. But it
is irredeemably cynical to believe that PACs always, or even usually, push
the voting buttons in Congress.

PACs and Pluralism

PACs are contemporary examples of what James Madison called factions. Through the flourishing of competing interest groups or factions,
Madison wrote in *Federalist* number 10, liberty would be preserved:
"Liberty is to faction what air is to fire, an element without which it would
instantly expire."[23]

In any democracy, and particularly in one as pluralistic as the United
States, it is essential that groups be relatively unrestricted in advocating
their interests and positions. Not only is unrestricted political activity by

22. National Republican Congressional Committee, "Working with PACs" (1982).
23. *The Federalist,* no. 10 (New American Library, 1961), p. 78.

interest groups a mark of a free society, but it provides a safety valve for the competitive pressures that build on all fronts in a capitalist democracy. It also provides another means to keep representatives responsive to legitimate needs. This is not to say that all groups' interests are legitimate, nor that vigorously competing interests alone ensure that the public good prevails. The press, public, and watchdog groups such as Common Cause must always be alert to instances in which narrow private interests can prevail over the commonweal. This generally happens when no one is looking.

Besides the press and watchdog organizations, there are two major institutional checks on the evils of factions, associations, and now PACs. The most fundamental of these is regular free elections with general suffrage. As Tocqueville commented:

> Perhaps the most powerful of the causes which tend to mitigate the excesses of political association in the United States is Universal Suffrage. In countries in which universal suffrage exists, the majority is never doubtful, because neither party can pretend to represent that portion of the community which has not voted.
>
> The associations which are formed are aware, as well as the nation at large, that they do not represent the majority: this is, indeed, a condition inseparable from their existence; for if they did represent the prepondering power, they would change the law instead of soliciting its reform.[24]

PAC critics frequently make the point that certain segments of the electorate are underrepresented in the PAC community. Senate Republican leader Robert Dole has said, "There aren't any poor PACs or Food Stamp PACs or Nutrition PACs or Medicare PACs."[25] Yet without much support from PACs, food stamps, poverty and nutrition programs, and medicare do exist. Why? Because the recipients of governmental assistance constitute a hefty slice of the electorate, and votes matter more than dollars to politicians. Furthermore, many citizens outside the affected groups have also made known their support of aid to the poor and elderly, making yet a stronger electoral case for these PAC-less programs.

The other major institution that checks PAC influence is the two-party

24. Alexis de Tocqueville, *Democracy in America* (Vintage Books, 1954), vol. 1, p. 224.

25. Quoted in Drew, "Politics and Money, Part I," p. 147.

system. While PACs represent particular interests, the political parties build coalitions of groups and attempt to present a national perspective on policy. They arbitrate among special-interest claims, and they seek to reach a consensus on matters of overriding importance to the nation. The parties are among the most important of the unifying forces in an exceptionally diverse country. If interest groups and their PACs are useful to a functioning democracy, then the political parties must be considered essential.

In the last few years the parties, after decades of decline, have begun to achieve rehabilitation. But there is a long way to go. Reforms to bolster the parties also have a useful side effect: they temper the excesses of PACs by reducing their proportional effect on the election of public officials.

Reforms That Would Do More Harm Than Good

A number of legislative proposals have been made to restrict the total contributions a congressional candidate can receive from PACs to a fixed amount ($70,000 under the Obey-Railsback bill that passed the House in 1979, and $100,000 in the proposal by Senator David Boren of Oklahoma that was under consideration in 1986).[26] Like many reforms, this idea has a certain superficial appeal. But the hidden costs and consequences would be enormously destructive.

Such a limitation on PAC gifts would unfairly benefit incumbents. While incumbents as a group raise far more PAC money than do challengers, in competitive races (where there is a good chance for the incumbent to lose) challengers sometimes match or outraise incumbents among PACs. The extra PAC money is usually much more useful to a little-known challenger than to a well-known incumbent. A cap on PAC gifts

26. The Obey-Railsback bill and other proposals are described in Michael J. Malbin, "Looking Back at the Future of Campaign Finance Reform: Interest Groups and American Elections," in Malbin, ed., *Money and Politics in the United States: Financing Elections in the 1980s* (Washington, D.C.: American Enterprise Institute for Public Policy Research, 1984), pp. 235–38. In Boren's 1986 bill, the $100,000 limit applied to House candidates only. For Senate candidates, between $175,000 and $750,000 would have been allowed, depending on the size of the state. Limits for both House and Senate candidates were to be adjusted upward in cases of runoffs and contested primaries. Boren's more extensive 1987 bill (S.2)—at least in its first version—dealt only with Senate elections and proposed some public financing. PACs were to have no role in the general elections of candidates receiving public funds. In the primaries (or primaries and general elections of candidates *not* receiving public funding), the $175,000–$750,000 limits applied to total PAC gifts.

would mean that challengers would have less chance to raise enough money to defeat vulnerable incumbents. The "PAC cap" would in reality be a "challenger cap."

Limitations on PAC gifts would also have other unintended consequences. Reducing the flow of PAC funds would help wealthy candidates. Currently, candidates can spend unrestricted personal funds on their own election; to limit opponents' access to cash would obviously further increase the wealthy candidates' advantage. It is ironic, in light of the support given to PAC limits by labor-oriented Democrats, that a PAC cap is likely to hurt labor and Democratic candidates more than the business interests and Republicans. Democratic candidates depend on PAC funds more heavily than do Republicans because the relatively impoverished Democratic party cannot supply them with as much money as the well-financed Republican party committees can offer their party's nominees. Moreover, as former Democratic National Committee political director Ann Lewis points out, "Once labor bumps up against the ceiling they can't go back to their members and expect to channel large individual donations (to favored candidates). Our people don't have that kind of money, whereas the corporate PAC people can double their contributions by going to their executives and asking them to send personal donations (to candidates) of $1,000 each."[27] Some PAC limitation proposals also call for reducing the maximum gift of $5,000 per election that a candidate can now receive from any one PAC. This is another move sure to hurt labor disproportionately, since labor PACs tend to "max out" far more frequently than corporate and trade committees. Actually, this type of PAC limitation has already occurred as a result of inflation: a 1974 gift of $5,000 has now been reduced in value by about half.

The most disturbing consequence of further limits on PAC contributions would be an inevitable increase in the role of independent expenditures (see discussion below). Independent expenditures are the least accountable form of political spending, and have often been used to finance viciously negative advertising. They are hardly something campaign finance reformers should want to encourage. PACs are established organizations with the proven ability to raise money; if their capacity to make direct contributions is restricted, they will find other useful ways to spend their funds. Reformers may be able to squeeze PAC cash out of candidates' election accounts. They will not succeed in forcing it out of the

27. Interview with Ann Lewis, July 22, 1983.

political system. Other activities will simply come to the fore, such as unreported "soft money" gifts to parties in states without restrictions on political contributions by corporations or unions, Washington lobbying campaigns, and political education and involvement programs galore.

No doubt encouragement of large individual gifts from PAC-affiliated persons would also become widespread. Such donations, of course, are not as easily traceable as PAC gifts are. Martin D. Franks, the Democratic Congressional Campaign Committee's former director, speculated that "with a PAC limit, instead of getting one check from Lockheed corporation's PAC we'll get five $1,000 checks from housewives in the San Fernando Valley with no mention that their spouses are executives with Lockheed. In that sense PACs serve an efficient bookkeeping and disclosure purpose."[28] Senator Boren, a prominent champion of PAC limitations, is himself a good case study. Boren virtuously refuses all PAC money, but a detailed investigation revealed that fully a quarter of Boren's million-dollar war chest raised in 1983 and 1984 came from executives and employees of the energy and banking industries.[29] The total was probably larger, since many contributions from "homemakers" were reportedly made by women closely related to corporate executives who had contributed under their own names.

Finally, an overall PAC limit might increase the chances that legislative votes could be swayed by PAC gifts. If both the railroads and the trucking industry, for instance, tried to make a contribution to a congressman, but only the railroads succeeded before the incumbent's PAC limit was reached, might not the legislator be more beholden to railroad interests as a result of this scheme? Allowing the congressman to accept donations from both the railroads and their natural competitors maintains some balance among competing interests.

One of the leading PAC critics, Representative David Obey, Democrat of Wisconsin, dismisses all arguments that increasing limits on PACs is self-defeating because PACs will find ways, often more harmful, to circumvent the restrictions. "To me," he says, "that is like saying, 'Don't cure heart disease, because the guy might get cancer.'"[30] But considering

28. Interview with Martin Franks, August 25, 1983.
29. "The Financing of David Boren," *Campaign Practices Reports*, vol. 13 (May 5, 1986), pp. 1–5.
30. Quoted in Herbert E. Alexander and Brian A. Haggerty, *The Federal Election Campaign Act: After a Decade of Political Reform* (Washington, D.C.: Citizens' Research Foundation, 1981), p. 74.

all the problems that would be introduced by further PAC limits, a better medical analogy might be: Don't use a cancer-causing drug on a cold.

Reforms That Make Sense

As I have discussed, one sure way to lessen the importance of PACs is to shore up competing institutions and to increase the pool of alternative money. To begin with, the $1,000 limit on an individual's contribution to each candidate per election should be raised to recover its loss to inflation since 1974. Both the $1,000 cap and the companion limit of $25,000 on what an individual is permitted to donate to all candidates in a calendar year should be permanently indexed to the inflation rate. Restoring the value of individual contributions will offset somewhat the financial clout of the PACs.

Much more vital is the need to enhance the financial flexibility of the political parties. While individuals and PACs represent particular interests and further the atomization of public policy, the parties encompass more general concerns and push the system toward consensus. Their role is absolutely central to American democracy's future health and success; thus the parties should be accorded special, preferential treatment by the campaign finance laws. The original Federal Election Campaign Act of 1971 (FECA) was not especially generous to the parties, though neither was it particularly injurious, considering that it allowed coordinated expenditures by the party on behalf of a slate of candidates, and established relatively liberal limits on contributions and expenditures for parties. The 1979 amendments to FECA helped by allowing state and local parties to spend unlimited amounts on materials for volunteer activities and get-out-the-vote drives. The most useful party advantage of all under current law may be the greatly reduced postage rates allowed party mailings, funded by a congressional subsidy.

But parties can be aided still further. The current limits on contributions to party committees ($20,000 a year for an individual and $15,000 for a multicandidate PAC) should be substantially increased. Additionally, contributors should be permitted to underwrite without limit the administrative, legal, and accounting costs parties incur. A modest level of public funding from general tax revenues or some of the surplus existing in the Federal Election Campaign Fund (derived from the income tax check-off) should be provided each year to the national party committees for party-building activities, or, alternatively, taxpayers should be permitted to take a tax credit for their gifts to parties (see below).

It would be wise, too, for Congress to reclaim a portion of the public's airwaves and require that television and radio stations turn over a dozen five-minute blocks of prime time each year to both the state parties and another dozen blocks to both national parties (rather than to individual candidates) so that more generic, institutional advertising can be aired even by the relatively underfinanced Democrats.[31] (Politicians should still be free to make unlimited additional purchases to promote their individual candidacies.) The parties should have wide discretion in determining the uses to which the time is put. They may wish to conserve it all for the general election, or they may allocate some of it to help the party's endorsed slate in the primary.

The relative failure of the Democratic party at fund raising, so far at least, stands in the way of more substantial reforms. Republican National Committee chairman Frank Fahrenkopf is surely correct in wondering "why the United Auto Workers or NCPAC can spend an unlimited amount of money supporting or opposing candidates for federal office [by means of independent expenditures] and not the Republican or Democrat parties."[32] At some point the amounts party committees can give or spend on behalf of their nominees should be considerably increased, but this will probably not be acceptable until the Democratic party becomes better funded. The long-term objective is clear: beef up the parties so that PACs will be limited indirectly. Candidates and the political system will then benefit from the infusion of more party funds and power, and the influence of PACs will decrease without their being shackled by unfair and unworkable restrictions.

Public Finance Proposals

President Theodore Roosevelt first proposed in 1907 that the cost of campaigns be borne by the federal treasury, and since 1976, as a result of the Watergate scandals, presidential campaigns have been publicly fi-

31. See Sabato, *The Rise of Political Consultants*, pp. 326–28. Incidentally, allocation of free time to parties rather than to individual candidates would solve the problem of time availability in large metropolitan areas combining dozens of congressional districts and candidates.

32. As quoted in "A Shopping Guide for Contributors to the GOP Cause," *First Monday*, vol. 13 (November–December 1983), p. 9.

nanced. But three major attempts in the late 1970s to extend the presidential system to congressional races fell short.[33] More recently Senators Boren and Byrd have seriously proposed partial public financing of Senate campaigns, but it is questionable whether such a bill can be enacted in the foreseeable future.

If and when public financing of congressional elections is passed, it should be designed in ways that benefit the political system. Public funds should be given to candidates as *floors* rather than as *ceilings*. Under this system, every congressional candidate at the primary election level who can raise a qualifying amount (say $50,000) in small contributions (perhaps $250 and under) should be eligible for matching funds from the federal treasury for all similar small gifts, up to a maximum per candidate of something between $50,000 and $75,000. Then in the general election, congressional nominees of the major parties would receive a flat amount (a floor) in public funds (perhaps $150,000) to ensure that they had the minimum financial base needed to conduct a modern campaign. Beyond that, in both the primary and general election, they should be permitted to raise as much as they can in unrestricted fashion from PACs and individuals. This approach guarantees at least basic competition in each district and augments the ability of candidates to communicate with voters while preserving for individuals, PACs, and interest groups a rightful and legitimate role in elections. A ceiling on expenditures, by contrast, almost certainly benefits incumbents since challengers must usually spend a great deal more than average to defeat an incumbent. Moreover, a ceiling restricts the flow of communications between candidates and voters and unfairly minimizes the direct participation of PACs in the political process. And as is true of other limitations on PAC contributions, a public-funds ceiling would squeeze PAC money into less accountable and less desirable channels, such as independent spending. A public-funding scheme should also transmit treasury money through the national or state political parties, permitting them to keep a certain percentage for their own administration and party-building activities and perhaps also allowing them some degree of flexibility in allocating funds to their nominees.

33. See "Election Reforms: Delay and Defeat," *Congressional Quarterly Almanac 1977* (Washington, D.C.: Congressional Quarterly, 1978), p. 798; "Public Financing, Campaign Spending Bills," *Congressional Quarterly Almanac 1978* (Washington, D.C.: Congressional Quarterly, 1979), p. 769; and "Carter Election Package Fails to Advance," *Congressional Quarterly Almanac 1979* (Washington, D.C.: Congressional Quarterly, 1980), p. 551.

Realistically, these reform measures do not now have a good chance of enactment. Congressmen are probably not going to subject themselves to additional leverage by their parties, nor are they going to do any favors for their opponents by enacting public-funding floors that favor challengers rather than ceilings that favor themselves. Representative Richard Cheney, Republican of Wyoming, said it best: "If you think this Congress, or any other, is going to set up a system where someone can run against them on equal terms at government expense, you're smoking something you can't buy at the corner drugstore."[34]

Probably the best form of public financing with a reasonable chance of passage is the tax credit option. The 1986 tax reform bill eliminated the 50 percent tax credit for all contributions to candidates, PACs, and political committees of up to $50 for an individual and $100 on a joint return. A useful and feasible reform would restore the old credit and increase it to 100 percent, but only for contributions to political parties, or to House and Senate candidates from the contributor's own state, not for gifts to PACs. Special-interest groups should not be restricted as they go about fulfilling their legitimate purposes, but their political activities should not be subsidized by the taxpayers.

Reforming the tax credit incentive in this way would remove the inducement for giving to PACs and augment the motivation for party giving. It would also encourage candidates to expand their base of small, in-state contributors rather than simply concentrating on national PACs and large individual donors. And while challengers would benefit from a form of public financing that increases the electoral money supply without capping expenditures, incumbents would perhaps be in a better position to take advantage of the small-donor tax credit because of their superior resources and higher name recognition. Not incidentally, recent elections have underlined the need to stimulate more small individual contributions. Gifts of under $100 to House general election candidates declined from 36 percent of all campaign money in 1978 to 18 percent in 1982 and 15 percent in 1984.[35] Increasing the tax credit for small gifts would encourage participation from more citizens while providing another indirect check on PACs.

34. Quoted in Richard A. Armstrong, "Election Finance and Free Speech," *Newsweek,* July 18, 1983, p. 11.

35. See Richard P. Conlon, "The Declining Role of Individual Contributions in Financing Congressional Campaigns," *Journal of Law and Politics,* vol. 3 (Winter 1987), p. 491. Individual contributions of all sizes have also declined as a proportion of money raised. Whereas House and Senate general election candidates secured 66 percent of their funds from individuals in 1978 and 59 percent in 1980, individuals provided only 53 percent in 1984.

This reform might also help to stem another unhealthy development, the aggregation of large personal debts accumulated by candidates (especially nonincumbents) during their campaigns. By 1984, 12 percent of all money raised by Senate candidates and 8 percent of all funds secured by House candidates were in the form of loans, either borrowed from banks or given from their own personal fortunes.[36] These loans can place elected representatives under great pressure once in office, as they raise money to repay the banks or themselves.[37]

The Importance of Disclosure

Probably the most universally supported and certainly the most successful provision of the campaign finance law is the disclosure requirement, under which PACs and candidates are required at various intervals to reveal their contributors and their expenditures. Disclosure provisions not only expose the motives and decisions of PACs and politicians, but also alert competing interests to the need for mobilization.

Disclosure is no cure-all, however. As David Adamany has pointed out, the disclosure laws generate more information than can be mastered by the media or the voters.[38] The volume of financial disclosure reports filed with the Federal Election Commission is crushing. Despite inadequate funding, the FEC does an admirable job in making the information available to press and public, but it is usually well after election day before any thorough analysis of the data can begin, which is too late to affect the election results. Still, disclosure serves many useful purposes, from permitting postelection enforcement of the laws to allowing connections to be made between campaign contributions and votes cast on the floor of Congress. Disclosure itself generates pressure for more reform. When campaign finance was out of sight, it was out of most people's minds; now that the trail of money can be more easily followed, indignation is only a press

36. Data from Federal Election Commission.

37. See Edward Roeder, "Huge Campaign Borrowing Is Corrupting Elections," *Washington Post,* April 14, 1985; and "Banks and Political Lending," *Washington Post* editorial, April 16, 1985. It is certainly true that fund-raising pressure is a constant of life for all congressmen, whether they have debts or not. But personally secured loans are particularly worrisome, since they present the opportunity for the lending banks to assert undue influence—although they are strictly regulated on this score. In the case of a loan from a candidate's personal monies, postelection PAC and individual gifts can go right into a congressman's pocket (as he repays the loan to himself).

38. David Adamany, "PAC's and the Democratic Financing of Politics," *Arizona Law Review,* vol. 22, no. 2 (1980), pp. 597–98.

release away. Disclosure is the single greatest check on the excesses of campaign finance, for it encourages corrective action, whether judicial or political. It is such an essential and welcome device in American democracy that it should be broadened to bring to light a number of abuses or perceived abuses in the PAC community.

No PAC practice is so distasteful as the distortion and deception found in many direct-mail solicitations, especially from the ideological committees. PACs using any form of direct-mail fund-raising should be required to enclose a copy of all letters with their periodic FEC reports. Direct-mail fund-raising is notoriously prone to exaggeration and deceptive promise. Robert Timberg documented a number of such cases in a newspaper series on PACs. The Life Amendment PAC, an antiabortion organization, sent out a letter begging for money to save the seat of antiabortionist Representative Henry Hyde, Republican of Illinois, who was described as being in mortal danger of defeat. In fact Hyde, who had no prior knowledge of the letter and repudiated it, was in a safe Republican district. Another antiabortion group calling itself "Stop the Baby Killers" promised in 1979 to give maximum contributions to candidates opposing a number of "Political Baby Killers" (liberal Democratic congressmen), and to pay for polls, in-kind campaign consultants, and campaign training seminars for volunteers. In truth, the group made not a single contribution of any size to a candidate in 1979 or 1980, conducted no polls, and held no campaign seminars. What happened to the $189,000 the group raised? About $146,000 was used to pay three for-profit direct-mail firms with ties to the organization itself.[39]

The political right wing has no monopoly on such travesties. Other disturbing examples come from the ideological left. Of the nearly $1.7 million raised by Congressman Edward Markey's two PACs (the U.S. Committee Against Nuclear War and the National Committee for Peace in Central America) from 1982 to 1986, less than 3 percent was contributed to candidates sympathetic to the Massachusetts Democrat's causes. Markey's PACs broke repeated promises to 50,000 contributors that their money would be used to train and elect liberal contenders, lobby legislators, and conduct polling, canvassing, and phone banks.[40]

---

39. See Sabato, *The Rise of Political Consultants,* pp. 220–67; and Robert Timberg, "The PAC Business," *Baltimore Sun,* July 11–19, 1982.

40. See Steven Waldman, "The Hiroshima Hustle," *Washington Monthly,* vol. 18 (October 1986), pp. 35–40; and John Robinson, "Problem PACs: Groups Take In More Than They Contribute," *Boston Globe,* October 2, 1986, pp. 1, 6.

The FEC has received many complaints about fraudulent political fund-raising, and this may be only the tip of the iceberg. Unless a reporter happens to receive a copy of a questionable solicitation or a contributor takes it upon himself to trace his money through the FEC, little is heard about most direct-mail pieces.

Just as private charities are required to do in many states, PACs using direct mail should be forced to disclose in each letter and on each contributor card how much of all money raised is devoted to fund-raising and administrative costs. Granted, prospecting for direct-mail donors is a necessary and expensive first step in the process, but it takes only a couple of paragraphs to explain this to letter recipients. They may not like what they read and consequently may refuse to give, but they are entitled to know how their money will be spent if any degree of accountability is to exist. Furthermore, all PACs, not just those using direct mail, should be required to report their list of candidate selections to their contributors. Most PACs already do this, but the ideological PACs are usually exceptions.

Beyond PACs, broadened disclosure is needed in other areas. Both national parties have a "building fund" to pay the costs of the headquarters facilities. Corporations, unions, and individuals contribute millions of dollars to these funds, which, for the most part, remain hidden from public view.[41] Tens of millions have been similarly given in "soft money"—donations channeled through the national and state parties that normally would be illegal under federal election law because the money comes directly from corporate or union treasuries or exceeds maximum contribution limits. This "soft money" remains barely legal because it is spent primarily by the *state* parties in states where direct corporate or labor union treasury contributions are permitted, ostensibly to affect only non-federal races. The distinction, of course, is artificial since voter registration and turnout programs inevitably influence all contests on the ballot.[42]

Finally, some presidential candidates, as well as some large PACs, have established tax-exempt foundations that exist primarily to prepare the

41. See Thomas B. Edsall, "Firms, Lobbies Provide Much of Democrats' Funds," *Washington Post*, August 12, 1986; and Edsall, "Corporate Chiefs Put Heart Into Contributions to GOP, " *Washington Post*, August 29, 1986.

42. Ibid. See also Herbert E. Alexander, *"Soft Money" and Campaign Financing* (Washington, D.C.: Public Affairs Council, 1986); Ronald Brownstein and Maxwell Glen, "Money in the Shadows," *National Journal*, vol. 18 (March 15, 1986), pp. 632–37; "Common Cause Fights FEC over 'Soft Money,' Reagan Trip," *Campaign Practices Reports*, vol. 13 (July 14, 1986), p. 3; and Steven Emerson, "Soft Money Hits Hard in '86 Races," *U.S. News and World Report*, July 21, 1986, p. 18.

groundwork for their sponsors' White House bids. Yet these foundations can accept unlimited donations from groups and individuals and do not have to disclose the identities of any donors.[43] Some potential candidates have voluntarily revealed their foundations' benefactors, but they should not have the choice. This subterfuge should be exposed and disclosed.

Particularly if these reforms are adopted, the perpetually starved Federal Election Commission must be funded at a much more generous level to accommodate the increased crush of paper that comes with broad disclosure.[44]

The Dilemma of Independent Expenditures

It is not easy for a liberal Democratic senator who was a prime target of the National Conservative Political Action Committee (NCPAC) in his 1982 reelection race and the former chairman of NCPAC to find common ground, but the issue of accountability in independent spending is apparently an area on which they agreed. Senator Paul Sarbanes, Democrat of Maryland, testified: "The independent PACs operate outside of [the] framework of accountability and simply become hit artists on the political scene." The late John "Terry" Dolan, former NCPAC chairman, was quoted as saying, "I'm against independent expenditures . . . because they decrease accountability. . . . I think candidates should be accountable for charges that are brought up."[45]

Voters cannot hold candidates accountable for the charges made about their opponents by an independent group, and that is only the beginning of the nettlesome problems caused by independent expenditures. Under federal election law an independent expenditure is money spent by an individ-

---

43. Democratic presidential candidates Gary Hart and Bruce Babbitt and Republican candidates Jack Kemp and Pat Robertson have all maintained tax-exempt foundations in recent years. Robertson's Freedom Council, which was dissolved in October 1986, has perhaps been the most controversial. See Thomas B. Edsall, "Robertson Group Ruled Tax Exempt," *Washington Post,* June 7, 1986; "A Tax Exempt Campaign?" *Washington Post* editorial, June 9, 1986; and Jeff Garth, "Tax Data of Pat Robertson Groups Are Questioned," *New York Times,* December 10, 1986.

44. The FEC—intentionally underfunded and hamstrung by Congress to keep it relatively toothless—needs an infusion of funds even if no new responsibilities are added. Among other things, disclosure needs to be more prompt and accessible (particularly as election day approaches), but the FEC currently lacks the resources to accomplish this.

45. Testimony of Sen. Paul S. Sarbanes in *The Federal Election Campaign Act of 1971,* Hearings before the Senate Committee on Rules and Administration, 98 Cong. 1 sess. (Government Printing Office, 1983), p. 157; and Alexander and Haggerty, *The Federal Election Campaign Act,* p. 86.

ual or a group to support or defeat a candidate without consultation with, or the cooperation of, any candidate or campaign. In other words, the expenditure truly must be independent, and if it is, there are no limits on the amount that can be spent.[46] Since independent spending is unlimited, it undermines a basic intent of the campaign finance laws. The frequent use of negative, even vicious, messages and tactics by independent groups makes any sort of civility in politics much more difficult to achieve. And since most of their cash is raised by direct mail, the groups' minimal contact with their contributors leaves them unaccountable to their own donors as well as voters at large.

Despite these widely acknowledged difficulties and the opposition to unlimited independent expenditures by political figures as diverse as Barry Goldwater and George McGovern, every attempt to rein in the independent groups has so far failed. For instance, the Federal Election Commission made a determined but unsuccessful try to enforce a key provision of the Presidential Campaign Fund Act that bars PACs from spending more than $1,000 each on behalf of a presidential nominee who has accepted public financing.[47] The proximate cause of the failure was the Supreme Court's 1976 decision in *Buckley* v. *Valeo*.[48] The Court held that PACs and individuals acting completely on their own can advocate a candidate's election or defeat without limit. But the real obstacle to this reform is the First Amendment to the U.S. Constitution guaranteeing free speech, on which the *Buckley* decision was based. However noxious the independent groups' activities may be, to stifle their right to free speech would be a dangerous and blatantly unconstitutional error.

Even though independent spending itself should not be restricted, its unfortunate effects can be tempered somewhat. Once again, strengthening the financial role of political parties in elections as well as increasing the pool of small individual givers through tax credits would indirectly help to reduce the importance of independent spending. Beyond that, requiring the disclosure of direct-mail letters, candidate selections, and fund-raising

46. For a background discussion of independent expenditures, see Rodney Smith, "Federal Election Law, Part II: What You Can Get Away With!" *Campaigns and Elections,* vol. 3 (Fall 1982), pp. 24–28. See also Alexander, *Financing the 1980 Election,* pp. 129, 168, 370, 378, 387–90.

47. See Alexander, *Financing the 1980 Election,* p. 388; and Maxwell Glen, "Independent Spenders Are Gearing Up, and Reagan and GOP Stand to Benefit," *National Journal,* vol. 15 (December 17, 1983), p. 2631. In March 1985 the Supreme Court upheld a lower court ruling that declared unconstitutional the $1,000 limitation on independent spending by any PAC in a presidential election (*FEC* v. *NCPAC,* 105 S. Ct. 1459 [1985]).

48. 96 S. Ct. 612 (1976).

costs (as proposed above) might also take the wind out of the sails of some independent expenditure groups.

Several reform bills have been introduced in Congress to provide candidates with free response time when independent groups attack them or support their opponent. For example, several legislators have championed provisions awarding aggrieved candidates either free radio and television advertising (courtesy of the broadcasters) or a grant from public funds equal to the amount of the independent expenditure whenever independent spending against them tops $5,000.[49] However, the former proposal may itself be of questionable constitutionality, because it would discourage broadcasters from accepting independent ads by forcing them to provide free equal response time. And the latter proposal overlooks the ingenuity and aggressiveness of the independent groups. NCPAC actually welcomed the idea, announcing that it would simply run $100,000 in ads attacking a favored candidate and urging that he be defeated for lowering taxes, opposing busing, and standing for a strong defense.[50] Besides identifying its candidate with a litany of popular positions, NCPAC's independent salvo would then trigger another $100,000 in free time for him. "We don't have a perfect solution," admits Common Cause's Fred Wertheimer, who has backed the reform proposals. "There's always going to be a problem with independent expenditures."[51] Perhaps the fact that many independent spending campaigns failed or even backfired in 1984 and 1986 will serve as some consolation to those concerned by this vexing phenomenon.[52]

Honoraria and Other Fees

Those who fear the vote-buying potential of PAC money might better direct their attention to the $6.9 million awarded in 1985 by interest groups

49. This was one provision of the "Clean Campaign Act of 1983," H.R. 2490. Senator David Boren's 1986 reform amendment contained a somewhat similar provision. See *Congressional Quarterly Weekly Report*, vol. 44 (August 16, 1986), pp. 1887–90; and "Senate Approves Boren Amendment, Delays Taking Final Action on Bill," *Campaign Practices Reports*, vol. 13 (August 13, 1986), pp. 1–4.

50. See the prepared statement of John T. Dolan in *Federal Election Campaign Act of 1971*, Hearings, p. 377.

51. Interview with Fred Wertheimer, September 21, 1983.

52. See Frank J. Sorauf, "Caught in a Political Thicket: The Supreme Court and Campaign Finance," *Constitutional Commentary*, vol. 3 (Winter 1986), pp. 97–121; Richard E. Cohen, "Spending Independently," *National Journal*, vol. 18 (December 6, 1986), pp. 2932–34; Maxwell Glen, "Spending Independently," *National Journal*, vol. 18 (June 21, 1986), pp. 1533–37; and "Michigan 3: Mudslinging Round II," *Political Report*, vol. 9 (July 18, 1986), pp. 13–14.

directly to legislators, not as campaign contributions but as "speaking fees" and honoraria. This sum represented a 300 percent increase over the 1984 total, and further steady increases are expected; as one prominent Washington lobbyist put it, "It's the wave of the future."[53] While PAC and other campaign contributions are devoted to the legitimate public purpose of democratic elections, honoraria are placed directly in the pockets of lawmakers for their private enrichment. Not surprisingly, the most powerful and influential congressmen receive the highest fees,[54] and most of them need only make a brief appearance at a breakfast seminar or executive luncheon to collect their money.

Under current rules the legislators themselves devised, members of Congress can accept up to $2,000 per appearance; House members can take up to 30 percent of their annual salary in honoraria, and senators are allowed 40 percent of their salary. Even more disturbing is the latest enticement interest groups are offering legislators (and sometimes their families): all-expense paid trips to resorts around the world.[55] The sponsoring groups reimburse the legislators for travel expenses incurred in connection with their speaking engagements at vacation centers, in addition to the regular honorarium. PAC contributions may receive media attention, but honoraria and free trips should more properly be the focus of attention for those worried about undue influence and corruption in the legislative branch.

Congress ought to restrict severely or eliminate honoraria and special-interest junketing. Such fees and trips are often excused as necessary supplements to income for a Congress that will not pay its members the substantial salaries they deserve. That the need is present is not disputed; but political cowardice cannot justify the tolerance of implied corruption.

The Root of All Evil

While the reforms suggested here will help to build a better system of campaign finance and to balance some of the influence now enjoyed by

53. Burt Solomon, "Bite-Sized Favors," *National Journal*, vol. 18 (October 11, 1986), pp. 2418–22; and Jerald V. Halvorsen, vice-president for government affairs at the American Trucking Association, Inc., as quoted in ibid. See also "Pocket Money," Common Cause press release, May 20, 1987, pp. 1–7.

54. "The 1985 Honoraria Scorecard," *Common Cause Magazine,* vol. 12 (July–August 1986), p. 42.

55. See Sheila Kaplan, "Join Congress—See the World," *Common Cause Magazine,* vol. 12 (September–October 1986), pp. 17–23.

political action committees, they clearly will not radically alter a system whose current defects are serious but not a threat to the health of American democracy. The reforms I have put forward are moderate and feasible; they address the weaknesses in campaign finance without risking deleterious side effects. The medicine, I hope, fits the disease.

PACs are not the chaste and innocent political cheerleaders or selfless civic boosters that their proponents often contend they are. Neither are they the cesspools of corruption and greed that some of their critics depict. PACs will never be popular with idealistic reformers because they represent the rough cutting edge of a democracy teeming with different peoples and conflicting interests. Indeed, PACs may never be hailed even by natural allies; it was the business-oriented *Wall Street Journal,* after all, that editorially compared Washington, D.C., to "the mutants' saloon in 'Star Wars'—a place where politicians, PACs, lawyers, and lobbyists for unions, business or you-name-it shake each other down full time for political money and political support."[56]

Viewed in perspective, the root of the problem in campaign finance is not PACs, it is money. Americans have an enduring mistrust of the mix of politics and money (particularly business money). As Finley Peter Dunne's Mr. Dooley put it:

> I never knew a pollytician to go wrong ontil he's been contaminated be contact with a business man; . . . It seems to me that th' on'y thing to do is to keep pollyticians an' business men apart. They seem to have a bad infloonce on each other. Whiniver I see an alderman an' a banker walkin' down th' street together I know th' Recordin' Angel will have to ordher another bottle iv ink.[57]

As a result of the new campaign finance rules of the 1970s, PACs superseded the "fat cats" of old as a symbol to the public of the role of money in politics. PACs inherited the suspicions that go with the territory. Those suspicions are valuable because they keep the spotlight on PACs and guard against their exercising undue influence.

It may be regrettable that such supervision is required, but human nature—not anything that is unique about PACs—demands it. One final example will suffice as proof. Forty-six members of Congress chose not to seek reelection in 1986. This would not be noteworthy in the area of

56. "Cleaning Up Reform," *Wall Street Journal,* November 10, 1983.
57. Finley Peter Dunne, *The World of Mr. Dooley,* edited with an introduction by Louis Filler (New York: Collier Books, 1962), pp. 155–56.

campaign finance except for a scandalous and little-noted "grandfather" clause in federal election law permitting any member of Congress who was in office on January 8, 1980, to keep any remaining campaign contributions for personal use after leaving office.[58] Many congressmen have not been shy about converting cash given them by PACs and individuals for their reelection races into supplementary pensions or personal slush funds. One former House member purchased a new Cadillac as a "going away" gift to himself. Others have bought everything from furniture to flowers. Interest-free loans are particularly popular, since congressmen must pay tax on campaign money converted to personal use, but not on loans. Most of the members, however, have simply pocketed the money. "I used it to help tide me over," said one, while another only "wished it had been more."[59]

Representative Andrew Jacobs of Indiana, though "grandfathered," is seeking to abolish the "golden parachute" loophole. Explained Jacobs: "These funds are given for a *purpose*—to get elected—not to provide a civil service retirement fund. We already have a very generous one. When I think of those who have engaged in this sort of practice, only the word 'sleazy' comes to mind."[60] Surely the offending clause should be repealed, and excess campaign funds returned pro rata to contributors or donated to charity (without congressmen being allowed to take a charitable tax deduction).[61] Of course, repeal of the provision will not come easily, since over 200 current representatives—a majority of the House—are beneficiaries of the clause. Moreover, many of Congress's leaders are among the "grandfathered" representatives. This singularly seedy clause reveals again the hidden baggage that can be tucked away in campaign finance reform.

Repeatedly over the years, campaign finance laws have yielded "surprises," some intentional and some not. When all is said and done, it is Congress—not PACs or campaign-finance academics or public-interest lobbyists—that passes campaign finance laws. And Congress, left to its own devices, will always aim to take care of its own. In the field of political money, the best advice remains "caveat reformator": let the reformer beware.

58. The clause was contained in the 1979 amendments to the Federal Election Campaign Act.

59. Kevin Chaffee, "Money Under The Mattress: What Congressmen Don't Spend," *Washington Monthly*, vol. 16 (September 1984), pp. 32–38.

60. Quoted in ibid., p. 37.

61. To reduce administrative costs, pro rata refunds of contributions could be limited to those who gave more than a nominal amount (perhaps $100).

CHAPTER EIGHT

Election Fraud: .
An American Vice

ROBERT GOLDBERG

ELECTION FRAUD, or vote fraud as it is commonly called, may be defined as any activity that has the effect or intent of subverting the rights of voters to cast ballots free of intimidation or improper influence and to have their votes accurately counted without dilution by illegal ballots. It takes four main forms: vote buying, fraudulent registration (often to facilitate multiple voting by "repeaters"), fraudulent use of absentee ballots, and falsification of election counts.

It has been said that election fraud is the price we pay for our nation's open system of elections. But although it has been practiced by politicians for hundreds of years, relatively little fraud seems to be committed in the United States today. Perhaps part of the reason is that it lacks political utility. Although the impact of successful vote fraud is difficult to measure, such evidence as exists indicates that it has not made much difference in the actual outcomes of elections. In most cases, fraud on a truly massive scale is needed to guarantee that a candidate or party will actually win an election. As a result, vote fraud is a rather inefficient activity on which to expend limited political resources.

Some of the remedies offered for further reducing fraud may do more damage than the disease itself. Efforts to purge registration lists of infrequent voters, for example, may reasonably be interpreted as aimed at cutting political participation by blacks and other minorities. Changing laws to make registration or absentee voting more difficult inevitably would diminish voting by the poor, the elderly, and the infirm.

Nevertheless, even small amounts of fraud committed over a long time or sporadic instances of widespread fraud can foster cynicism and distrust among the electorate. The public concern therefore is clear: How open can an election system be without risking unacceptable fraud? And will current proposals to make registration and voting easier, including some in this book, have the effect of undermining the integrity of elections?[1]

An Old American Custom

There are some accounts of vote fraud in the early years of the Republic, but the problem does not seem to have become serious until the Jacksonian era. By the 1820s most states had dropped property qualifications for voting, which caused the ranks of eligible voters to swell. The abandonment of the caucus system of nominating presidential candidates made it necessary for ambitious politicians to seek broader public support. When Andrew Jackson first ran for president, unsuccessfully, in 1824, only 355,000 votes were cast, chiefly because many states were regarded as political fiefdoms to be delivered to particular candidates (Tennessee and Pennsylvania to Jackson, Massachusetts to Adams, Virginia to Crawford, Kentucky to Clay, and so forth). By 1828, when Jackson conducted a genuinely national campaign and was elected, the vote increased to 1,155,000. From 1828 to 1848 the vote in presidential elections trebled, while the population did not quite double.[2]

"As poor farmers and workers gained the ballot," Richard Hofstadter observed, "there developed a type of politician that had existed only in embryo in the Jeffersonian period—the technician of mass leadership, the caterer to mass sentiments. . . . Generally subordinated in the political corporations and remote from the choicest spoils, these leaders encouraged the common feeling that popular will should control the choice of public officers and the formation of public policy."[3] These democratic sentiments helped foster the Jacksonian notion that public patronage and other government resources should belong as spoils to the victorious party and party leaders. Almost overnight the stakes of governance became enormous.

1. See chaps. 5 and 6. The Committee on Law and the Electoral Process of the American Bar Association is currently preparing a report on vote fraud and guidelines for reform that will deal extensively with this issue.
2. Richard Hofstadter, *The American Political Tradition and the Men Who Made It* (Knopf, 1951), p. 49.
3. Ibid.

Under the new system of politics, vote fraud grew common. In New York pro-Jackson Democrats based at Tammany Hall mobilized immigrant voters to inflate turnout. "Cart-loads of voters, many of whom had been in the country less than three years, were used as repeaters." Some enthusiasts were detected voting at six different places. Jackson's opposition responded in kind. In 1831 "the National Republicans . . . foisted upon the voters a Jackson electoral ticket containing forty-three names instead of the legal number, forty-two, thereby invalidating each of these ballots voted. This trick, it was calculated, lost to Jackson more than a thousand votes."[4]

During the 1840s, vote fraud in such cities as New York, Philadelphia, Chicago, and to a lesser extent Boston was part of a larger struggle for social power. Riots, gang warfare, and economic discrimination were other manifestations of the social turmoil of the time. Local politicians used neighborhood volunteer fire departments as political bases and sources of muscle. Political parties provided frameworks for coalition building. Police officers, who depended on party leaders for their jobs, often served as poll watchers. Under such circumstances, election fraud was bound to flourish.[5]

After the Civil War, rapid growth of cities gave further impetus to political corruption. The Tweed Ring that controlled New York in the 1860s and 1870s based its power in part on manipulation of recently naturalized Irish immigrants. "In the three weeks prior to the election of 1868," Martin Shefter states, "the judges allied with the Tweed Ring naturalized several thousand new citizens, and expanded the number of registered voters in the city by more than 30 percent. . . . The cost of bringing . . . the immigrants into the political system was high. . . . It was especially high because the Ring was structurally weak. Tweed was unable to command the obedience of other politicians; instead he was compelled to purchase with cash bribes the support of state legislators, county supervisors, and even his immediate associates."[6]

Tweed's need for payoff money required stealing from the municipal treasury on a scale that eventually drove the city into bankruptcy. A new regime at Tammany led by "Honest John" Kelly slated blue-ribbon candi-

4. Gustavus Myers, *The History of Tammany Hall*, 2d ed. (New York: Dover Publications, 1971), pp. 73, 90–91.

5. Conrad Weiler, *Philadelphia: Neighborhood, Authority, and the Urban Crisis* (Praeger, 1974), pp. 37–39.

6. Martin Shefter, "New York City's Fiscal Crisis: The Politics of Inflation and Retrenchment," *Public Interest*, no. 4 (Summer 1977), pp. 102–03.

dates for city offices, reduced corruption to manageable proportions, and created what Shefter has called the "modern Tammany machine."[7] For fifty-five years, from the reign of Kelly through that of Richard Croker to that of Charles Murphy, the Manhattan-based Tammany club controlled the Democratic party in New York and the city government. To preserve this rule, district leaders were kept under tight control. Able Tammany bosses held corruption in general and vote fraud in particular within limits that the public and the business community were willing to tolerate. Only after Murphy's death in 1925 did Tammany increasingly resort to election fraud and alliance with the underworld to hold on to power. When Fiorello LaGuardia set out to break its dominance in the 1930s, he helped rally support for reform by staging confrontations with Democratic poll workers who routinely fixed election results.[8]

Election fraud was by no means limited to major cities. In Pennsylvania the formidable Republican state machine built by Matthew Stanley Quay gained its victories in part through multiple voting and illegal registration in small upstate cities and rural townships.[9] Vote buying and stealing were also common in the rural areas of southern Ohio and southern Indiana. In Tennessee the Democratic machine in Memphis distributed funds through party leaders in rural counties to ensure success for its candidates in state elections. Various sources have reported general acceptance of election fraud in Kentucky and West Virginia. In Texas, V. O. Key found evidence in the 1940s that party workers in many parts of the state continued a long tradition of manipulating ballot box results.[10]

As in the cities, some predominantly rural machines seem to have avoided vote fraud or at least kept it to a minimum. In Louisiana, for example, the predominantly rural machine created by Huey Long in the 1930s relied mainly on state patronage and social services rather than on buying votes to preserve its dominance. The Long forces and the rival New Orleans city machine struck a bargain to avoid election day pilfering.[11]

To the extent that party machines were able to control entire electoral systems, fraud was potentially a significant problem. Much has been made of the encouragement of fraud caused by the parties' printing and distribut-

7. Ibid., p. 104.

8. Arthur Mann, *LaGuardia Comes to Power* (Lippincott, 1965), pp. 118–20.

9. James A. Kehl, *Boss Rule in the Gilded Age: Matt Quay of Pennsylvania* (University of Pittsburgh Press, 1981).

10. V. O. Key, Jr., *Southern Politics* (New York: Vintage, 1949), p. 274.

11. Harry T. Williams, *Huey Long* (Knopf, 1969), p. 629.

ing their own ballots in the nineteenth century. Actually, as the Tammany example suggests, control over election judges and polling places seems to have been more important. By the same token, political competition, both interparty, as in the rivalries of the Jacksonian period, and intraparty, as in the cases of Louisiana and New York City, limited the extent of fraud.

Election Fraud Today

By the 1930s vote fraud had become less common. One theory holds that politicians began to find it inefficient or dishonorable or both. While such methods of getting votes as rewarding workers with patronage, manipulating government services, and distributing "walking around money" on election day remained morally acceptable and seemed politically effective, vote stealing, in this view, had become neither. Frank Kent, a veteran political journalist, wrote in 1928 that "vote buying, like cheating in the count, has practically gone out of fashion. Both are still practiced in some cities but in the main these days the count is honest and the vote buying is indirect rather than direct. . . . There is in every state a certain amount of repeating and some padding of the registration lists, but in the main elections in the country to-day are reasonably honest and the bribing of voters is almost a lost political art, practiced now only in a desultory fashion in certain sections."[12]

The toughening of election laws and the introduction of mechanical voting devices during waves of state and municipal reform in the 1930s and 1960s could reasonably have been expected further to reduce the scope of fraud. Yet just as professional politicians had adapted to direct primaries and nonpartisan elections, so too their successors adjusted to new prohibitions on electioneering at the polls and to mechanical balloting. Mechanical balloting actually facilitated straight ticket voting and made rigging election returns easier for politicians controlling all aspects of an electoral system.

While fraud is less pervasive today than it was even twenty years ago, it persists in some parts of the country. Examination of recent court cases involving election law violations and federal inquiries into vote fraud, and interviews with election officials, national and local journalists, and politicians, have led me to compile the following nonexhaustive list of places

12. Frank R. Kent, *Political Behavior* (William Morrow, 1928), pp. 200–01.

where significant election fraud appears to remain common: most of Chicago, parts of New York City and Philadelphia, parts of Alabama and Mississippi, central Georgia, northern Florida, some counties in South Carolina, the mountain counties of North Carolina, much of West Virginia, southern Texas, the southeastern river counties of Ohio, the Ohio Valley counties of Indiana, eastern Kentucky, and eastern Tennessee. Different kinds of fraud are prevalent in different places, responding to demographic variations.

Fraudulent Registration

Registration of persons who do not exist or do not meet voter qualifications takes place most frequently in large cities such as Chicago and Philadelphia where high population densities and mobility make accurate verification of registration extremely difficult. In Chicago a check of voter lists in 1982 found persons registered from addresses occupied by city parks, railroad tracks, vacant lots, and factories. In 1983 an investigative reporter for a Chicago television station registered Macho Newman and Claudia McLay as Democrats. Both new voters were French poodles.[13] In Brooklyn between 1968 and 1982, Democratic party workers in several precincts regularly used fictitious names to create large numbers of voter registration cards, which they filed with the Board of Elections. Fraudulent votes were cast under these names by crews of repeaters, who received up to $40 for their work. In 1974 this technique accounted for approximately 3,200 votes cast in the Democratic primary.[14]

Registration of illegal aliens apparently is common in some cities. The U.S. attorney for the Northern District of Illinois estimated in 1983 that more than 80,000 illegal immigrants were registered in Chicago.[15] This practice has also been found to be widespread in parts of East Los Angeles, despite California's reputation for electoral purity. Illegal immigrants often register as voters to obtain some form of personal identification. But once on the rolls, they are available to be voted by local politicians.[16]

13. *Voting Rights Act: Criminal Violations,* Hearings before the Subcommittee on the Constitution of the Senate Committee on the Judiciary, 98 Cong. 1 sess., Chicago, Illinois, September 19, 1983, pp. 52, 54.

14. "Grand Jury Reports in the Matter of Confidential Investigation of 84-11," Brooklyn District Attorney's Office, September 5, 1984, p. 14.

15. *Voting Rights Act,* Hearings, p. 52.

16. Ibid., p. 53.

Some voters register in more than one locality or precinct. In 1982 an investigation found more than 1,000 persons who were registered both in Chicago and adjacent areas of Indiana. Another inquiry in 1982 found 36,000 persons registered in two or more precincts in Chicago. In a South Philadelphia ward in 1975 the Democratic ward leader registered and voted more than 100 people who were also registered in other parts of the Philadelphia metropolitan area, including Camden, New Jersey, where the ward leader himself maintained his principal residence.[17]

Fraudulent Use of Absentee Ballots

Theft or purchase of absentee ballots is a favored form of vote fraud in rural counties of the South and Midwest where small populations make inflated registration or repeater voting relatively easy to detect. Fraudulent use of absentee ballots takes three main forms: applying for ballots under names of registered voters who are deceased or no longer reside in the locality, purchasing them from voters who have obtained them legitimately, and altering them before they are counted.

In one vote fraud case that led to federal prosecution in 1981, Democratic party workers in Dillon County, South Carolina, obtained absentee ballot applications from well over 1,000 voters. After the ballots were mailed to the voters, the party workers returned to encourage support for the approved slate. A local party leader paid the workers $10 for each correctly cast ballot, part of which they shared with the voters. The organization candidate for sheriff in Dillon County received 94 percent of the absentee votes.[18]

In Alexander County, North Carolina, two employees of the sheriff's office and one employee of the county clerk's office were convicted in federal court of conspiring to cast absentee ballots in the November 1982 election, taken out in the names of residents of the Belle View Rest Home who were "of advanced years, feeble both physically and mentally." With the help of the home's manager, the employees obtained the signatures of the elderly residents, the majority of them forged, on letters of application for absentee ballots and then had similarly fraudulent signatures notarized on the election forms returned with the ballots. By this means they were able to deliver votes to reelect their respective employers.[19]

17. Interview with Craig Donsanto, director, Election Crimes Branch, Public Integrity Section, Criminal Division, U.S. Department of Justice, January 6, 1987.

18. *U.S.* v. *Carmichael,* 685 F. 2d 905 (4th Cir. 1982).

19. *U.S.* v. *Odom,* 736 F. 2d 106 (4th Cir. 1984).

Vote Buying

Paying voters to cast ballots for approved candidates or slates is the simplest form of election fraud and arguably remains the most common, especially in economically disadvantaged areas. In parts of the South, according to the head of the Justice Department's Election Crimes Branch, politicians preserve minority white control of local government through a combination of buying votes and intimidating voters. In Duval County, Texas, stronghold of the machine that produced the disputed votes that sent Lyndon Johnson to the Senate in 1948, the county welfare director was recently convicted of distributing food vouchers in exchange for votes for a slate of candidates in a Democratic primary.[20] Institutionalized vote buying has been repeatedly exposed in Clay County, North Carolina, several counties in southwestern Louisiana, the river counties of southwestern Indiana, and Mingo County, West Virginia.

The case of Mingo County is probably extreme but appears far from unique. The race for sheriff in Mingo County is always hotly contested because the sheriff influences the awards of school bus and gasoline contracts in addition to holding responsibility for local law enforcement. As a result, according to a national journalist who has covered politics in the county, candidates for sheriff have to pay at least $10 a vote to have a chance at election.[21]

Poverty helps account for persistence of vote buying in some areas. Mingo County, for example, has long been economically depressed. Improved economic conditions, however, do not necessarily bring vote buying to an end. In Clay County, North Carolina, where vote buying has reportedly been widespread for half a century, rising personal income does not seem to have dampened the incidence of electoral fraud. As recently as 1982, the sheriff of Clay County was convicted of buying votes, and the FBI estimated that about $30,000 was spent illegally at the polls.[22]

Falsifying Election Returns

Rigging election counts is often combined with the other three forms of fraud. Recently in Chicago, election officials and a local precinct worker

20. *U.S.* v. *Garcia*, 719 F. 2d 99 (5th Cir. 1984).
21. Interview with Kenneth Bode, NBC political correspondent, February 9, 1987.
22. Mark Barrett, "Voting for Dollars: WestVote Failures," *Asheville Citizen-Times*, June 14, 1987, and "Voting for Dollars: Brewer Leaves Office 'Disillusioned,' " *Asheville Citizen-Times*, June 18, 1987.

discarded ballots actually cast in their polling place and created their own vote count. The maneuver depended on their ability to use fraudulent registration cards to cover the falsified return. Although the count was computerized, the precinct captain simply ran a straight Democratic ballot through the computer 198 times and then for the sake of credibility ran through a straight Republican slate 6 times.[23]

Election returns can also be falsified by forging voter cards with the names of people who did not actually cast ballots to substantiate fake results. In New York City, voting irregularities of this kind in a recent election almost caused the courts to set aside the results.[24]

One-Party Dominance and Election Fraud

Not surprisingly, vote fraud often occurs in places where one party has maintained almost total dominance of government for an extended period. This situation has led some political scientists to conclude that lack of effective political opposition encourages the party in power to practice fraud at the polls. The virtue of a two-party system, V. O. Key wrote, "is not that there are two groups with conflicting policy tendencies from which the voters can choose, but that there are two groups of politicians" providing a "continuing group of 'outs' which of necessity must pick up whatever issue is at hand to belabor the 'ins.' " Under this theory fraud is unlikely when two strong parties keep close watch on each other.[25]

The areas discussed earlier in which vote fraud remains common are indeed almost all controlled by one party. This, of course, does not answer the chicken-or-egg question: Does one-party rule produce fraud or does fraud help create one-party rule? The former answer is somewhat undermined because development of a two-party system in an area where fraud has been traditional has not, immediately at least, seemed to produce a purer brand of politics. The emergence of the Republican party as a credible competitor for state offices in North Carolina in the past twenty years, for example, has reportedly made vote buying by both parties even more flagrant. Key himself pointed out that when Democratic hegemony

23. *Voting Rights Act*, Hearings, pp. 6–9.
24. "Grand Jury Reports," Brooklyn District Attorney's Office, p. 16.
25. Key, *Southern Politics*, pp. 309–10.

in the South was threatened by Republican-Populist fusion campaigns in the 1890s, fraud tended to increase.[26]

Intense two-party competition in Illinois and Pennsylvania has not saved either from significant vote fraud in some areas. In both states, however, statewide two-party competition masks one-party dominance in many localities. In Illinois the Democrats dominate Chicago while local Republican organizations have maintained supremacy in many downstate counties. Similarly in Pennsylvania, once a one-party Republican state, Democrats in recent years have firmly controlled Philadelphia and Pittsburgh while Republicans have usually held the upper hand in most upstate counties. In both states many local organizations have insulated themselves against statewide two-party competition. Continuation of vote fraud, therefore, does not necessarily contradict the explanation based on one-party dominance.

The strongest argument against the theory that one-party dominance induces election fraud is that in some states and localities that have had one-party systems for a long time vote fraud has never seemed much of a problem. One party or the other has generally been dominant in many parts of New England and in parts of the belt of northern states extending from the Great Lakes to the Pacific coast, but reported cases of vote fraud in either region have been rare.

Election Fraud and Political Culture

Another explanation for the prevalence of vote fraud, most fully developed by Daniel Elazar, is that certain kinds of local culture are more likely to tolerate it. Elazar defines political culture as a framework of shared social values and assumptions about how these values should be promoted through political action. This framework gives rise to social mores that govern actual political behavior. Americans, he maintains, share a broad common political culture, but within this common national culture are three distinct subcultures, which he calls moralistic, traditionalistic, and individualistic. Each subculture instills a somewhat different view of how political power should be gained and used.

The moralistic subculture, according to Elazar, judges each political act

26. Ibid., p. 443.

by the "degree to which it promotes the public good." It expects "honesty, selflessness, and commitment to the public welfare" from "those who govern." Politics is seen as "a matter of concern for every citizen, not just for those who are professionally committed to political careers."[27]

The traditionalistic subculture regards the primary goal of politics as "the continued maintenance of the existing social order." To achieve this end, it favors confining "real political power to a relatively small and self-perpetuating group drawn from an established elite." Most citizens are expected to take little part in politics and may not even be encouraged to vote.[28]

The individualistic subculture views public life as a division of the economic marketplace. Politics, like any other business, "competes for talent and offers rewards to those who take it up as a career." Politicians are regarded as seeking office "as a means of controlling the distribution of the favors or rewards of government rather than as means of exercising governmental power for programmatic ends." The public is expected to tolerate a good deal of corruption and graft as part of the price for getting things done.[29]

Elazar claims these political subcultures grew out of "very real socio-cultural differences found among the peoples who came to America over the years. . . . Because the various ethnic and religious groups that came to these shores tended to congregate in the same settlements and because, as they or their descendants moved westward, they continued to settle together, the political patterns they bore with them are today distributed geographically."[30]

Under Elazar's theory, election fraud should be harshly condemned in areas characterized by moralistic subcultures, generally tolerated by traditionalistic subcultures, and almost expected under individualistic subcultures. The theory does not account for all differences in attitudes toward vote fraud: Why, for instance, have traditionalistic Virginia and individualistic Detroit generally maintained clean elections? It does, however, give a broadly accurate guide to varying degrees of tolerance and incidence of election fraud. In the moralistic states of New England and the states from the Great Lakes to the Pacific Northwest largely settled by New England-

27. Daniel Elazar, *American Federalism: A View from the States* (Thomas Crowell, 1966), pp. 90–91.
28. Ibid., p. 93.
29. Ibid., p. 87–89.
30. Ibid., p. 94.

ers and moralistic Scandinavians, vote fraud seems rarely to occur. Traditionalistic subcultures in Louisiana, Mississippi, Texas, North Carolina, West Virginia, Kentucky, and Tennessee coincide with substantial incidence of fraud. And fraud seems most prevalent amid the individualistic subcultures of Chicago, New York City, and Philadelphia. In Ohio and Indiana, fraud is much less common in the northern rural counties settled from New England than in the traditionalistic counties of the Ohio Valley or the individualistic cities. In California the moralistic tone of state politics has been matched by a record of clean elections—although incidents of election fraud have begun to occur in parts of Los Angeles in recent years.

Does Fraud Matter?

Electoral fraud is not a clear and present danger to practical democracy in most parts of the United States today. Election laws dealing with it appear adequate, though in some areas these laws are not enforced with particular rigor.

Whether election regulations should be significantly weakened to encourage voter turnout is another matter. Even a little fraud damages public morale and may determine outcomes in close elections. In some areas the prevailing moral climate would probably maintain honest elections under a less restrictive system; but in others the tendencies toward fraud against which the Progressive era election reforms were directed still exist. Local electorates are probably the best judges of the laws they need to keep vote fraud to a minimum.

Attitudes toward vote fraud seem to have some roots in political culture. Since cultures change slowly, proposals to increase voter turnout by enactment of federal laws to ease federal election regulations should be approached with caution.

Holding the electorate to a higher standard of conduct through voter education and aggressive monitoring of elections, activities in which political parties as well as volunteer civic groups and the media should play important parts, may be the best hope for breaking patterns of fraud where organized political competition is slight or nonexistent. Recent reductions in the incidence of vote fraud in Chicago and the growing discontent with vote buying in West Virginia suggest that public watchdog agencies and highly visible prosecution and conviction of politicians involved in vote fraud can have salutary effects, even in areas where political cultures have

PART FOUR

The Role of Parties

CHAPTER NINE

Strengthening the National Parties

JAMES L. SUNDQUIST

Political parties have always occupied an ambiguous position in American public life. They are profoundly mistrusted—yet accepted. Their constant maneuvering for petty advantage is reviled and ridiculed, but millions of people call themselves either Democrats or Republicans and cherish the ideals of their party with a religious fervor. Parties have been credited with such supreme achievements as saving the Union and rescuing the country from the Great Depression. But they have also been accused of placing partisan advantage ahead of the national good, of failing to conceive farsighted programs, of running away from problems and responsibilities, and sometimes of deep and pervasive corruption.

It was the last of these that led, during the Progressive era, to a passionate reformist crusade to destroy the strength and influence of the party organizations that, at the end of the nineteenth century, had reached their zenith of power and plunder. Throughout this century the Progressive reforms have been serving that purpose, until by now the objective has been largely accomplished. Governmental administration has been cleansed of the grosser forms of corruption—in most places, anyway—but in the process the party organizations have been shorn of much of the patronage that had given them their armies of loyal workers. The direct primary gradually reduced, and by today has virtually eliminated, the organizations' control of, or even influence on, nominations for office, including the presidency itself. By law some states prohibit party organizations from making endorsements in primaries or from participating at all in nonpartisan general elections for mayors and city council members. With their organizations thus stripped of both nominating functions and active workers, political parties have in most places lost the motivation and the competence to organize, finance, and manage general election campaigns as well, and these responsibilities in contests for major offices have gravitated to a new and growing professional elite of private campaign management and consulting firms.

But as the traditional political party organizations die—whether victims of reformist zeal or of simple obsolescence—what becomes of the functions that political parties have performed well, at least at times, and that only the parties can perform? Are there, indeed, such functions? A new school of reformers is now answering that question emphatically in the affirmative. "Our political party system," proclaims the Committee for Party Renewal (CPR), ". . . is in serious danger of destruction. Without parties there can be no organized and coherent politics. When politics lacks coherence, there can be no accountable democracy. Parties are indispensable to the realization of democracy. The stakes are no less than that."[1] And the Committee on the Constitutional System (CCS), in its 1987 report, declares that "the weakening of parties in the electoral arena has contributed to the disintegration of party cohesion among the officials we elect to public office," and that "the decline of party loyalty and cohesion at all levels of the political system" is a principal cause of "the failures and weaknesses in governmental performance."[2]

Anyone who would renew or remold an institution must have a model. The ambiguity in the popular attitude toward political parties and the confusion as to the role they should play arise from a conflict between two models of the American governmental system that has been left unsettled throughout the whole two centuries of national life. The first model was embodied in the Constitution, with James Madison its principal designer. It contemplated a national government without national political parties. But when the founding generation assumed responsibility for operating the new government, it discarded that model almost at once and embraced an

1. Statement read by James MacGregor Burns, then chairman of the committee, at the Jefferson Memorial, Washington, D.C., September 2, 1977. The committee, formed in 1976, is composed of political scientists and Democratic and Republican party activists.

2. Committee on the Constitutional System, *A Bicentennial Analysis of the American Political Structure* (January 1987), pp. 3, 5. The committee, organized in 1981, is made up of present and former members of Congress, former executive branch officials, academics, and others concerned with structural weaknesses in the government. Its cochairs are Lloyd N. Cutler, former White House counsel; C. Douglas Dillon, former cabinet member; and Senator Nancy Landon Kassebaum, Republican of Kansas.

alternative conception in which national parties occupied a central place. The nation's political leaders have ever since used parties as the means for gaining control of government and then for mobilizing the resources of the legislative and executive branches to enact and carry out programs. Yet the notion that organized parties, rather than unaffiliated and disconnected individuals, should take responsibility for the affairs of government—and be held accountable by the voters—has never been fully embraced in the country at large, and the Constitution has not been altered to accommodate it. Elements of both models are therefore reflected in America's institutional structures, political practices, and fundamental beliefs. And over the decades, the struggle to reconcile the models and achieve a workable blending of the two has come up against the hard fact that, in essential respects, the models are irreconcilable.

The Madisonian Model: A System without Parties

The Constitution that emerged from the Convention of 1787 made no place for parties. At that time, only the faint forerunners of modern political parties had appeared anywhere in the world. Factions had taken shape within legislative bodies in both the American states and in England, but they were not formally organized, and political organizations formed by citizens of the new states for purposes of particular elections were still local and rudimentary. Insofar as the Constitution's framers at Philadelphia referred to these groupings at all, they condemned them. They were usually termed factions or cabals rather than parties, and they were denounced as responsible for the "corruption" and "intrigue" of legislative bodies.

Accordingly, in designing the institutions of the new government, the men of 1787 deliberately sought to erect barriers against the development and influence of parties. Indeed, the basic tripartite structure of the government, as well as the division of the legislative branch into two houses, can be seen as having that essential purpose. The framers scattered power in order to forestall the evils of concentration in any individual or group, that is, in any one faction or party. They feared that a transient popular majority might be able to seize the House of Representatives and try to impose its will on the country, but they designed the Senate as a body of elder statesmen with long, overlapping terms who would rise above factionalism, and conceived the presidency, possessed of a veto in the legislative process, as the very embodiment of the nonpartisan ideal.

It was to ensure that kind of presidency that the framers, after extensive debate over the merits of the two obvious means of selecting a president—first, by the legislature, or second, by the people through direct election—ultimately rejected both. Either, they concluded, would encourage factionalism. "If the Legislature elect, it will be the work of intrigue, of cabal, and of faction," contended Gouverneur Morris of Pennsylvania at the midpoint of the Convention; ". . . real merit will rarely be the title to the appointment."[3] But others feared that factionalism and intrigue could come to dominate a direct national election. "The people are uninformed," argued Elbridge Gerry of Massachusetts. Their "ignorance . . . would put it in the power of some one set of men dispersed through the Union and acting in Concert to delude them into any appointment."[4] To render the presidential election free of factions, the framers invented their alternative, the electoral college. The electors chosen in each state would be public-spirited and eminent citizens who would have no other duty, and officeholders would be ineligible to serve. They would not meet as a body but would cast their votes separately, in their own states. "As the electors would be chosen for the occasion, would meet at once, and proceed immediately to an appointment, there would be very little opportunity for cabal, or corruption," reasoned Madison.[5] The electoral college, then, would function as a more elaborate version of a civic club's nominating committee or an institution's search committee. Merit, achievement, and competence alone would be the touchstones. Parties or cabals would be excluded.

In *Federalist* number 10, Madison advanced as one of the Constitution's central merits that it would tend "to break and control the violence of faction," which he equated with party. No more powerful diatribe against the evils of parties has been penned in the United States or perhaps in any country than his famous essay. In it he denounces "the violence of faction" as "this dangerous vice" that introduces "the instability, injus-

---

3. Max Farrand, ed., *The Records of the Federal Convention of 1787*, rev. ed., 4 vols. (Yale University Press, 1966), vol. 2, p. 29, proceedings of July 17, notes of James Madison.

4. Ibid., p. 57, July 19, and p. 114, July 25, Madison notes. He even identified one existing national organization that was "respectable, United, and influential" enough to have the power to elect the president—the Order of the Cincinnati.

5. Ibid., pp. 110–11, July 25, Madison notes.

tice, and confusion" that have "been the mortal diseases under which popular governments have everywhere perished." In the new American states, public measures were "too often decided, not according to the rules of justice, and the rights of the minor party, but by the superior force of an interested and overbearing majority." All this was due "chiefly, if not wholly" to "the unsteadiness and injustice, with which a factious spirit has tainted our public administrations."

Creating the new union would help in "curing the mischiefs of faction" by raising decisions to the national level. There they would be more likely to be in the hands of representatives "whose enlightened views and virtuous sentiments render them superior to local prejudices and to schemes of injustice." A "greater variety of parties" would lessen the chance that any one party could "outnumber and oppress the rest." "Factious leaders" in individual states could not "spread a general conflagration through the other states." In later papers, particularly numbers 47, 48, and 62, Madison extols the separation of powers as the means to forestall the "tyranny" and "sinister combinations" that would follow if all elements of the government were to be controlled by any one individual or political faction.[6]

The Responsible-Party Model

The opposing model for organizing a government recognizes not only the inevitability but the necessity of parties and assigns them the role that they everywhere seek and come naturally to assume. This is the model that has been adopted in various forms by most of the other advanced democracies of the world, and it is the one that inspires the recommendations of such contemporary American reformist groups as the CPR and the CCS.

In this model, political parties are formed because groups of people, each sharing a philosophy and a set of goals, desire governmental power in order to carry out their programs. In competition with one another, they present their programs to the people in an open and free election. The party or coalition that wins the support of a majority of the people gains control of the government and enacts its program. The minority party or parties form an opposition, with power to criticize, debate, and delay but

6. The authorship of number 62 has been disputed, but the weight of scholarly opinion now appears to ascribe it to Madison rather than Hamilton.

not to block. After a few years the voters in another election render a verdict on the majority's stewardship. If they approve what has been done, they return the ruling party or coalition to office. If they disapprove, they turn the incumbents out and entrust power to an opposition party or combination of parties. At all times, one of the parties, or a combination, is responsible for the government, possesses authority commensurate with its responsibility (subject to check by the judiciary if it exceeds its constitutional powers), and is fully accountable for whatever the government (except for the judiciary) does. In the metaphors of political science textbook writers, the political party is the tie that binds, the glue that fastens, the bridge or the web that unites the disparate institutions that make up the government. Without parties, democracy on a national scale simply could not work.

Yet one can readily perceive why Madison and his colleagues saw such a model as dangerous. If a majority party can win the whole of governmental power, what is to prevent it from oppressing the minority? As Madison saw it in *Federalist* number 10, the natural party division would be between "those who hold, and those who are without property," between "those who are creditors, and those who are debtors." He feared that a majority party made up of the propertyless would exhibit "a rage for paper money, for an abolition of debts, for an equal division of property." He put his faith in the geographical scale of the country and in the division of powers among the branches of government. Others, however, demanded more ironclad guarantees against the tyranny of the majority, and those guarantees emerged from the First Congress, under Madison's own leadership, as the Constitution's Bill of Rights.

In the European countries, as monarchs either surrendered their power or were deposed, institutions evolved according to the responsible-party model. The executive authority was assumed by the legislative body in the fusion of power known as the parliamentary system. The larger, always popularly elected, legislative house achieved a dominant position. If a party won a majority of that house, it attained a virtual monopoly of governmental power—limited only by such restraints as might be embodied in a written constitution, and by whatever residual powers that were assigned to a smaller, and often indirectly elected, second chamber. Most continental European countries also adopted proportional representation, which fostered a multiplicity of parties and hence reduced the likelihood that any one party might obtain undivided control of the government.

Yet, with these modifications the responsible-party model has prevailed throughout the democratic world save in America.[7]

Few would argue, surely, that the experience of Europe has borne out Madison's dread of party government. Tyrannies have appeared only when the forms of parliamentary government were abandoned or destroyed, not when they were sustained. The propertyless have used their majorities at times to redistribute to some degree the wealth of the propertied by raising taxes for welfare programs. Whether the redistribution has been carried beyond the bounds of sound macroeconomic policy in some countries will always be debated, but the electorate can, and often does, reverse unwise policies by transferring power to the opposition party. In any case, no country has ever approached the "equal division" or "leveling" that arose so often as the specter haunting the 1787 Convention. Tradition, a sense of justice, and no doubt above all the compelling desire to sustain public confidence and democratic political support have been sufficient to restrain all-powerful majority parties from trampling on the rights of the propertied or wrecking market economies.

The Clash of Models in America

George Washington, who presided over both the Convention and the new government in its earliest years, tried to lead in the nonpartisan manner that the Constitution contemplated, only to observe the rise of factionalism not only in the Congress but also within his own cabinet. His dismay is expressed in the celebrated passage from his farewell address in which—echoing *Federalist* number 10—he warned his countrymen "in the most solemn manner against the baneful effects of the spirit of party generally." In popular governments that spirit serves to "distract the public councils" and "enfeeble the public administration." It "agitates the community with ill founded jealousies and false alarms . . . foments occasionally riot and insurrection . . . opens the door to foreign influence and corruption." Nearly two centuries later, ironically enough, deeply partisan senators and congressmen still gravely arise in an annual ritual on the

7. And, some would add, except in France under its current constitution. Executive powers are divided uneasily between the president and the premier, who may be of different parties.

observance of Washington's birthday to read that address, with its denun-
ciations, to their colleagues, who have all been elected on party tickets,
have organized their respective chambers through party caucuses and
party-line votes, and have entrusted the conduct of legislative business to
party organizations and leaders.

Within four years of the first president's retirement a two-party system,
reflecting to a degree the propertied-landless and creditor-debtor cleavage
that Madison had identified as fundamental, was in full operation, with
two slates of candidates running nationally. The electoral college, conceived as a body of nonpartisan statesmen with complete discretion and
independent judgment, was hardly formed when it was reduced to what it
has since remained: a group of individuals performing a purely ministerial
role, each casting his vote for a presidential and vice-presidential candidate nominated earlier by a national party. "The election of a President of
the United States is no longer that process which the Constitution contemplated," one of the framers, Rufus King of New York, remarked in an
1816 Senate debate.[8] Parties, James Madison acknowledged in his retirement years, are "a natural offspring of Freedom."[9] By that time, of course,
Madison had been elected and reelected president as a party nominee.

In organizing their parties the nation's political leaders then as now
accepted the responsible-party concept. The parties have always asked for
full control of both the legislative and executive branches. Since early in
the nineteenth century they have presented their programs formally, in
official party platforms. Asking for total control over the two elected
branches, they have been eager to accept the total responsibility and accountability that would accompany it.

And the American people have seemed to accept the responsible-party
model too. For the first century and a half under the Constitution, when
the voters chose a president each four years they normally entrusted
control of Congress to the same party, thus making it fully responsible.
From the time the two-party system settled into place in Andrew Jackson's
time until the second election of Dwight Eisenhower, only two presidents—Zachary Taylor, elected in 1848, and Rutherford B. Hayes, in

8. *Annals of Congress,* 14 Cong. 1 sess., p. 216, reprinted in Farrand, *Records,* vol. 3,
p. 422. King was a delegate from Massachusetts to the Constitutional Convention, but
moved to New York the following year.

9. Note to his speech at the 1787 Convention on the right of suffrage, apparently written
about 1821, when he was preparing his record of Convention proceedings for publication.
Ibid., p. 452.

1876—had to confront immediately upon inauguration a House of Representatives organized by the opposition. Even the Senate, despite filling only one-third of its seats in any presidential election, had a majority of the opposition's party after only two quadrennial elections—those of 1848 and 1884.[10] In the nineteenth century these results might be discounted as largely an artifact of the election process itself. The parties printed separate ballots listing their slates, and the voter selected the ballot of the party he preferred and dropped it in the box. Yet after the government-printed secret ballot came into universal use early in this century, straight-ticket voting and the resultant single-party control of the government continued to prevail. A majority of the people clearly wanted the Republican party to be responsible for the entire government in the 1900s and the 1920s and the Democratic party in the 1930s and most of the 1940s. No president in the first half of this century had to confront upon inauguration a Congress of which either house was controlled by the opposing party, and few had the problem even after the normal setback to the president's party in the midterm election.

Meanwhile, the nation's leading students of government had rallied behind the idea of responsible parties. In 1950 the classic appeal for strengthening national parties as central instruments of government was issued by the sixteen-member Committee on Political Parties of the American Political Science Association under the title *Toward a More Responsible Two-Party System.*[11] To make a responsible-party system work as it should, said the committee, the parties needed stronger central institutional mechanisms—specifically, authoritative governing councils. Prefacing its recommendations for institutional change were some impassioned passages, the rhetoric that resonates today in the writings of the CPR and the CCS in defense of party government:

> Throughout this report political parties are treated as indispensable instruments of government. That is to say, we proceed on the proposition that *popular government in a nation of more than 150 million people requires political parties which provide the electorate with a proper range of choice between alternatives of action* (p. 15).

10. After the 1880 election, the Senate was composed of 37 Republicans, 37 Democrats, and two minor-party senators.

11. Supplement to *American Political Science Review,* vol. 44 (September 1950). The committee is known as the Schattschneider committee, after its chairman, E. E. Schattschneider.

In an era beset with problems of unprecedented magnitude at home and abroad, it is dangerous to drift without a party system that helps the nation to set a general course of policy for the government as a whole. . . . When the parties are unable to reach and pursue responsible decisions, difficulties accumulate and cynicism about all democratic institutions grows (p. 17).

Historical and other factors have caused the American two-party system to operate as two loose associations of state and local organizations, with very little national machinery and very little national cohesion. As a result, either major party, when in power, is ill-equipped to organize its members in the legislative and executive branches into a government held together and guided by the party program. Party responsibility at the polls thus tends to vanish. This . . . poses grave problems of domestic and foreign policy in an era when it is no longer safe for the nation to deal piecemeal with issues that can be disposed of only on the basis of coherent programs (p. v).

An effective party system requires, first, that the parties are able to bring forth programs to which they commit themselves and, second, that the parties possess sufficient internal cohesion to carry out these programs (p. 1).

A generation later the reader is struck by how casually the committee took for granted that both the legislative and executive branches would be controlled by a single party. One of the major parties would be "in power," and if it possessed "sufficient internal cohesion" it could "organize its members" in the two branches to carry out the party program. In the lifetimes of the committee members, that had always been the case. But within a few years the U.S. government would pass through a momentous transition: from one of single-party government nearly all the time to one of divided government most of the time. In 1956, for the first time in more than seven decades, the people denied to a newly elected president a Congress controlled by his own party, and they repeated that decision in four of the next seven presidential elections. As in 1956, in 1968, 1972, 1980, and 1984 they placed Republican presidents in the White House but sent Democratic majorities to the House of Representatives, and in the first three of those elections to the Senate as well. Neither party was given full responsibility with corresponding accountability.

Does this mean, then, that beginning at mid-century the people came to reject the concept of responsible party government that until then they appeared to have accepted? By no means. In each of the five elections that produced divided outcomes, a large majority of individual voters continued to support the entire ticket of one or the other major party. In 1984, for instance, the Democrats won control of the House because their candidates ran about 9 percentage points ahead of their presidential candidate, Walter Mondale, in contested races. Even if one were to assume that the net differential of 9 points was the result of 5 percent of the voters splitting their tickets to support Mondale and the Republican House candidate—an assumption that would surely be too generous—and 14 percent splitting their tickets in the opposite direction, for Reagan and the Democratic congressional candidate, the proportion of all voters splitting their tickets between the two offices would still be only 19 percent. The other 81 percent, by their votes, would have sustained the concept of responsible party government.[12]

Yet if politicians and voters alike support that doctrine, one may ask why the Democratic and Republican parties have not developed the national machinery and the national cohesion that the Committee on Political Parties considered so essential. The committee did not identify the "historical and other factors" that left both parties "ill-equipped" to organize coherent government, but the basic cause is readily apparent: the scale of the country required a federal rather than a unitary government, and a federal structure of government was bound to be reflected in a corresponding party structure, each national party formed as a league of state parties. And the state units making up a national party would be as diverse as the states themselves—in the ethnic and religious backgrounds of members and leaders, in their interests and concerns, and in their ideologies and philosophies of government. Thus throughout its history the Democratic party has been deeply split between its northern liberals and its conservative southern elements, and the Republican party has had its northeastern industrial and its western agrarian wings. These schisms were so deep that at times the parties formally split, as when Theodore Roosevelt and his

12. The figure of 9 percent (rounded up from 8.7 percent) is provided by Rhodes Cook of *Congressional Quarterly*. The estimate of 19 percent is supported by polling data. In the seven presidential elections from 1956 through 1980, the University of Michigan Center for Political Studies found that from 13.2 percent of the voters (in 1960) to 26.7 percent (in 1980) split their tickets between presidential and congressional candidates. John A. Ferejohn and Morris P. Fiorina, "Incumbency and Realignment in Congressional Elections," in John E. Chubb and Paul E. Peterson, eds., *The New Direction in American Politics* (Brookings, 1985), p. 100.

supporters left the Republicans in 1912 to form the Bull Moose party, and the States' Rights Democrats seceded from the national Democratic party in 1948.

Under these circumstances, a state governor or party chairman in either party could see the development of a strong, centralized national organization as portending only trouble. An authoritative national party would impose its policy positions on the entire party, even in states where they would be unpopular. It might try to influence the choice of party nominees within the state, which to the degree it was successful would lessen the power of state leaders. True, a state party might sometimes want to identify with an enormously popular president, but at other times it would wish to dissociate itself. To preserve its freedom to take either course, its leaders have had to insist on state party autonomy within a weak federal structure.

Those who advocate the responsible-party model have been, generally, those who want more from government. To move toward that model would enhance the possibility of a bolder and more vigorous government able to concert its powers to overcome the deadlock and indecisiveness conduced by the Madisonian structure. Those who want less government have been, on the whole, understandably happy with the Madisonian model as a barrier to governmental activism. Yet the Madisonian model stands impartially in the way of activists of every stripe. And now that conservatism has become, in the Reagan era, hardly less activist than liberalism—its statesmen as eager to dismantle the welfare state as the liberals were to build it, and anxious to write conservative social values into law and carry out a forceful foreign policy—the responsible-party model may have a new appeal over a broadened range of the political spectrum.[13]

The remainder of this chapter is addressed to those who, whether liberal or conservative and for whatever reason, would wish to nudge the nation's institutional system in the direction of the responsible-party model. Without arguing the case further, the discussion will pass from considering *whether* political parties should be strengthened to *how* that might be achieved.

---

13. See, for example, Paul M. Weyrich, "A Conservative's Lament," *Washington Post*, March 8, 1987. Weyrich, a leading organizer of New Right activism, cites the difficulty of making foreign policy decisions because of executive-legislative conflict and concludes, "As conservatives, we have to help the nation face a stark choice: either modify our institutions of government to play the game of great power, or move back toward our historic, less active foreign policy."

Responsible Parties in a Divided Government

The responsible-party model presupposes single-party control of the executive and legislative branches. By definition, if two parties divide control, neither can be responsible. Whatever happens is the result of conflict, negotiation, and compromise between political opponents, and each can point the finger at the other if things go wrong.

If divided government is to be the nation's destiny most of the time—as it will have been for twenty-two of the thirty-four years from the election of 1954 through 1988—strengthening the parties is in fact a dubious objective from the viewpoint of responsible-party advocates. Stronger parties confronting each other from their respective redoubts in the White House and on Capitol Hill would reduce rather than enhance the prospects for governmental unity. Conflict would intensify. In 1981 Ronald Reagan was able to redirect the course of government only because the Democratic majority in the House of Representatives split and enough Democrats followed the leadership of the Republican president to give him a working majority for the essential elements of his party's program. How would a united, disciplined Democratic majority in the House have conducted itself that year? We cannot deduce the answer from anyone's experience, of course, because the only times within memory that a Democratic House majority has approached anything that could be called unity and discipline has been when it has submitted to the leadership of a strong and popular fellow partisan in the White House, notably in the early years of Woodrow Wilson, Franklin D. Roosevelt, and Lyndon Johnson. But if the position favored by the majority of House Democrats in 1981 can be taken as the likely position of a united party, that party would have deadlocked the Reagan program and plunged the country into a long-drawn-out struggle. Negotiations would have ultimately taken place, presumably, but if the bargaining had extended into 1982, much of the Reagan program would surely have been lost, for by that date the economic slump had robbed the president of much of his popularity and even the Republican Senate had rebelled against his economic program. Beginning in 1982, even a disunited Democratic majority in the House was able to block further Reagan initiatives aimed at dismantling governmental programs, to curtail much of the expansion he sought in defense expenditures, and to limit his intervention in Nicaragua.

Those who advocate responsible-party government, then, must at the outset find a way to mitigate the three-decades-old phenomenon of divided

Table 9-1. *The Fraying of Republican Presidential Coattails, 1952–84*

	1952 Republicans	1952 Democrats	1956 Republicans	1956 Democrats	1968 Republicans	1968 Democrats	1972 Republicans	1972 Democrats	1980 Republicans	1980 Democrats	1984 Republicans	1984 Democrats
Presidential vote (percent)	55.1	44.4	57.4	42.0	43.4	42.7	60.7	37.5	50.7	41.0	58.8	40.6
House members elected												
Total	221	213	201	234	192	243	191	244	192	243	182	253
South[a]	6	99	7	99	26	80	34	74	39	69	43	73
Outside South	215	114	194	135	166	163	157	170	153	174	139	180
South plus border[b]	13	117	11	120	32	97	38	93	47	84	50	88
Outside South and border	208	96	190	114	160	146	153	151	145	159	132	165
Percent outside South and border	68.4	31.6	62.5	37.5	52.3	47.7	50.3	49.7	47.7	52.3	44.4	55.6

a. The South is defined as consisting of the eleven states that made up the Confederacy: Virginia, North Carolina, South Carolina, Georgia, Florida, Alabama, Mississippi, Tennessee, Arkansas, Louisiana, and Texas.

b. The border states included here are Kentucky, Missouri, and Oklahoma. All were carried by Republican presidential candidates in the six elections, with two exceptions. Kentucky went Democratic for president in 1952 by 700 votes and Missouri in 1958 by 3,984 votes, or 50.1 percent.

government. And here they are sure to be frustrated. Changes in the electoral system to prevent the division of the government can be conceived, but the prospect of their adoption is close to zero.

Two approaches are possible. Because divided government is the result of ticket-splitting, a requirement that voters choose between party slates, or "team tickets," consisting of a party's candidates for national office (presidency, vice-presidency, Senate, and House) would virtually assure the president's party control of the House and usually of the Senate also—as was the case in the nineteenth century when the ballot was printed in the form of party tickets. A second approach would be to award the party that won the presidency enough bonus seats in the Congress to assure a majority of both houses. Republicans might be expected to see some merit in devices such as these, for either would have converted them from the minority to the majority party in Congress during much of the past three decades. But Democrats would give no such proposal a second glance, for that very reason. Even Republican members of Congress could be expected to reject them. The team ticket would involve the risk that the individual member's fate would be tied to that of an unpopular presidential candidate (remembering Barry Goldwater), while the addition of bonus members would reduce the status and influence of the members elected in their states and districts in the accustomed manner.[14]

Then what of the possibility that divided government might disappear through the normal course of events as suddenly as it appeared? Until the 1970s that indeed appeared to be the prospect. As shown in table 9-1, Democratic control of the House in the Eisenhower era and in the first Nixon term could be attributed directly to the historical accident of the Solid South. When in 1956 Dwight Eisenhower became the first winning presidential candidate in eighty years to fail to carry with him enough of his party's candidates to control the House, he did pull in a healthy plurality of 59 members from outside the South. But that was more than offset by the 92-seat margin that the Democrats maintained in that region—even though Eisenhower carried five southern states. When Richard Nixon won a much narrower presidential victory in 1968, his party's margin in the North and West was likewise narrower, 166 seats to 163, but it did exist. The 3-seat edge was, of course, overwhelmed by a Democratic majority of

---

14. These proposals as well as some less far-reaching measures to the same end are discussed in "Forestalling Divided Government," chap. 4 of my *Constitutional Reform and Effective Government* (Brookings, 1986).

54 from the South. In 1972 the Republican majority outside the South disappeared—despite the party's much more lopsided victory in the presidential race. Yet if one also excludes three border states—Kentucky, Missouri, and Oklahoma—that have been regularly carried by winning GOP presidential candidates but whose rural areas had traditionally voted as solidly Democratic as the South itself, the rest of the country still gave Nixon a tiny Republican majority in the House.

The Senate reflected much the same pattern. In 1952 Eisenhower brought a Senate controlled by the GOP. After his even greater landslide in 1956, Eisenhower confronted a Senate in Democratic control by a 49–47 margin, but the Democrats' monopoly over Senate seats from the South accounted wholly for this result. After the 1968 election, in which the presidential votes were almost evenly divided, the Republicans held exactly half the seats outside the South. In winning the presidency in 1972 the Republicans also won 18 of the 34 Senate seats at stake, including 4 of 9 in the South.

Examining these figures, one could conclude that if the politics of the South and the border states ever came to resemble those of the rest of the country, the likelihood of divided government would be considerably reduced. The nation might not return to the pre-1954 decades, when the president's party invariably controlled Congress following each presidential election, but it would come close to that pattern. A Republican president could expect a Republican House of Representatives, if only by a small margin, and he would have a reasonable chance of a GOP Senate as well, depending on the party's share of the holdover members.

The South, moreover, appeared to be conforming its politics to the national pattern. Southern voters first found it acceptable to vote Republican for president in the 1950s, with Eisenhower; thirty years later voting Republican for other offices had become respectable, too. The GOP was still not organized in depth in much of the South, and the Democrats maintained their grip on the state legislatures and the rural courthouses. But the Republicans were able to bring their strength in the Senate to exactly half the region's members (11 of 22 after the 1982 election), increase their House representation from the South to 37 percent (43 of 116 in 1984), and elect governors in all but two southern states—Georgia and Mississippi.

Meanwhile, however, something else was happening in the rest of the country regarding the House of Representatives. While President Eisenhower had coattails strong enough to pull in a large majority of Republican representatives from the North and West, and Richard Nixon was still able to bring in bare Republican majorities outside the South and border states, in the 1980s that was not possible for Ronald Reagan. Table 9-1 shows that the loss of presidential coattail power apparent in the Nixon years continued at an astonishing pace in the 1980s. President Reagan won reelection in 1984 by an even larger margin than did Eisenhower in either 1952 or 1956, but the proportion of Republican House victories outside the South and border states fell by 24 percentage points compared with 1952. That translated into 76 fewer seats, or barely three-fifths of the number won in 1952. If the most popular Republican president in modern times could not even come close to breaking the Democratic lock on the House of Representatives that has held solid except for four years (1947–48 and 1953–54) since 1930, one may well ask what Republican leader possibly can.

GOP campaign committees place their faith in two possibilities. First, they attribute the continuing Democratic ascendancy in the House in large part to the power of incumbent members to win reelection for virtually as long as they desire, and they point out that sooner or later every incumbency must end.[15] How have the Republicans fared, then, in capturing seats that have become open through the retirement of incumbents? Not very well, obviously, for in the period of continuous Democratic control since 1955 all but 9 Democratic House seats have been open at least once, and the party's margin is larger now than when the period began—even though the people have chosen Republican presidents during most of that time.

In the past four elections, when the most popular of all those presidents has been the party's leader, the Republicans did win a slight majority of the open seats, 78 to 72.[16] But the party had held 68 of the seats being vacated, leaving a net gain of 10. If the Republicans were able to maintain the relatively high rate of approval they enjoyed in the Reagan years, it would

15. For analyses of the power of incumbency, see the chapter by Thomas E. Mann in this volume. Also see Ferejohn and Fiorina, "Incumbency and Realignment." More than 90 percent of House incumbents running for reelection are regularly returned to office. In 1986 the proportion was 98 percent, with only 8 incumbents suffering defeat out of 393 who sought reelection.

16. Open seats are defined as those that are vacated by the incumbent for any reason—death, resignation, retirement, or defeat in a party primary. Technically, the Democrats won only 71. One of the seats vacated by a Democrat was won by an independent, but the seat reverted to the Democrats at the next election.

take more than three decades of picking up open seats at the rate of the 1980s for the party to gain the 40 seats it needs for a House majority. Even that projection assumes that the Republicans would remain as high in popular favor throughout that period as they have been in the 1980s, an assumption that defies both history and logic and ignores the recent drop in public confidence in the GOP.

Second, officials of the Republican National Committee place much of the blame for their minority position on the gerrymandering of district boundaries by Democratic state legislatures. But the scholarly studies summarized by Thomas Mann in chapter 12 do not confirm either that the redrawing of district boundaries after recent censuses has cost the GOP more than a few seats—mainly in California—or that even judicial intervention promises them much of a gain. The courts might prove reluctant to upset districting schemes that have become honored by tradition if they can be defended as having some measure of rationality—and most can, since there are various approaches to "objective" apportionment that produce different results but rest on equally defensible criteria. In the absence of court intervention, Republican hopes for significant gains through reapportionment are remote. Of the states that have more than one district, the GOP now controls both houses of the legislature and the governorship, which is necessary to give them complete control of the apportionment process, in only five, and those states have only eleven Democratic representatives. Ironically, seven of these are in Indiana, elected despite the fact that the Republican party had control of reapportionment after the 1980 census and drew a plan for the state's ten districts designed to give it maximum partisan advantage.

At bottom, the Democratic party's dominance of the House of Representatives for more than half a century reflects the fact that it has been the majority party in the country during that entire period. In 1984, after the second Reagan landslide, the Democrats held 58 percent of all state legislative seats, and that proportion was increased in 1986. The party is similarly preponderant in city halls and county courthouses, which along with the legislatures are the training ground for appealing candidates for Congress. Clearly, it will take another powerful swing of the pendulum to give the Republicans the strength in depth that would be necessary to produce a majority in the House of Representatives—and, if moving at all, the pendulum now is swinging toward the Democrats. One must reach the disappointing conclusion, then, that the responsible-party model is liable to be irrelevant for a long time as far as the Republican party is concerned.

It may continue to elect its presidential candidate most of the time, but the consequence will be divided government, not government by a party able to enact its program and take responsibility for it. Strengthening the GOP as an organization is still a desirable goal, but only for the marginal improvements that it might bring in the capability of the candidates the party offers and the effectiveness of those it elects.

To strengthen the Democratic party, however, would contribute directly to the effectiveness of party government whenever the Democrats again elect a president, for they can expect at that time to control Congress also.

The Obstacles to Strengthening Parties

The fundamental barrier to strengthening political parties is the survival in popular culture of the Madisonian model. Rejected almost unanimously by the country's political elite for two centuries, the Madisonian ideal of a factionless government has never lost its hold on the public. Factionalism is derided, and wherever possible averted, in the multitude of private organizations with which individual citizens are familiar. Why then, they ask, must politicians divide into factions that spend their energies in re-crimination and petty squabbling rather than getting together to do what is best for the country?

The machines that were the target of antiparty legislation nearly a century ago have by now virtually disappeared, and the strongest political organizations in the country are those held together not by public jobs and other forms of patronage but by ideology and philosophy. Yet the antiparty rhetoric of the Progressive era still rings loudly in political campaigns. Both Jimmy Carter and Ronald Reagan trumpeted their antiestablishment sentiments, and candidates at every level still find their road to victory by running against a party organization wherever one exists—the "man against the machine." So advocates of stronger parties must struggle against the widespread and often prevailing view that powerful party organizations are more a menace than a boon.

A second obstacle, related to the first, is the self-interest of individual politicians. A stronger party is by definition one with a stronger center, possessing some institutional means of fostering unity and cohesion. But for reasons stated early in this chapter, the individual politician who does not aspire to national leadership usually finds more to lose than to gain by strengthening the center. With a loose, decentralized structure the state or local leader can follow the national party and its leaders when their policies are popular at home or defy them when they are not. The self-interest of thousands of politicians is a centrifugal force within the party structure that is operative constantly; centripetal political forces develop now and then, but most of the time they are overbalanced.

Recent Progress toward Stronger Parties

Yet advocates of stronger parties are the beneficiaries of one profound trend in American politics and one series of deliberate actions, and both of these give hope.

The promising trend is that the two major parties have both become, and are still becoming, more homogeneous ideologically. This trend is the simple consequence of the party realignment that began in the 1930s and has been working its way, gradually but inexorably, through the political system. Simply put, the minority wings, once strong enough to disrupt the internal unity of the two parties, have been dying out. The "four-party system" James MacGregor Burns condemned a generation ago for producing "the deadlock of democracy" is now much more nearly a genuine two-party system.[17]

First to fade were the progressive Republicans. The progressive wing of the GOP, which spanned the generations from Theodore Roosevelt through the La Follettes and George Norris to Nelson Rockefeller and George Romney, was powerful enough as recently as twenty years ago to contest seriously for the presidential nomination. But the progressive Republicans are now an ineffectual remnant. Their counterparts, the conservative Democrats, have been vanishing as well, although more slowly. Virtually confined to the South since the New Deal era, they have from the 1960s been gradually losing their base there to the burgeoning Republican party. As conservative Democrats have ended their careers one by one—usually through retirement rather than defeat—their successors have typically been either conservative Republicans or Democrats cut in the mold of their national party. Thus Republicans occupy the seats once held by such archconservative senators as Harry F. Byrd and A. Willis Robertson of Virginia and James O. Eastland of Mississippi, while new Democratic senators arriving from the South tend to be moderates, such as Terry

17. Burns, *The Deadlock of Democracy* (Prentice-Hall, 1963).

Sanford of North Carolina and Bob Graham of Florida, or even bear the liberal label, like Wyche Fowler of Georgia. A corresponding transformation has taken place in both parties in the House.[18]

The deliberate actions are those taken by congressional Democrats over the past two decades to impose discipline on party dissenters. Any article on strengthening political parties written earlier than twenty years ago would have opened and closed with a call for destruction of the seniority system in the Congress. That has now been accomplished on the Democratic side. As long as seniority was automatically honored, any Democrat, no matter how out of step with the majority of the party in Congress, could acquire all the plenary power of a committee chairmanship through mere longevity. Through that device some of the Senate and House committees most crucial to the enactment of the Democratic party's program were turned over to conservative Democrats who voted regularly with the Republicans against the majority of their own party. Sooner or later the situation was bound to prove intolerable. Finally the revolution occurred: liberals in the House forced through the party caucus a series of rules changes that not only scrapped seniority but reduced the arbitrary power of committee chairmen. The revolt was solidified in 1975 when the caucus deposed three chairmen. And it has continued to exercise disciplinary power. In 1987 the caucus voted to remove Les Aspin of Wisconsin from the chairmanship of the House Armed Services Committee, reversing itself only after Aspin humbly promised to accept its guidance on major questions of military policy.[19] The caucus has also assumed, and exercised, the power to instruct the Democratic committee majorities to bring specific measures to the House floor.

With this power of discipline, the caucus has been revived as an instrument for building policy consensus. In their drive to assert control over party policy, the liberals won a demand for regular monthly party caucuses plus additional meetings on petition of fifty members—a dramatic departure from the once-every-two-years tradition that had prevailed for a quar-

18. The homogeneity of the congressional Republicans has, of course, been demonstrated throughout the Reagan years. But Democratic unity has also improved; see A. James Reichley, "The Rise of National Parties," in Chubb and Peterson, eds., *New Direction,* p. 197.

19. House and Senate Republicans also permit departures from seniority in selecting chairmen or ranking minority members of committees, but no member has yet been penalized. In a contested case in 1987, Senate Republicans upheld seniority in assigning Jesse Helms of North Carolina to the ranking minority post on the Foreign Relations Committee.

ter of a century. The caucus has proved to be an effective consensus-building mechanism, particularly in the long and acrimonious debate over the Vietnam War when the passion of the antiwar Democratic majority eventually persuaded some reluctant senior party figures to abandon their support. Since then it has expressed itself on a wide range of measures, including the issues of defense policy that led to Aspin's pledge of conformity. In early February 1987 the caucus denounced the Reagan administration's resumption of underground nuclear testing and urged the administration instead to begin negotiations with the Soviet Union for an agreement banning such tests.

Institutional change has occurred less formally in the clublike Senate, but the arbitrary power of Democratic committee chairmen has been effectively curtailed there as well. Within the committee structures in both houses, democratic norms now prevail.

Finally, the new Democratic party rule that guarantees seats in the quadrennial presidential nominating convention to 80 percent of the party's members of Congress may prove to be an important move in the direction of greater party cohesion. While most members will no doubt be guided by the sentiment of their states' voters as expressed in primaries and caucuses, and while they are unlikely to vote as a bloc in any case, their influence will be enhanced. In a close convention contest a determined network of House and Senate leaders could conceivably be decisive in selecting a nominee experienced in dealing with Congress, as opposed to an outsider like Jimmy Carter whose misfortunes in his relationships with the legislators and the rest of the party establishment spurred the rules revision.

So, whenever the next Democratic president is elected, advocates of responsible-party government may yet expect to see a close approximation to their model. Given reasonable luck in the presidential nominating lottery, today's more homogeneous Democratic party should be able to attain a degree of cohesion under presidential leadership that observers of the party system have not seen—except for the honeymoon years of Lyndon Johnson—in half a century.

Perhaps that cohesion will provide a satisfactory enough version of responsible-party government. But if additional measures to strengthen parties could be taken, the possibilities are worth considering. Any such measures, however, are sure to be difficult. If they were easy, they would already have been adopted, for those who lead the two national parties would assuredly prefer to lead stronger organizations.

The Limited Opportunities for Further Action

The first obvious possibility for further action is for the majorities in Congress to impose party discipline not merely to get measures out of committee but to get them passed. The means to that end is the binding caucus, which both houses last used with full effectiveness in the first Congress of the Wilson administration, in 1913–14. Through that device two-thirds of the Democratic caucus could bind the entire membership to vote with the majority.[20] When the rule was invoked, however, the Democrats laid themselves open to attack by the Republican opposition and its supporters in the media and elsewhere, as well as by independents revolted by the spectacle of coercion. Rule by "King Caucus" developed into a major political issue. Chastened by the public reaction and by intraparty opposition as well, Senate Democrats abandoned the device after the Wilson era. The House party discarded it, too, after a brief revival in the early New Deal period. Any proposal for its reintroduction would undoubtedly arouse an even more adverse response in today's climate of political individualism, which makes the suggestion futile at the outset.

Another instrument employed by strong parties in other countries also appears beyond consideration in the United States. That is control by the national party, in one or another degree, over the selection of candidates for the national legislature. On reflection, it has to appear anomalous that anyone, no matter how ideologically opposed to the program and philosophy of the Democratic or Republican party, may run for Congress as the party's candidate, take his or her seat with the party upon election, and receive choice committee assignments as a matter of right from the party caucus. Yet neither party has ever developed mechanisms at any level for screening candidacies. Even to design such a mechanism would be difficult. Some have suggested that the copyright laws be made the vehicle, with only persons authorized by the national party allowed to use the party label. But the idea of national control of nominations has too antidemocratic a ring—smacking, like the binding caucus, of thought control—ever to acquire noticeable support. In emergencies, like the one that developed in Illinois in 1986 when two unacceptable candidates won Democratic nominations for state office, the party can devise extraordinary remedies,

---

20. Except for those who formally communicated their intention not to be bound, citing one or more of several permissible grounds. That privilege was, however, not often invoked.

as the Democrats did in that case by organizing a temporary new party. Moreover, the principal reason for advocating control of candidacies disappeared on the Democratic side when the seniority system was scrapped, for while a dissenter can win committee assignments, he or she can now be denied on ideological grounds the power of a chairmanship. This, if the issue arises, would be the easier solution for the GOP as well.

In its 1950 report the American Political Science Association Committee on Political Parties proposed creation of a national council in each party to set party policy as a means for moving toward a more responsible two-party system. The council, to consist of about fifty members from both inside and outside government, would draft the preliminary party platform and, after its adoption by the convention, interpret it. The council would also make recommendations "in respect to congressional candidates," and perhaps presidential candidates as well. But any such proposal also founders on the rock of self-interest. Why would a president and leading legislators who had won governmental office through arduous election campaigns voluntarily share their policymaking power with outsiders and submit to their restraints? That was the experience when the Democratic National Committee, influenced by the APSA committee report, established its Democratic Advisory Council after the 1956 election. The party's congressional leaders simply declined to join.[21] The council issued well-considered policy pronouncements, but it spoke for only a segment of the party and could not serve its purpose as an institution to unify the party.

There remains one other instrument of discipline: money. Dependent as legislators are on campaign contributions, the power to grant or deny financial assistance can in theory be a powerful disciplinary tool. The national Republican party in recent years has demonstrated the capacity to raise and distribute an enormous treasury. The Democrats' capability is by no means comparable, but it has been improving. Is money a potential means, then, for tightening party discipline within Congress to achieve responsible-party government?

In theory, yes. In practice, probably not to a significant degree. Because discretionary power over congressional campaign funds would be a powerful device to achieve central control, the resistance that arises

21. However, two members of the party's liberal wing in the Senate—Hubert Humphrey and Estes Kefauver—did join the Advisory Council at the outset. Senators John F. Kennedy and Stuart Symington joined late in 1959.

against central control of any aspect of party organization would in this case be commensurately potent. But even if discretion were granted to the national party committees, their self-interest would steer them away from exercising it as an instrument of party discipline. The overriding objective of the national party in congressional campaigns is to win a majority of seats. To this end, the party's self-interest is to support any candidate with a chance of victory, and to support most generously the candidates in the closest races, where additional spending is most likely to pay off in victories. In the heat of a campaign the national party officials making money decisions do not ask about the voting regularity of a party's incumbents or extract voting promises from nonincumbents. They ask only about election prospects. They take polls and are guided by the numbers.[22]

So it is that in these days of Republican opulence no complaints have been heard that the national party has been using its funds in a discriminatory fashion to penalize legislators who have deviated from the Reagan party line. After the 1986 election the party was proud to announce that it had "maxed out" on every candidate, that is, given the maximum amount permissible by law to its nominee in every race. No one was disciplined. Indeed, one true believer in party discipline, Patrick J. Buchanan, the White House director of communications, could complain after the election that President Reagan had been "travelling the nation as no other president before him, fighting to save the Senate for . . . Republicans, throwing his arm around men—some of whom had cut-and-run on him in every major engagement he has fought since he came to the White House."[23]

In any case, cash contributions to congressional campaigns by national party committees are now so tightly limited by law that the potential for monetary discipline is not great. In House campaigns a party committee is treated as just another political action committee limited to contributing the same $5,000 a race (in Senate contests the ceiling is $17,500). Com-

22. A national party committee under presidential control might on occasion be tempted to intervene in a party primary against a recalcitrant member (despite the unhappy experience of President Franklin Roosevelt in his attempted "purge" of anti–New Deal Democrats in 1938). Early in 1986 President Reagan's political operatives were reportedly encouraging Governor Richard L. Thornburgh of Pennsylvania to challenge Senator Arlen Specter in that state's 1986 Republican primary. While the White House ultimately turned away from that course, it may have achieved a measure of discipline for a limited time through the threat to support Thornburgh. Significantly, the Senate Campaign Committee did not participate in threatening an incumbent senator.

23. *Washington Post*, December 8, 1986.

pared with what the array of PACs can put into closely contested races, these sums are a pittance, particularly in the case of the senior members of key committees who—if any member needed discipline—might need it the most. Any major influence by party committees has to be exerted indirectly, through advice given by party officials to friendly PACs, rather than directly through the party's own funds.

The limits on party contributions could, of course, be raised by new legislation, but the Democrats are hardly likely to use their Senate and House majorities to enhance the advantage that the richer Republican party would get from freer spending. And if a large share of congressional campaign funds were to come from the public treasury, that would not change matters either. In the bill introduced in January 1987 as S. 2 by Democratic Senators David L. Boren of Oklahoma and Robert C. Byrd of West Virginia, the majority leader, the public funds would be distributed among candidates by formula, with the party not even serving as a channel.[24]

Money, then, is not likely to become the powerful centralizing force within the parties that at first sight might appear possible. The handling of money has yielded to, and been conformed to, the prevailing pattern of decentralization in the party structure. And it is likely to remain that way, no matter how the sums at the disposal of the parties might be increased. The members of Congress who would write any public financing law and who already have the decisive voice in determining the national parties' policies for distributing congressional campaign funds will see to that.

Deliberate attempts, then, to strengthen political parties run counter to deep-seated public attitudes, to the self-interest of the politicians who would have to initiate change, and to the structure of governmental and political institutions, including the electoral system. The feasible actions have already been taken—notably the crucial decisions in the 1970s to assert majority rule within the congressional parties. There is a solid basis for hope, however, in political trends beyond the influence of even the political elite itself—the continuing realignment of the party system that is producing the homogeneity on which party cohesion and strength at the governmental level must rest.

If, when one party again wins single-party control of the presidency and Congress, it succeeds in coping effectively with the problems of the coun-

24. For more extensive suggestions on how changes in campaign finance laws might be used to strengthen parties, see chap. 7 in this book.

try, the value of the responsible-party concept will have been demonstrated and the model will win a wider public acceptance. More people will then see the role of parties as those who believe in the responsible-party model see it—as institutions crucially necessary to formulate governmental programs, to enact and execute those programs, and to account for them to the electorate afterward.

Only such a period of success can provide the necessary popular support for institutional changes that will further the same ends. In the meantime, such changes of any consequence will simply have to wait.

CHAPTER TEN

Party Reform
and the Public Interest

EVERETT CARLL LADD

*Since everything is made to serve an end, everything necessarily serves
the best end.* —Voltaire, *Candide*

*A disposition to preserve, and an ability to improve, taken together, would
be my standard of a statesman.* —Edmund Burke, *Reflections on the
Revolution in France*

EDMUND BURKE'S perspective, and those Voltaire assigns to Pangloss,
are in one superficial regard similar: both are aligned against the restless
search for perfection. But here the similarity ends. Pangloss is a fool,
Burke a wise man. This is obviously not the best of all possible worlds.
Suggesting that it is negates one of the most precious of human attributes,
the drive to improve. Burke recognized that success in preserving
institutions of lasting value depends upon an ability and readiness to
remedy their defects. Nonetheless, he saw clearly that *change* and
improvement may be as different as night and day. Unless proposals are
scrutinized to determine whether they are indeed likely to make things
better, passion for change will be self-defeating and counterproductive.

Lest I be branded as Panglossian, let me make clear that I am keenly
aware that American parties and elections do not approach perfection; my
skepticism about much of the case for change stems only from my
conclusion that it has not earned the right to be considered *reform*.

Many desirable results simply aren't achievable through institutional
engineering. Electing more Washingtons and Lincolns undoubtedly would

222

make the presidency work better, but there is no institutional means to this end. Other political problems have *institutional* sources, but their roots are not in *political* institutions. Our educational system may, for instance, be deficient in the training it imparts to political leaders and citizens. I refer specifically to the relative absence of rigorous instruction aimed at providing deep historical understanding and awareness of the moral and philosophical bases of American nationality.

This latter subject is huge and most of it lies well outside the scope of this study. It is relevant to suggest, however, that if there are problems in the quality of contemporary political leadership, they may have far less to do with the recruitment processes of the electoral system than with the training processes of the educational system.

Calvin Coolidge, delivering a speech on July 5, 1926, in Philadelphia, upon the 150th anniversary of the Declaration of Independence, observed, "Under a system of popular government there will always be those who will seek for political preferment by clamoring for reform. While there is very little of this which is not sincere, there is a very large portion that is not well informed." To assess properly where we are as a polity and what responses we must make to present challenges, the president went on, we must better understand what aspects of our founding are the vital heritage:

> They [the founding generation] were a people who came under the influence of a great spiritual development and acquired a great moral power. No other theory is adequate to explain or comprehend the Declaration of Independence. It is the product of the spiritual insight of the people. We live in an age of science and of abounding accumulation of material things. These did not create our Declaration. Our Declaration created them. The things of the spirit come first. Unless we cling to that, all our material prosperity, overwhelming thought it may appear, will turn to a barren sceptre in our grasp.[1]

Coolidge was, of course, issuing a call for political renewal—and one that belies the now-common conception that his political philosophy is well captured by the laconic observation that "the business of America is business." Throughout his major addresses the thirtieth president showed deep historical awareness. That he possessed it probably had little to do with how presidents were then recruited and much with what churches,

1. Calvin Coolidge, *Foundations of the Republic: Speeches and Addresses* (Charles Scribner's Sons, 1926), pp. 453–54.

colleges, and other institutions then taught. Calvin Coolidge received at Amherst in 1891–95 much the same kind of training as James Madison received from John Witherspoon at Princeton in 1769–71. Without arguing that the overall quality of contemporary leadership falls below the level of most earlier periods—except that of the founding era, which surely far surpassed our own—one can wish that our educational system, dwarfing in available resources that of any earlier era, might find a way to develop more of the historical and philosophical understanding that previous educational systems, though far less elaborate, managed to convey.

Defining the National Interest

Does our system of parties and electoral arrangements need fixing to enable it to better advance what is variously called the common, public, or national interest? Before exploring this question, I should note that American political science has had a simply terrible time grappling with the idea of the public interest. Robert Dahl and Charles Lindblom have insisted that in most instances the meaning of the national or public interest is "left totally undefined. . . . Often enough a precise examination would show that it can mean nothing more than whatever happens to be the speaker's own view as to a desirable public policy."[2] Frank Sorauf nominated the term "public interest" as a leading candidate for inclusion in "a list of ambiguous words and phrases 'which never would be missed'."[3] According to Howard Reiter, radical political scientists (in whose company he places himself) "argue that in any society dominated by class interests, like the United States, there can be no general interest that unites all classes, and the concept of a 'public interest' is a sham intended to fool the lower classes into supporting the interests of the upper classes."[4]

Other scholars have found the concept of a public or national interest highly meaningful, of course, and I put myself in their ranks.[5] In discus-

2. Robert A. Dahl and Charles E. Lindblom, *Politics, Economics and Welfare* (Harper, 1963), p. 501.
3. Frank Sorauf, "The Conceptual Muddle," in Carl J. Friedrich, ed., *The Public Interest* (Atherton Press, 1962), p. 190.
4. Howard L. Reiter, *Parties and Elections in Corporate America* (St. Martin's Press, 1987), p. 63.
5. See, among recent writers, Virginia Held, *The Public Interest and Individual Interests* (Basic Books, 1970); and Richard E. Flathman, *The Public Interest: An Essay Concerning the Normative Discourse of Politics* (Wiley, 1966).

sing their political aspirations, most people seem to find the conception natural and essential. Probably this is because, as Daniel Bell and Irving Kristol argued in introducing their magazine, *The Public Interest,* "there has never been a society which was not, in some way, and to some extent guided by this ideal."[6]

For the purposes of this chapter, I content myself with a few basic distinctions. Most people seem able to distinguish between interests that are broadly shared and those that are quite narrow. For example, obtaining a system that provides high-quality public education reflects a broader constellation of interests than does preserving a special tax write-off for Uptight Motors, Inc. Furthermore, some interests are fundamental and enduring; pursuit of immediate goals that threaten basic long-term objectives is counter to the national interest. Most Americans regard their country's security and an environment conducive to the extension of liberty and democracy around the world as key elements in the national interest. It includes, too, a healthy, growing economy that extends economic opportunity. And surely, most Americans see it in the national interest that successful popular governance be obtained.

Does our system of parties and elections do as much as any other could to serve such broad, enduring ends? Or does it sacrifice them by being too responsive to claims that are narrow, particularistic, shortsighted, and short term?

The Argument for Disciplined National Parties

Specific criticisms of the parties and election system for insufficiently serving the pursuit of broad public interests cannot be separated from more general criticisms of the entire American system of widely dispersed and decentralized governmental authority. Most arguments that have been advanced throughout this century for strengthening political parties' control over nominations and the policy process stem from one underlying assumption: the separation of powers and all its ramifications need mitigation through the intermediary of relatively disciplined and integrated parties.

6. Daniel Bell and Irving Kristol, "What Is the Public Interest?" *The Public Interest,* vol. 1 (Fall 1965), p. 5.

In *Congressional Government,* first published in 1885, Woodrow Wilson stated forcefully the argument that the American system and its extreme dispersion of authority frustrate the achievement of national interests. "As at present constituted," he wrote, "the federal government lacks strength because its powers are divided, lacks promptness because its authorities are multiplied, lacks wieldiness because its processes are roundabout, lacks efficiency because its responsibility is indistinct and its actions without competent direction. . . . Nobody stands sponsor for the policy of the government."[7]

In this view, the system hampers pursuit of the national interest by making it virtually impossible for government to frame the kind of coherent, integrated approaches to complex policies that are required. The policy incoherence bred of separation of powers was one thing in 1793, when the federal government did very little and could take a long time doing it. It was already something quite different, Wilson thought, by the late nineteenth century when, he observed, "the sphere and influence of national administration and national legislation are widening rapidly." Wilson was then a strong advocate of responsible party leadership and an admirer of the British parliamentary system with its disciplined parties and responsible ministries. He stopped short of advocating its application in America as a remedy for the ills he observed, but he lamented the weaknesses of the American "committee system of government" with its ineffectual parties.

Wilson's early advocacy of responsible party government was modified considerably by the turn of the century. In writing the preface of the fifteenth printing of *Congressional Government* in 1900, he argued that the nation's plunge into international politics had produced "greatly increased power and opportunity for constructive statesmanship given the President . . . [and that as a result] the Executive . . . will have very far-reaching effect upon our whole method of government." Those views were fully developed in *Constitutional Government,* first published in 1908.[8] Wilson did not, of course, abandon his commitment to the goal of more coherent national leadership. Presidential leadership would replace party leadership in linking all the power centers of our constitutionally separated government.

7. Woodrow Wilson, *Congressional Government: A Study in American Politics* (Johns Hopkins University Press, 1981), pp. 206–07.
8. Woodrow Wilson, *Constitutional Government in the United States* (Columbia University Press, 1908).

The prevailing view in American political science since the Second World War has been that presidential leadership is insufficient without disciplined parties. In 1950, for example, the Committee on Political Parties of the American Political Science Association issued its call for a system of stronger parties able to meet the national need "for more effective formulation of general policies and programs and for better integration of all of the far-flung activities of modern government."[9]

The American system's dispersion of authority has often been faulted for retarding political accountability and popular control. Giving the public effective means of control over a big, complex government is difficult, yet vital in any country that takes democracy seriously. A century ago, Wilson lamented that "the average citizen may be excused for esteeming government at best but a haphazard affair upon which his vote and all of his influence can have but little effect. How is his choice of a representative in Congress to affect the policy of the country as regards the questions in which he is most interested?"[10]

Contemporary American political science for the most part sees the strengthening of parties as essential for extending popular control over government and ensuring greater responsiveness of public institutions to popular wishes. Only strong parties can so organize issues that the public can speak effectively on them. If they make elected officials in some sense collectively rather than individually responsible to the electorate, parties greatly expand the public's capacity to reward and punish.

Similarly, stronger and more disciplined parties have been seen as an important but elusive potential antidote to extreme congressional individualism and the opening it offers the swarm of special interests. The 1950 APSA report made this case. "The value of special-interest groups in a diversified society . . . should be obvious," its authors argued. "But organized interest groups cannot do the job of the parties. Indeed, it is only when a working formula of the public interest in its *general* character is made manifest by the parties in terms of coherent programs that the claims of interest groups can be adjusted on the basis of political responsibility. . . . [The proliferation of interest groups and the extension of their sway] makes necessary a reinforced party system that can cope with the multiplied organized pressures."[11]

9. American Political Science Association, *Toward a More Responsible Two-Party System,* supplement to *American Political Science Review,* vol. 44 (September 1950), p.16.

10. Wilson, *Congressional Government,* pp. 331–32.

11. APSA, *Toward a More Responsible Two-Party System,* p. 19.

Strong parties are needed not only to curb special interest influence by forcing them "to pick on people their own size" but also to help the underorganized many have their proper say in competition with the highly organized few. E. E. Schattschneider gave classic statement to this argument: "The flaw in the pluralist heaven is that the heavenly chorus sings with a strong upper-class accent."[12]

If one stays within the body of theory and political argument I have been reviewing, one is hard put to quarrel with it. Surely the American governmental system, built upon federalism and separation of powers, does greatly divide and disperse political authority. Indeed, in the parliamentary sense of the term, the United States really does not have a *government* at all. The president has significant authority, but he and his executive subordinates are rightly called the *administration,* not the *government;* Congress's role is so great that it would have to be part of the government for there to be a government. In this dispersed and decentralized scheme, barriers aplenty are erected to coherent, centrally developed policies. And interest groups are indeed presented with multiple points of access at all levels. It is very messy, and presidents are not alone in finding it frustrating.

The American governmental order has dictated a special type of party system. Given federalism, the parties historically were organized on state lines, and even when individual state parties were robust and disciplined the national party system remained fragmented. Given separation of powers, the case for party discipline evident in parliamentary systems could never be made, and party factions had a variety of bases from which to maintain their independence. Given the extreme individualism that has always distinguished American political culture, calls for greater collective party authority have rarely struck a responsive chord among the public, and succeeding waves of "reform" have had the principal result of further extending political individualism. The "reforms" of the 1960s and early 1970s in Congress, for example, left individual members even more advantaged vis-à-vis the House and Senate leadership.

All in all, today's party system does not reduce the effects of the constitutionally dictated separation of powers: rather it reflects them and, in so doing, magnifies them. American political parties are not well equipped for developing comprehensive policy positions, presenting them

---

12. E. E. Schattschneider, *The Semisovereign People: A Realist's View of Democracy in America* (Holt, Rinehart, and Winston, 1960), p. 35.

to the electorate, and seeing them through into legislated programs that might be voted up or down in the next election.

Distinction between Change and Reform

Although it is hard to argue with much of the above so far as it describes how the U.S. system works, it is not hard to reject the argument that these conditions present a prima facie case for a particular set of institutional changes being in the public interest.

No one who pays close attention to politics would dismiss out of hand every call for change in our parties and elections system. I do maintain, however, that the more substantial recently proposed changes fail to show real promise of making things better by such national-interest standards as more responsive democratic government and wiser long-term policies.

I should acknowledge that my current judgment in this regard differs to some extent from that of times past. I have always been skeptical about claims that proposed changes should be readily recognized as reforms. Often, the changes do not in fact make things better—and within a few years of their enactment the cry is raised loudly that the reforms must themselves be reformed. Nonetheless, I did at one time accept much of the argument in favor of stronger parties and an improved presidential nominating process. With regard to the latter, I offered my own elegant blueprint for change, which included a bigger role for party and elected officials in conjunction with a single, nationwide presidential primary.[13] While I remain comfortable with much of the earlier analysis, I think I yielded too readily to the underlying notion that successful institutional tinkering is easily conceived.

Tinkering

Proposed changes differ as to their comprehensiveness. Some are potentially far-reaching, such as arguments for strengthening the national parties. Others are much more limited, such as proposals for altering the schedule of presidential primaries. My concern with the latter sort of proposals is in part the familiar one about unintended consequences—that

13. Everett Ladd, "A Better Way to Pick Our Presidents," *Fortune,* May 5, 1980, pp. 132–42.

they often result in two steps forward and two steps back, or sometimes two-and-one-half steps back. They advocate change that has merit but also disadvantages.

The continuing discussion of the scheduling of presidential primaries is a good case in point. Concern has been voiced about the implications of small states (Iowa and New Hampshire) leading the parade of caucuses and primaries, permitting their Republican and Democratic electorates, which are far from national microcosms, to receive undue weight. Are there unfortunate implications in giving one state or region, whose social and political outlook differs from the other sections, so much weight in establishing early momentum? All manner of suggestions have been made to cope with such scheduling problems. For example, some have urged a series of four primary dates, with all states holding primaries assigned to one or another so that no region dominates any date. This has some merit: New Hampshire and Iowa would get less attention, and a more representative collection of states would lead things off. But there are drawbacks: for example, candidates would be forced to campaign simultaneously in four scattered sections of the country, putting enormous burdens on them, especially on those who start with less funding and organizational resources. By leading off, manageable little Iowa and New Hampshire enable less well known and well heeled candidates to gain attention through presenting their wares to real people in real election settings. If a candidate with modest resources and no national reputation manages to impress a fair number of voters in these small states, isn't this laboratory experience of considerable interest to the country?

In offering in 1980 "a better way to pick our presidents," I argued for combining in the election system large doses of two differing, even conflicting, elements: peer review by party leaders and a strong voice for rank-and-file voters. The former would be achieved by providing that one-third of all national convention delegates be chosen wholly outside the primaries in their capacity as party officials and officeholders. The remaining two-thirds would be chosen in state delegate-selection primaries held in every state on a single day—for example, the third Tuesday in June. Each state's delegates would be divided among the candidates in proportion to the candidates' respective shares of the state's total vote, with perhaps a threshold of 10 percent of the vote required before one gets any delegates.

Under this system, a candidate who ran strongly in the national primary would almost surely add enough support from party leaders to be nominated on the first ballot. If he received 60 percent of the primary vote, for example, across the fifty states, he would go to the convention assured of roughly 40 percent of the first-round convention ballots—that is, 60 percent of the two-thirds of the delegates chosen through the primary. It would be surprising if he couldn't pick up another 10 percent from the party officials. Otherwise, the convention would go on to further balloting, with no delegates bound but all aware of voter preferences. Bargaining and negotiation would finally produce the nominee.

These arguments, advanced in the spring of 1980, still seem sound to me seven years later. I am less inclined to argue confidently on behalf of their implementation today, however, for two differing sorts of reasons. First, I am now more skeptical about the desirability of imposing upon the states and parties any national reform of presidential nominee selection, even assuming the political readiness in Congress to legislate such change. Respect for the federal character of presidential selection and for the private associational nature of the national parties requires that Congress not presume to tell the states and the parties that delegate-selection primaries must be held on a given date and delegates chosen according to one nationally set standard.

It is entirely appropriate, of course, to try to educate and persuade the parties to consider certain approaches, like those that build a greater measure of peer review into the selection process. And here, it should be noted, recent developments give one reason to be modestly satisfied. I refer, in particular, to the Democrats' decisions to increase the numbers of party leaders and officeholders selected ex officio as convention delegates. Such gradual change, based on the lessons of experience, is wholly consistent with the modest Burkean approach to reform.

My second reason for quarreling with my earlier position is related but still distinct. Our laudable enthusiasm for making things better may lead to urging the parties to tinker constantly with their procedures. This argument is something more than insisting on a need to be sensitive to "the unintended consequences of purposive social action." It is also more than insisting upon the need to recognize that every system of presidential selection has its own weaknesses and biases. It involves the judgment that there is a vital national interest in achieving order, stability, and predictability in election machinery, of the kind discussed by James Ceaser in chapter 2. Electoral reform should be approached from a perspective that recognizes how important it is to settle on something and stick with it.

I have made this same argument with regard to the endless stream of proposals for improving campaign finance. Like Michael Malbin, I have concluded that our present arrangements for funding elections do not work badly and certainly are not guilty, as is so often charged, of giving certain special interests a corrupting financial influence.[14] Some of the changes made in the 1970s through the Federal Election Campaign Act and its amendments do seem to have improved things, as in providing for a far more complete public accounting of who receives how much in campaign contributions from whom; and undoubtedly some further improvements can be made. The greater improvement now would come from securing bipartisan agreement on an election finance scheme that, while no doubt falling short of perfection, would meet a few basic objectives—thereby bringing to an end the long period of partisan skirmishing.

If the United States does not resist the urge to tinker with campaign finance every few years, this area may become for us what election laws were for France during the Fourth Republic—subject to regular change guided by nothing more substantial than immediate partisan advantage. Before every election during the Fourth Republic, a key battle was fought on what election law would prevail in the balloting. Several variants of proportional representation were used, for example, each differing substantially in its implications for how votes would get translated into seats in the National Assembly. After a twenty-year hiatus, electoral law skirmishing resumed in France in the mid-1980s, when the Socialists put through changes designed to reduce expected losses. If this kind of opportunistic manipulation comes to pass in American campaign finance law, popular confidence is bound to suffer. People in a democracy need to believe that the basic rules governing the way they choose their leaders have a durability that reflects an underlying propriety and legitimacy. Constant change suggests that rulemaking is a shallow, cynical, political game.

We should, then, resist the temptation to tinker continuously. Changes sometimes have to be made, and interested parties and groups will inevitably differ as to where their interests lie. But stability in electoral rules and procedures is in the national interest. The proper goal of reform is to remove electoral machinery as far as possible from partisan debate and

14. See, for example, Michael Malbin, "Looking Back at the Future of Campaign Finance Reform: Interest Groups and American Elections," in Malbin, ed., *Money and Politics in the United States* (Washington, D.C.: American Enterprise Institute for Public Policy Research, 1984), pp. 232–76; and Everett Ladd, "Campaign Spending and Democracy," *Ladd Report #4* (W. W. Norton, 1986).

endless tinkering. The U.S. single-member district, simple majority system seems to me to offer the model. It certainly has its biases, but both parties have learned to live with it, and the American electorate has come to see it as involving generally fair, justifiably permanent rules of the game.

Major Surgery

The American system in its entirety—including the separation of powers and the decentralized, undisciplined party system established within it—undoubtedly makes more difficult the enactment of programs that reflect some centrally inspired coherence. Even when a president wins a handsome public endorsement, he must immediately grapple with a fiercely independent Congress in which members of his own party as well as the opposition resist him at critical junctures. Compared with parliamentary systems with relatively disciplined parties, our system is surely disjointed and at times even incoherent.

Given that in other systems party factions have gained working control of the government and managed to enact their programs with less compromise and adjustment than is typically required in the United States, one must question whether the biases of the American system should be seen as disadvantageous. Arthur Schlesinger, Jr., argues that the key problem evident in the making of public policy in the United States is not that we are unable to enact a set of elegant programs because of the system of dispersed authority. "Our problem . . . is that we do not know what to do. . . . If we don't know what ought to be done, efficient enactment of a poor program is a dubious accomplishment—as the experience of 1981 demonstrates. [Schlesinger was critical of various economic proposals that the Reagan administration advanced and Congress enacted.] What is the great advantage of acting with decision and dispatch when you don't know what you are doing?"[15]

Schlesinger points out that as early as a century ago foreign visitors to the United States were leveling much the same criticisms of the American system as are made today. In *The American Commonwealth*, Lord Bryce summarized the British view that the American system was virtually incapable of settling major national questions. "An Englishman is disposed

15. Arthur M. Schlesinger, Jr., "Leave the Constitution Alone," in Donald L. Robinson, ed., *Reforming American Government* (Westview Press, 1985), p. 53.

to ascribe these failures to the fact that as there are no leaders, there is no one responsible for the neglect of business, the miscarriage of bills, the unwise appropriation of public funds. 'In England,' he says, 'the ministry of the day bears the blame of whatever goes wrong in the House of Commons. Having a majority, it ought to be able to do what it desires.'"[16]

Bryce also reported the response that he encountered among American political leaders. They insisted that Congress had not settled a number of major national questions not because of defects in institutional structure "but because the division of opinion in the country regarding them has been faithfully reflected in Congress. The majority has not been strong enough to get its way; and . . . no distinct impulse of mandate towards any particular settlement of these questions has been received from the country. It is not for Congress to go faster than the people. When the country knows and speaks its mind, Congress will not fail to act." Schlesinger endorses this general argument. "When the country is not sure what ought to be done, it may be that delay, debate and further consideration are not a bad idea. And if our leadership is sure what to do, it must in our democracy educate the rest—and that is not a bad idea either."[17]

Admittedly, this argument has a large subjective component. It is distrustful of the notion that an ascendant political faction is likely to be the repository of special wisdom and insight on what programs will best advance certain ends. Schlesinger seems to have come to this perspective as a result of his disagreement with certain Reagan administration policies. I find a recurring experience: the errors of a great many ascendant factions in many different governmental contexts have demonstrated that barriers to clear control of the government are generally conducive to sound long-term policy in the national interest.

When reasonably broad agreement is reached on a course of action, the American system seems perfectly capable of coherent and expeditious responses, even on complex policy questions. The Tax Reform Act of 1986 is a case in point. The conventional wisdom before its enactment was that it presented precisely the kind of situation where special interests inevitably dominate—a hyper-individualistic Congress wholly incapable of fending off special interest pleas, combined with complex, and hence invisible to the general public, tax code provisions. Yet no such thing happened. When substantial intellectual and political agreement was

16. James Bryce, *The American Commonwealth,* vol. 1 (Macmillan, 1918), pp. 153–54.
17. Schlesinger, "Leave the Constitution Alone," p. 54.

reached on the wisdom of a general course of change in tax policy, that change was swiftly and coherently established. (Whether we will live to regret it is, of course, another matter.)

Any governmental or electoral system can at times yield policy that passes muster by standards of enduring national interests—and similarly any can fail to do so. Judgments as to the adequacy of a particular system are inevitably colored by one's views of their recent yield. A case in point is the criticism of the British system advanced by some American political scientists, notably Pendleton Herring and Don K. Price, at the end of the 1930s. Leon Epstein notes that both Herring and Price thought that "Britain's disciplined party leadership had produced bad policy results during the 1930s, at the very time that American presidential leadership appeared to have been relatively successful."[18]

Herring's observations are worth considering as one contemplates whether our own system needs more party discipline and centralization. In Britain, Herring argued, "it is the whole tendency of the system that distinctive parties govern the nation in accordance with the class basis upon which their strength is organized. . . . The isolation of classes into separate parties prevents that modification of extreme points of view that is possible when different elements join in compromise. . . . One party machine rules while the opposition elements stand aside and hope for mistakes that will oust those in power." Herring found the American presidential system with its weak parties and dispersed power more attractive. "The chief executive is forced to seek middle ground. He cannot depend on his own party following. His measures are often supported by minority party members. The separation of executive and legislative branches gives both Congress and the president an opportunity to appeal to the voters."[19]

Epstein suggests that American political science has suffered from its infatuation through much of this century with its idealized picture of a British "responsible-party" system.[20] Shaken from their attraction to some degree by developments in the 1930s and again by recent British experience in formulating public policy, political scientists still have not suffi-

18. Leon D. Epstein, "What Happened to the British Party Model?" *American Political Science Review*, vol. 74 (March 1980), p. 10; Don K. Price, "The Parliamentary and Presidential Systems," *Public Administration Review*, vol. 3 (Autumn 1948), pp. 317–34; and Pendleton Herring, *Presidential Leadership* (Farrar and Rinehart, 1940), especially pp. 128–46.

19. Herring, *Presidential Leadership*, pp. 129–30.

20. Epstein, "What Happened to the British Party Model?"

ciently examined questions of the institutional capacity of the British system for encouraging sound broad-based policies. My own limited examination suggests that every party system in the advanced industrial democracies is a complex mix that reflects both the strengths and the weaknesses of the larger political-institutional system of which it is a part. Cross-national borrowing is a dubious venture.

Does the U.S. System Advantage Special Interests?

The United States has a plethora of interest groups intruding into the governmental process at all levels. Moreover, the number of groups operating at the national level has burgeoned over the last quarter century. From these developments it has been easy to reach the conclusion that the American system has given special interests a unique and excessive opportunity to shape policy.

Jack L. Walker challenges the view, however, that the explosion of interest group activity has anything to do with the characteristics of the American parties and election system. The factors he cites for the expansion of group activity are: (1) long-term increases in the level of education of the population, providing a large pool of skills on which various citizen movements can draw; (2) development of inexpensive yet sophisticated methods of communication; (3) a period of social protest beginning with the civil rights demonstrations of the early 1960s, which called many established practices into question and provided a strong stimulus for change; (4) the creation of massive new governmental programs; (5) subsequent efforts by governmental agencies and foundations to encourage links among the providers and consumers of the new programs; and (6) defensive response by groups that felt threatened by new regulatory legislation in areas like consumer protection, occupational health and safety, and environmentalism.[21]

A great number of developments outside the parties and election system have encouraged groups to organize, set up Washington offices, and try to bend programs and policies more to their wishes. It might still be true that

21. Jack L. Walker, "The Origins and Maintenance of Interest Groups in America," *American Political Science Review*, vol. 77 (June 1983), p. 397.

the American electoral system gives unusual opportunities to special interests; but upon examination this claim appears unsubstantiated. The experience of Western democracies indicates that different electoral and governmental systems stimulate different forms of interest group intervention; it does not establish that more centralized systems fare better in resisting special interests.

In France, notes Frank L. Wilson, "with deputies voting en bloc according to their parties' decisions, interest groups might be expected to redirect their pressure from the individual deputy to the party, but there is no evidence that this shift took place. Instead, interest groups redirected their activities toward influencing government and the bureaucracy."[22] Over half of the interest group leaders Wilson interviewed said that their groups rarely or never contacted the parties as such. These officials described contacts with ministers and civil servants as by far their most effective means of action; parliamentary lobbying ranked near the bottom of the list. Interest group interventions in France look different from those in the United States, but are not less influential.

In Britain decisionmaking is highly centralized in the government and in the parties. As a result, compared with the United States, parliamentary lobbying is relatively limited, though far from nonexistent. However, when interest groups form strong bonds with tightly disciplined parties in this centralized decisionmaking environment, the influence of these special interests over government policy may dwarf that achieved by their counterparts in the United States. No interest group or collection of groups has influence over the Democratic or Republican parties comparable with that of the labor movement over the Labor party in Britain. The British system may have special difficulty in responding to more general interests because of the extent of group involvement in party decisionmaking.

Elected officials of both parties in the United States routinely do business with a great variety of different interest groups. The reverse is true: most groups consider it in their interest to maintain access to people on both sides of the aisle and in the various sectors where decisions are made. The main result seems to be that groups rarely dominate any broad sector of national policy, although they may exercise great influence in narrower policy sectors where "iron triangle" relationships apply.

22. Frank L. Wilson, "French Interest Group Politics: Pluralist or Neocorporatist?" *American Political Science Review,* vol. 77 (December 1983), p. 905.

Does the System Diminish Public Control?

Calls for "reform" aimed at more disciplined and "responsible" parties have typically assumed that the public is frustrated by the wide dispersion of power in which no faction is able to gain clear control of "the government" and see its programs comprehensively enacted. The exact opposite seems to be the case. When public opinion polls ask Americans what they think about a system in which Republicans control the presidency and the Democrats control Congress, they invariably indicate their satisfaction.

Examining public opinion on many of the large contemporary issues, one gets a better sense of why divided control may not appear to Americans as either confusing or threatening. Again and again one finds a public that is highly ambivalent. For example, *Public Opinion* magazine has reviewed the opinions of Americans on various "role of government" questions. Over the last two decades the public has been continuously pulled in two directions. On the one hand, Americans make expansive claims for services of all sorts, many of which they expect government to provide. On the other hand, they see government as intrusive, clumsy, and problem-causing. Those who have wanted to cut back on domestic government have naturally chosen to emphasize the public's dissatisfaction with government's size and scope; those who want more government intervention stress the public's appetite for services.[23] The fact is that both dimensions have been prominent in American thinking over the last two decades; the story is the tension between the two viewpoints, not their resolution to the left or right or between the parties.

Given these ambivalent feelings, fractured party control may be seen as a highly effective vehicle of popular control. If the public has not made up its mind in what direction it wants to go or, more precisely, has decided it does not want to go consistently in any direction, what better vehicle than a system in which a loosely disciplined Democratic majority pushes one way through Congress and a loosely disciplined Republican coalition pushes the other way through the executive? An ambivalent public's control of policy is enhanced by a system of dispersed authority. Frustration seems to reside more with certain party elites than with the general public.

The relationship of a party system to the promotion of broad national interests will never be demonstrated with the final precision of the Pythag-

23. For data on the public's conflicting views of government, see *Public Opinion*, vol. 9 (March–April 1987), pp. 21–33.

orean theorem. There are too many slippery concepts, too many sources of variation in end results. Nonetheless, it is striking that over the past century, in which the American system of dispersed authority has been so much lamented, so little real evidence has been accumulated to support the argument that party discipline and centralized policymaking actually serve the national interest. Special interests do not appear less influential in parliamentary systems with disciplined parties. Centralized systems of policymaking show no signs of being able to regularly produce sounder results. The American public shows satisfaction, not frustration, with the system in which no party faction can dominate the course of public policy. The basic case for extensive reform of the American party system simply has not been established.

CHAPTER ELEVEN

How State Laws Undermine Parties

KAY LAWSON

STATE LAWS undermine political parties in almost every way imaginable. They make it difficult and sometimes impossible for parties to form and to get on the ballot, to control their own nomination processes, to define issues effectively, and to hold their elected representatives accountable. By weakening state and local parties, state laws undermine the national parties as well, depriving them of the base they must have to perform the functions strong parties perform in other nations. One cannot speak of party renewal or of electoral renewal without considering the need for reform of the election laws at the state level.

The problem is not, of course, the same in every state. By leaving the matter of regulating elections to the states, the writers of the Constitution guaranteed electoral chaos far beyond the political demands of federation. Lack of uniformity in state electoral codes is almost as serious an impediment to the operation of the party system and the creation of party government as the content of those codes. What political expediency demanded in 1787 to ensure acceptance of a new constitutional system has produced serious problems for the very operation of that system.

The Constitution did not in fact grant the states the power to regulate political parties. Parties were heartily despised in the late eighteenth century and were not even mentioned in the Constitution.[1] But the states *were* given the power to regulate elections, a power eventually interpreted

1. For the attitudes of early Americans toward political parties, see Richard Hofstadter, *The Idea of a Party System: The Rise of Legitimate Opposition in the United States, 1790–1840* (University of California Press, 1969).

to include the right to regulate parties. Even so, the first regulation of parties did not take place for nearly a hundred years, and widespread regulation did not begin until the end of the nineteenth century and the introduction of the Australian, or secret, ballot. Taking over the right to print ballots (which had formerly been printed by the parties) obliged the states to decide which parties qualified for inclusion. From there it seemed but a short step to requiring that parties show a minimum level of support to qualify and then to insisting they use secret ballots in their own elections of officers and candidates.[2] The floodgates to state regulation of parties were open.

The substance of such regulation will be examined here, but first it is necessary to state the assumptions on which this analysis is based. To begin with, one assumes that democracy means rule by the people, and further that to rule cannot mean merely to set limits every few years by entering a voting booth. Rule by the people means *quotidian citizenship*, which in turn means not merely having the behavioral skills to evaluate the performance of elected officials but also the structural means for conveying that evaluation continuously to them—and for making it matter—while at the same time not interfering unduly with their daily work.[3] Not everyone votes, even in the most participatory democracy, and it is even less likely that everyone will take part in institutions that permit participation between elections. But democracy is an empty term unless such institutions exist and are open to everyone.

Encouraging the development of such institutions is a delicate matter. In most democratic systems, including our own, they have usually taken the form of interest groups and political parties. Interest groups have been the preferred institution when single interests command political passions, but political parties have been more suitable for citizens with a wider agenda, as well as for group leaders seeking a wider arena in which to do battle and win support. When political parties work well, they make it possible for a wide range of interests to be articulated and aggregated, transformed into proposals, and combined into programs. Participants are

2. Advisory Commission on Intergovernmental Relations, *The Transformation in American Politics: Implications for Federalism* (Washington, D.C.: ACIR, 1986), pp. 124–26. Chapter 4, by Timothy Conlan, contains the best available summation of state laws on party nominations and internal party affairs, and I have drawn on it heavily. Chapter 7, by Cynthia Cates Colella, includes important information on state regulation of campaign finance.

3. I use the term *quotidian citizenship* to suggest citizenship that one can engage in, if one is so inclined, almost every day, and not just on election days.

able to nominate candidates to carry the programs to the public, evaluate those elected to office, and decide whether to offer them renomination. That renomination can be denied is a key factor in holding elected officials accountable, that is, in making quotidian citizen response to officeholders' performance *matter*.

This intimate connection between the work of parties and the work of quotidian citizenship has been all but broken in the United States. It is now popular, as well as accurate, to describe our parties as electoral machines, instruments to get out the vote for largely self-selected candidates who campaign on programs they and their advisers have created independent of party.[4] Signs of party strength are sought within the context of truncated functionalist analysis: strong parties are, it is said, those that keep the electoral machine running smoothly between elections as well as during them.[5] The weaknesses of the parties in articulating and aggregating interests, recruiting and nominating their own candidates, and devising programs for which such candidates can in fact be held accountable are regarded as no longer worth mentioning: such functions are no longer what parties are all about.

However, if parties no longer provide the arena in which the link between interests, programs, candidates, and government policy can be created, how else can that link be made? Political action committees may provide quotidian linkage between some special interests and policy processes. Candidates independent in all but name may momentarily forge rough links between themselves and the dominant interests of the day (*election* day). Pollsters may tell elected officials what the public thinks about selected issues (issues not selected by that public) at a particular time. But the one agency that might offer a more comprehensive, enduring, and reciprocal form of citizen linkage to government is the political party.

Thus, if one is interested in the nature and strength of that relationship, one must consider why and how parties in the United States have declined in their capacity to provide such linkage. Contemporary scholarship has

4. See, for example, Joseph A. Schlesinger, "The New American Political Party," *American Political Science Review*, vol. 79 (December 1985), pp. 1152–69.

5. A good recent example of this position is Xandra Kayden and Eddie Mahe, Jr., *The Party Goes On* (Basic Books, 1985). For these authors and others writing from a similar perspective, participation in parties does not mean using the parties as agencies of linkage but simply serving as "volunteers." And the fact that "politics appears to be becoming a more passive activity" is not alarming, because "it should be borne in mind that the percentage of the population who used to be active was always small" (pp. 192–93).

seriously slighted this area of study. Most students of party insist on their right—and responsibility—to study parties as they are, not as they should be. And democratic theorists, who routinely argue that democracies must encourage the free formation of such groups, seldom if ever examine the empirical data that indicate their own system does not. Nor have they recognized, even in theory, the need for democracies to take positive steps to ensure the well-being of parties. Indeed, they have often been more than ready to sanction laws designed to sap that vitality, seeing parties as intervening between the people and the state rather than as the best available means for forging links between them. Parties have as a result been formed ad hoc in response to the needs and ambitions of their members, and the general citizenry has been offered little or no guidance on how to improve party performance—or even why it is important to do so. This chapter explores how state laws have helped to undermine our parties; it is written in an effort to offer some partial remedy to the situation.

State Laws Inhibiting Formation of New Parties

If parties are to facilitate the linkage of citizens and their government, people must be able to find parties that welcome the expression of their views or, if necessary, be able to form new parties. Forming a new party means not only setting up an organization but also nominating candidates for public office, placing them on the ballot, and campaigning on their behalf.

State laws making it difficult to form new parties are often defended on the ground that they protect the two-party system. It is certainly true that having no more than two major parties is a decided advantage in achieving majority rule, especially when a nation's constitutional system provides for division of power both between national and state governments and among branches of the national government. A broadly based national party may do a fair job of putting back together what the authors of the Constitution, in their not always infinite wisdom, wrought asunder. But should pragmatic interest in more effective government override democratic values of free speech and association? And if so, to what extent?

In answer to these questions, many nations have decided that establishing an electoral system of single-member districts with plurality or runoff elections is an acceptable limitation on would-be new-party activists' rights of free association. Such a system makes it difficult for new or minor parties to win office but does not prevent them from competing and sometimes winning.[6] Where a runoff election is allowed, as, for example, in France, smaller parties are particularly encouraged to see what they can accomplish on the first round and to accept the constraints of electoral reality by going into alliance with stronger but ideologically adjacent competitors on the second.[7] The United States has single-member-district elections by plurality for congressional seats and for seats in most state legislatures. The majoritarian bias of the presidential electoral system is even stronger, operating first within the states (each in effect serving as a single-member district casting its bloc of electoral votes for a single candidate on the basis of plurality) and then at the national level, where the contest is decided by an absolute majority of state electoral votes or House decision.

However, this relatively strong legislative means of encouraging minor parties to combine with their stronger neighbors has not been deemed sufficient by many states. Such states have, in addition, made it extremely difficult for new parties to get on the ballot in the first place, although a party that is not able to compete in free elections cannot properly be said to be a party.[8] Until 1968 it was possible for a state to have no procedures at all for admitting new political parties to the ballot.[9] In eighteen states it is still impossible for a new party to qualify for the ballot before it has chosen its candidates, who must be listed on the ballot-access petition.[10] In 1971 in *Jenness* v. *Fortson* the Supreme Court upheld a Georgia law requiring a

6. For the impact of electoral systems on party systems, see Maurice Duverger, *Political Parties: Their Organization and Activity in the Modern State*, trans. Barbara North and Robert North, 2d ed. rev. (Wiley, 1959).

7. Kay Lawson, "The Impact of Party Reform on Party Systems: The Case of the RPR in France," *Comparative Politics*, vol. 13 (July 1981), pp. 401–19.

8. There is a wide range of definitions for a political party, but almost all of them include some reference to participation in elections. See Kay Lawson, *The Comparative Study of Political Parties* (St. Martin's, 1976); and Giovanni Sartori, *Parties and Party Systems: A Framework for Analysis* (Cambridge, England: Cambridge University Press, 1976).

9. *Williams* v. *Rhodes*, 393 U.S. 23 (1968).

10. In addition to the District of Columbia, the states are Colorado, Connecticut, Illinois, Indiana, Kentucky, Maryland (other than presidential elections), Massachusetts, Minnesota, Missouri, New Hampshire, New Jersey, New Mexico (other than presidential elections), New York, Pennsylvania, Rhode Island, Virginia, Washington, and West Virginia. See Richard Winger, "Why HR 2320 Is Needed," unpublished paper (1986), p. 6. Winger is editor and publisher of *Ballot Access News*, a good source of current information on the topic at hand, published at 3201 Baker Street, San Francisco, Calif., 94123.

separate petition for each third-party or independent candidate who wished to be placed on the ballot, containing signatures equal to 5 percent of the number of registered voters when the previous election was held for the office in question.[11] Although the Georgia law was changed in 1986, vastly improving the situation there for new parties, the ruling has been sustained in court cases brought in Louisiana, Florida, and Oklahoma. Since 1971 ballot-access requirements for new parties have been made substantially more difficult to meet in fourteen states.[12] In 1986 it was necessary to gather nearly 2 million valid signatures to get a single state-wide candidate of a new party on the ballot in all fifty states. Richard Winger has calculated that "if every state were to have ballot access laws similar to those upheld in *Jenness* v. *Fortson*, it would take 5,850,849 valid signatures to get a third party presidential candidate on the ballot of all states."[13]

Furthermore, until the late 1960s many states also required that a certain portion of qualifying signatures be gathered in each county of the state. After the Supreme Court ruled such a procedure unconstitutional,[14] nine states simply shifted to laws requiring that a certain number of signatures be gathered in each of a certain number (or all) of the state's congressional districts. The new laws are in fact more restrictive than the old, inasmuch as most voters know the county but not the number of the congressional district in which they live. Nevertheless, the requirement has recently been upheld in court.[15]

It has also been declared constitutional for states to prohibit those who voted in either major-party primary from signing a petition to get a new party on the ballot—Texas has such a law—and to impose restrictions on who can circulate petitions—in Virginia no one may circulate a petition outside his or her own congressional district.[16] Texas requests signers to furnish their registration numbers on such petitions; Alabama, Arkansas,

11. *Jenness* v. *Fortson,* 403 U.S. 431 (1971).

12. The states are Alabama, Arizona, Arkansas, Idaho, Indiana, Kansas, Kentucky, Louisiana (for office other than president), New Mexico, North Carolina, North Dakota, Oklahoma, Pennsylvania, and Virginia. Winger, "Why HR 2320 Is Needed," p. 30.

13. Ibid., p. 4.

14. *Moore* v. *Ogilvie,* 394 U.S. 815 (1969).

15. *Libertarian Party of Virginia* v. *Davis,* 766 F.2d 865 (1985); and *Libertarian Party of Missouri* v. *Board,* 764 F.2d 538 (1985). The nine states are Michigan, Missouri, Montana (using legislative districts instead of congressional districts), Nebraska, New Hampshire, New York, North Carolina, Virginia, and Wisconsin.

16. *American Party of Texas* v. *White,* 415 U.S. 767 (1974); *Storer* v. *Brown,* 415 U.S. 724 (1974); and *Libertarian Party of Virginia* v. *Davis,* 766 F.2d 865 (1985).

New York, and Virginia require them to give their precinct numbers. Fifteen states require signers to assert that they will vote for the party whose petition they are signing or that they are members of that party, and fifteen have laws stipulating when such signatures must be gathered. In Maine, Ohio, and California new parties must qualify by January of the election year.[17]

Gathering the requisite number of signatures within the time allowed does not guarantee success. Signatures must be validated, and it is usually the new party that must pay the costs of such validation. Florida charges ten cents a signature to check the ballot-access petitions of a third party. Since more than 167,000 valid signatures are presently required, this means a minimum of $16,700 in filing fees.[18] Although federal courts ruled in 1972 and again in 1974 that states with filing fees must provide alternatives for candidates who cannot afford to pay them, they have since been reluctant to acknowledge plaintiffs' allegations of inability to pay.[19]

Finally, getting on the ballot for one election does not necessarily mean staying on the ballot. In *Jenness* v. *Fortson* the Supreme Court also indicated that it is constitutional to require a minor party to continue petitioning until it has polled 20 percent of the national vote for president or 20 percent of the state vote for governor. Alabama has initiated the 20 percent rule, and seven other states require 10 percent. Maryland requires that 10 percent of all those registered indicate affiliation with the party.[20]

Despite such restrictive legislation, more than 160 minor-party candidates for statewide office were placed on ballots in 1986, winning more than 9 million votes.[21] Nevertheless, the laws have been effective in keeping minor parties off the ballot in election after election. They may even be contributing to a condition widely deplored: a constituency domi-

17. In the first case, the fifteen states are California, Delaware, Hawaii, Illinois, Indiana, Maryland, Nevada, New Jersey, New Mexico, New York, North Carolina, Ohio, Oregon, Utah, and West Virginia; in the second case, the fifteen states are Arkansas, Florida, Georgia, Illinois, Massachusetts, Michigan, Minnesota, Missouri, New York, Oklahoma, Pennsylvania, Rhode Island, Texas, Virginia, and Wyoming. Winger, "Why HR 2320 Is Needed," p. 6.

18. This provision was upheld in *Libertarian Party* v. *State of Florida*, 710 F.2d 790 (1983).

19. *North Carolina Socialist Workers Party* v. *North Carolina State Board of Elections*, U.S. District Court, Middle District, Winston-Salem Division, case no. C-80-132-WS; *Hoyle* v. *Monson*, 606 P.2d 240 (1980); and Winger, "Why HR 2320 Is Needed," p. 1.

20. Ibid., p. 6. The seven states that require 10 percent of the vote are Colorado, New Jersey, North Carolina, Oklahoma, South Dakota, Virginia, and Wyoming.

21. *Ballot Access News*, vol. 2 (January 21, 1987).

nated by a single major party. There was only one candidate on the ballot in the general election in one-eighth of the nation's congressional districts in 1984. In 1983 and 1984, nearly 38 percent of state legislative elections had only a single major-party candidate.[22] Yet districts where one major party is so dominant that the other major party sees no point in contesting might well be receptive to shades of opinion not allowed on the ballot at all. Thus one must question whether ballot-access legislation is not only unconstitutionally limiting the rights of American political activists to form new parties but also denying the presumed right of any citizen in a democracy to a meaningful choice in open, free elections.

That which state laws take away from the minor parties with the left hand is not necessarily given to the major parties with the right hand. Restricting the incentives to form new parties and limiting their access to ballots does, of course, work to the advantage of the major parties. But to function as agencies of linkage between citizen and state, parties must be able not only to form and compete but also to choose their own candidates, define their stances on issues and develop programs, wage effective campaigns on behalf of their candidates, and hold their successful elected representatives accountable. Existing state laws have the effect of undermining the work of the major parties in each of these domains.

Undermining the Nominating Function

If there is one area where it is well understood that state law has undermined parties, it is nominations. Almost everyone acknowledges that introducing the primary election, and thereby permitting voters who have never attended a party meeting and indeed never taken any certifiable interest in party affairs to determine a party's candidate, is an excellent means of reducing the power of parties. In fact, giving the power of selecting party candidates to the voters can be seen as a form of legalized theft. A party label is a product the party itself has produced, usually through years of work by committed activists. Yet that label is not granted the status of private property. On the contrary, persons who have had nothing to do with making it may come along, take it, and give it to

22. Democrats failed to file candidacies in 11 percent; Republicans in 27 percent. Richard Winger, "What Difference Does It Make If Third Parties Are Kept Off the Ballot?" unpublished paper (1985).

whomever they choose. In two states—Florida and California—party committees have not even been allowed to endorse the candidates they would prefer to see win the prize.[23]

The primary not only undermines parties by taking away the nominating function but also ensures the function will be performed so poorly that popular respect for partisan politics will be yet further reduced. People who vote in primaries are often so unrepresentative of the parties' supporters in the general electorate that they choose candidates who cannot be elected even with a party label firmly stitched to their lapels.[24] Choosing a candidate who will win majority support in the general election is a difficult job, as those who took the trouble to engage actively in political parties in the days before primaries were instituted readily learned. Voters in primaries not only have no chance to develop the necessary expertise, but often have no interest. They naturally would rather decide which candidates they individually prefer, demoting questions of electability to second rank.

In a democracy all political processes must be open to citizen participation, and those who wish to participate in candidate selection must be allowed to do so. But this does not mean that the sensitive and difficult task of selecting a party candidate must be performed by individual voters marking ballots in the isolation of the voting booth on primary election day. It does not mean that the state should require a form of participation that ensures the job will be badly done.

Furthermore, the establishment of primary elections has made it more difficult for Americans even to think of a party as an organization that might be joined. Nothing much is going on inside local party meetings, where they are still held. Even in states with closed primaries, one can take part in candidate selection simply by registering a personal identification as Republican or Democrat. A key motive for more active participation in the parties has disappeared.

Yet despite their obvious deleterious effects on the parties, primaries

---

23. Eight states (Colorado, Connecticut, Delaware, New Mexico, New York, North Dakota, Rhode Island, and Utah) require or formally sanction parties to issue endorsements before the primary; the remaining states have no law on the question. ACIR, *Transformation in American Politics*, p. 148.

24. Whatever the format (closed, open, or blanket), voter turnout in primaries is low—only about 25 percent of the turnout in general elections outside the South—and those who bother to participate are often unrepresentative both demographically and ideologically of the party identifiers in a state and of the total electorate. Ibid., p. 100.

were introduced in some southern states as early as the 1870s and by 1955 could be found in every state in the Union for at least some state offices.[25] The initial motive for establishing them was almost always to weaken the dominant party or the dominant faction within that party. In many cases, primaries were regarded as a means for combating corrupt interests that had used the party to gain control of local or state governments. Laws that made it possible for voters to choose party nominees also made it possible for candidates not supported by party activists to capture the nomination and, subsequently, control of the party itself.

In the early years the usual procedure was for the party or faction out of power—or independent or third-party candidates (the more rigorous ballot-access laws not yet having been enacted)—to campaign on a reform ticket and then, once elected to party or government offices (or both) in sufficient number, to work for the enactment of a primary law, thereby setting up the means to destroy the power of the hitherto dominant leadership. In the process they also largely destroyed the parties. This loss was generally of small concern to the reformers. Rather than considering how to restore existing parties as agencies of linkage, they placed all their hopes for quotidian citizenship in devices of direct democracy. These included not only the primary but also the referendum, the initiative, and the recall election. Such instruments may be said to provide linkage because they permit immediate popular control of government through frequent voting. But they also offer golden opportunities for demagogic manipulation of the voter by well-financed special interests. The linkage established may therefore become little more than a charade of quotidian citizenship.

Despite the civic shortcomings of the primary system, it is now firmly embedded in the American electoral process. The states have made few efforts to temper its undermining effects on parties. One such effort is, however, worth mentioning: the sore-loser law. Twenty-six states prohibit primary losers from running in the general election as independents or as the candidates of another party.[26] Such laws are intended to ensure that everyone competing for a party's nomination is truly committed to that party and none other. Independent candidates are deterred from using the party's primary as a jumping-off place. While it is true that such laws do help protect the primaries of established parties from invasion by independents, the more straightforward way to accomplish that goal would be to

25. Ibid., p. 97.
26. Ibid., p. 151.

make it easier for independents to form their own parties and get on the general election ballot, as discussed above. Sore-loser laws do not address most of the injuries done to parties by the creation of primaries. Passing such a law is like offering a Band-aid to a person you have just shot—it will not hurt, but it will not do much good either.

Establishing primaries and, in some cases, prohibiting party endorsements before the primary are serious limitations on the nominating rights of the parties. An even more serious limitation on those rights is created by state and local laws mandating nonpartisan local elections. Approximately 74 percent of the nation's cities require nonpartisan local elections, in which parties are forbidden to take any meaningful part. The argument for such laws is usually that local parties would be aligned on the basis of state and national issues, and therefore too little focused on local interests. "There is," the saying goes, "no Republican or Democratic way to collect garbage." This argument lacks face validity, but even if it were true, should it not be up to the voters to decide?

If American parties are ever to serve as agencies of linkage between citizen and government, that linkage must begin at the local level. Americans take pride in a tradition of strong commitment to local government, and civics textbooks claim that participating at the local level is good training for broader-based citizenship. Yet voter turnout in local elections is even lower than in national elections. The United States is unique among the world's democracies in its commitment to nonpartisan local elections. Reestablishing partisan politics at the base would surely strengthen the parties, providing them with a foundation of activism rooted in community life. It might very well also reawaken voter interest in local affairs and help stimulate quotidian citizenship at all levels of government.

Limiting Campaign Functions

The most serious regulation of parties' activities in campaigns comes from federal law, particularly with respect to campaign finance (see chapter 7). But state laws have significant effects in this domain as well. States have acted to regulate campaign finance, to weaken the importance of parties as definers of the issues, and to make voting for straight party slates more difficult.

Campaign Finance

Although the states have entered campaign finance regulation with enthusiasm, very few of the regulations impinge directly on parties. In fact, the net effect of state campaign finance laws may be more positive than negative for parties. Only Massachusetts, Oklahoma, and South Dakota limit the amount an individual contributor may give to a political party during an election season.[27] Since twenty-five states limit the amount that may be given to individual candidates or political action committees or both, this leniency vis-à-vis parties can have the effect of making it easier to give large sums to a party than to other political entities. In addition, approximately one-fifth of the states provide some form of public financing for parties (most commonly by a tax checkoff of $1 or $2, more rarely by tax add-on provisions; and Indiana allocates a portion of automobile license fees). Of these, only one, Utah, has imposed expenditure limits.[28] In a unique arrangement, Alaskans get a $100 tax credit for a wide variety of political contributions, including contributions to "groups attempting to influence ballot proposition votes" and dues to "nonprofit political organizations" (presumably parties could be either).[29]

Obviously, the states could be doing much more to help parties financially. However, two scholars have made the argument that state funding may be contrary to parties' long-run interests, because such funding encourages them to become overly dependent on public funds.[30] Even if the evidence they cite for the need to protect the parties from state largesse is fragmentary and not very persuasive, the fact remains that in this area state law has at least not been excessively hostile to the parties.

Defining Issues

As other chapters in this book make clear, the role of parties in defining campaign issues has been reduced by several factors that have little to do

27. For Massachusetts the limit is $1,000, for Oklahoma $5,000, and for South Dakota $3,000. Ibid., pp. 310–15.

28. California and Maine have provisions allowing taxpayers to add on to their tax bill a contribution to the party of their choice, and Indiana contributes a portion of license plate fees to the parties. The rest permit taxpayers to indicate on their tax returns whether they wish to have the state contribute $1 (or in some cases $2) to a political party and if so to which one. Ibid., pp. 300–01, 310–15.

29. Ibid., p. 303.

30. John Bibby, Testimony before the U.S. Advisory Commission on Intergovernmental Relations, Washington, D.C., June 6, 1984; and Jack L. Noragon, "Political Fi-

with state law. But there are two ways in which state legislation has directly weakened parties' contributions to this activity. The first, discussed earlier, is the requirement of primaries. Although even after introduction of the primary some state parties continued to hold hearings on issues and formulate party programs, the advent of the primary clearly gave candidates additional reason to feel free to pay less attention to their party's platform than to the advice of their consultants and major contributors. If supporting the party's program is not seen as helpful in winning votes in the primary, such loyalty is not likely to be expressed. The party's work in building its program then becomes an exercise in futility.

State laws establishing the initiative, which gives citizens the right to place measures directly on the ballot, also undermine the parties' function of defining issues. Twenty-six states have some form of initiative, popular referendum, or both.[31] The weakening effects of the initiative for parties are subtle and difficult to document. Like the primary, the initiative seems at first merely a wondrous way to expand ordinary citizens' participation in government. As one scholar has pointed out, "Discussions of direct legislation often stop short because of the 'sacred' nature of direct democracy. Critics of the process are characterized as favoring smoke-filled rooms [and] party bosses."[32] Debate over the value of the initiative is normally seen by both sides as between advocates of direct democracy and champions of representative democracy. Given the current weakness of the parties, the notion that grassroots parties might themselves provide for more direct as well as more meaningful popular participation in government is viewed as almost laughable.

Nevertheless, it is becoming increasingly clear that the initiative has had the practical effect of augmenting, not reducing, elite control of legislation. The poor, who might reasonably hope for meaningful linkage to the political process through a strong grassroots party system, have little access to the initiative process. Initiatives qualify for the ballot only when a

nance and Political Reform: The Experience with State Income Tax Checkoffs," *American Political Science Review*, vol. 75 (September 1981), pp. 680–81, both cited in ibid., pp. 306–07.

31. David B. Magleby, "The Initiative and Popular Referendum Reconsidered: Election Law, Popular Rule and Legislative Accountability," paper presented at the Conference on Electoral Reform in California: The Current Agenda, University of California–Davis, Institute of Governmental Affairs, 1985, p. 13. In some of these, such as Massachusetts, the system used is the indirect initiative, a process that gives state legislatures a period of time to respond before petitioners can take their measure to the voters.

32. Ibid., p. 10.

stipulated number of valid signatures has been obtained. The number required may be as low as 2 percent of the total population (North Dakota) or as high as 15 percent of the votes cast in the last general election (Wyoming). In any event the task is large and difficult and is routinely performed by paid signature gatherers. Only six states ban collection of signatures by paid solicitors. The poor simply "lack the money to hire the initiative industry."[33]

Furthermore, the initiative process tends to do a remarkably bad job of defining the issues. Some of the propositions that make it to the ballot are patently unconstitutional, as subsequent court decisions have made clear. The wording of the propositions is often confusing. Campaigns for and against the initiatives, usually conducted by high-priced consultants, play upon this confusion, and often reduce the debate to competition between meaningless or deliberately misleading slogans.

Despite these and other consistently documented shortcomings, the idea that the initiative is "democratic" and that political parties are not continues to be widely accepted. Energies that might be directed toward making the parties more meaningful arenas for the articulation and aggregation of interests are instead consumed by battles for and against badly worded, possibly unconstitutional, and often special-interest-serving ballot proposals.

Straight Party Voting

At the conclusion of a campaign, voters must often choose between candidates for a wide range of national, state, and local offices. Faced with a list of unfamiliar names of persons running for seemingly unimportant positions in government, the normal tendency for many voters is simply to pass. Both candidates and voters are therefore helped—as, obviously, are the parties—by state laws that place means for straight party voting on the ballot. Such mechanisms permit the voter to choose, with a single stroke of the pen or pull of the lever, all the candidates of a single party. Only twenty-one states provide for such straight party voting. In the others, offices must be voted for one by one.[34]

---

33. Ibid., pp. 14–16. The six states are Colorado, Idaho, Massachusetts, Ohio, South Dakota, and Washington. David B. Magleby, *Direct Legislation: Voting on Ballot Propositions in the United States* (John Hopkins University Press, 1984), pp. 38–39.

34. ACIR, *Transformation in American Politics,* p. 152.

Internal Party Governance

As I have shown, the rights of activists to form effective party organizations, choose their own nominees, and articulate and publicize their points of view on the issues that matter to them are all seriously undermined by large and complex bodies of state law. State regulation of internal party governance is generally even more restrictive.

Forty-five states regulate parties' internal affairs in one way or another. Only Alaska, Delaware, Hawaii, Kentucky, and North Carolina have thus far managed to refrain.[35] Thirty-six have laws determining who may choose members of the state central committees (and of these, all except Pennsylvania and South Carolina also regulate who may choose members of local party committees). Thirty-two have laws determining who may be members of state central committees. Of these, all except Pennsylvania also regulate who may be members of local party committees, as do an additional three states—Connecticut, New York, and Rhode Island—that have nothing to say regarding the composition of state central committees.

The substance of state regulation of parties' internal affairs varies considerably. Regarding choice of members of party committees, state laws require that local committee members be chosen either by the voters, usually at the time of the primary election (twenty-eight states), or through party caucuses or conventions (seven states). Similarly, state committee members may be chosen by the voters (nine states) or by local committee members, usually from among themselves (twenty-seven states).[36]

Many states regulate details of internal party governance. Twenty-eight states include the rules for state party committees in their electoral codes, covering such matters as when and where the committee must meet, how it shall fill vacancies, whether proxies may be used, how members must be notified in advance of meetings, what constitutes a quorum, how and whether executive committees may be formed, and what shall be the powers and duties of both officers and members. The list of state prescrip-

35. Of these, seventeen regulate local parties only. The remaining twenty-eight regulate the procedures of both state and local parties. Ibid., pp. 128–44.

36. The key question for the composition of local and state party committees is whether elected officials must, may, or must not form part of the membership of the committee. The bias is strongly against allowing elected officials to take part. Laws forbid their membership on state committees in twenty-seven states and on local party committees in thirty. Only five states mandate their participation in state committees; only four in local party committees. Sixteen states have passed laws requiring state central committees to have equal numbers of men and women. Ibid., pp. 129–31, 136–37.

tions regulating local party committees is, if anything, even more extensive.[37]

Do all these laws undermine the parties? Some would argue yes, because all interfere with the right of free association, that is, with the right of parties to determine their rules for themselves, without any supervision from outside. Others prefer to distinguish between good and bad state regulations of parties' internal affairs. Good laws, in this interpretation, are those that make the parties stronger, such as laws in seven states (Iowa, Maine, Nevada, North Dakota, Tennessee, Utah, and Vermont) requiring that local committee members be chosen at party conventions or party caucuses rather than by the voters at large. But it is not always clear that a "good" regulation is in practice supportive of parties. For example, some argue that laws requiring state central committees to include elected officials (as in California, Colorado, Florida, Kansas, and North Dakota) are "good" laws, since excluding such officials is likely to "weaken the ties between elected officials and party leaders."[38] However, in California the parties have recently gone to court to fight the degree of control state legislators have been given over their state central committees by such a provision, suggesting that there can, in this case, be rather too much of a good thing.[39]

Agenda for Change

State laws seriously undermine the development and strength of political parties in the United States. Laws that effectively prevent new parties from forming and gaining strength, deny them control over their nomination processes, reduce their capacity to campaign effectively on behalf of their candidates and their programs, and exercise unreasonable and unnecessary control over their internal affairs should be either abolished or greatly changed. It is, however, one thing to prescribe what changes should be made, another to consider how such changes might be achieved. I will take up each in turn. First the desirable changes:

---

37. Laws in some states prohibit local committees from using the unit rule, and in some they stipulate party affiliation and residency requirements for committee members. Ibid., pp. 132–33, 136–37.

38. Ibid., pp. 130–131, 136.

39. Kay Lawson, "Challenging Regulation of Political Parties: The California Case," *Journal of Law and Politics,* vol. 2 (Fall 1985), pp. 263–85.

—The system of single-member districts with a plurality required for election is sufficient restraint on the multiplication of parties. If several parties form despite the encouragement such an electoral system provides for groups to combine into two electoral forces, it is a clear sign that sincerely held opinions, all deserving of representation on the ballots if not in the final arenas of power, are too divided for such combination. Ballot-access laws should be redesigned to ease the creation of new parties and improve their capacity to present candidates to the public.

—Control over their own nomination processes should be returned to the parties. If parties themselves choose primary elections, the state should be allowed to enter into the process, but state assistance with internal party elections should be as optional as state assistance with campaign expenditures. Limitations on campaign expenditures are not allowed unless public financing is accepted. Similarly, interference with the nomination process should not be allowed unless public assistance in holding primary elections is accepted. Even then, state control should be as limited as possible, and not be extended to matters beyond the actual machinery of the election.

—Parties should be free to participate in local elections exactly as they do in state and national elections. All state laws or constitutional provisions calling for nonpartisan local elections should be abolished.

—The limit on the amount that may be contributed by an individual or group to a political party should never be less than $10,000 (adjusted for the cost of living). At the same time, effective limits should be put on PAC contributions to candidates. It should be recognized that "independent expenditures" are a myth; the expenditures are in fact contributions. As such, they should be subject to the same limitations as all other contributions. Reducing the role of political action committees in campaigns will give more scope to that of political parties (see chapter 7).

—The initiative should be abolished altogether or seriously reformed, either by requiring larger majorities or by giving the legislature a chance to act first, once the necessary number of signatures has been acquired. This latter system, known as the indirect initiative, has not worked well in states where it is provided as an alternative to the direct initiative. To be an effective reform, it must be the only available system.[40]

—Voting a straight ticket should be made possible in every state.

—All state laws regarding who may select and who may serve on party

40. Magleby, "Initiative and Popular Referendum Reconsidered," pp. 23–24. See this paper also for other suggestions for reform of the initiative.

committees should be rescinded. These are matters for the parties to decide. All state laws interfering with parties' conduct of their internal affairs should be abolished. Parties must, like other organizations, abide by state and federal laws forbidding discrimination, theft, and corruption. No special laws for parties are necessary.

So much for the changes that *should* be made. Let me turn now to what might actually be done. First, one must remember that decades of miseducation have given strong popular sanction to most of the laws here recommended for abolition. Widespread support for the two-party system among Americans has promoted casual disregard for the rights of minor parties to free association. The hallowed status enjoyed by Progressive "reforms" among the public protects both the primary and the initiative. Antiparty sentiment, another product of progressivism, is well entrenched. Fear of the return of corrupt, boss-ridden parties, which have not been seen in most cities or states for more than fifty years (and in some cases never did exist), makes it easy for state legislators to maintain a vast body of debilitating legislation regulating parties' internal affairs.

The strength of popular sentiment is reinforced by that of individual ambition. Most of the legislation that weakens parties is designed to keep power in the hands of the powerful. However little attention they may pay to their own parties, state legislators, running as Republicans or Democrats, do not want the competition of minor parties' candidates. In primary states the incumbents are those who have succeeded in wooing those who vote in the primaries, often without having had to pay much attention to the party or its program. They have little interest in suddenly finding themselves truly accountable to a strong, well-informed, issue-oriented organization of activists. The direct initiative provides a process legislators can often use for their own purposes. By serving as sponsors of ballot propositions they are sometimes able to help persuade the public—through a media blitz—to put legislation on the books that their perhaps better-informed colleagues in the legislature would be certain to reject. Furthermore, no legislator is likely to believe that voting against the initiative would be a useful way to gain new friends and supporters. And finally, laws that make it difficult for parties to determine their own internal affairs clearly make it easier for elected legislators to keep the parties weak and under control.

Does this mean that change is impossible? Not at all. But it is naive simply to list the changes that should be made. Most of the antiparty law has not only been made by legislators, it will be maintained by legislators.

As things stand now, there is simply no point in asking them, "Please, sirs and madams, may we have *less*?" Lobbying is not the answer.

There are, however, three other routes open to those who seek to reduce state regulation of parties: education, judicial activism, and local and state party self-reform. The first is fairly obvious. Those who believe in the importance of parties within the democratic system must do a better job of explaining the role stronger parties could play and the ways the system could be improved. They must work harder to explain the negative effects of progressivism, particularly the primary election and the initiative. This is difficult work, given the antipathy toward the present parties, but it is essential if they are ever to assume a more acceptable form.

Judicial activism is a path many have already begun to follow with considerable success. Arguments that legislators and the public are unlikely to heed may very well find a more sympathetic audience in the courts, accustomed as they are to listening carefully when the question at issue concerns constitutional principles of free speech or free association. State laws that appear particularly vulnerable on these grounds include those mandating excessive requirements for ballot access, depriving parties of control over their nomination processes, denying them the right to take part in local elections, and imposing unnecessary restrictions on how they conduct their internal affairs, including how their ruling committees are selected and composed. Although the courts have ruled that all rights can, under certain circumstances, be limited, they have also made it clear that the burden of showing the need to do so is on the state. Recent rulings have suggested the courts are not impressed with the arguments of the states that many of the kinds of restrictions mentioned here are in fact necessary to serve the public interest.[41] Litigation is slow and costly, but it is one of the most promising routes for freeing the parties of excessive state regulation.

41. As I have noted elsewhere, whereas early party-related litigation focused on the national parties, including state government response to national party rules, more recently the focus has been on excessive state regulation of state parties. Particularly of note in this latter regard are *Crussel* v. *Oklahoma State Elections Board* (1980), *Ferrency* v. *Austin* (1980), *Republican Party* v. *Tashjian* (1985), and *San Francisco Democrats* v. *March Fong Eu* (1986). See Kay Lawson, "The Decline of Arena in the U.S.: The Real Reason for Party Renewal," in Thomas E. Cronin and Michael Beschloss, eds., *Democratic Leadership* (Prentice-Hall, forthcoming). For a detailed study of the early history of party-related litigation in the courts, see John Moeller, "Recent Involvement by the Federal Courts in the Operation and Role of Political Parties," paper prepared for the 1983 meeting of the Midwest Political Science Association.

Finally, state and local parties could themselves be doing a far better job of self-reform, particularly in making changes that would make it easier to gain the public acceptance necessary for yet further reforms. Having accepted the truncated image of themselves as electoral machines, the parties have, not surprisingly, done their best job of self-reform in improving campaign support for the candidates, adopting many of the fund-raising and vote-getting techniques of modern political consultancy.[42] Such steps are commendable and should be continued, but by themselves they do not, for reasons explored at the beginning of this chapter, suffice to renew parties. The parties need to undertake changes that expand their role, not merely those that make them better at doing the little that presently remains for them to do.

One such change would be to participate much more strongly, even under present state restrictions, in defining issues at the local and state level and in seeking means to hold both candidates and elected incumbents accountable to the party's program. The lines of accountability between party and candidate are blurred, especially in those states where nominations have been taken out of the party's control. No party enjoys helping the opposition by calling public attention to what it sees as the inadequacies of those who have gone into office bearing its name. But winning elections is not, finally, as important as winning them with candidates one can believe in, a fact of political life that recent events in national presidential politics have been bringing home to all Americans, including party activists. Incumbents who disappoint their parties should be told so and, where possible, denied renomination.

Furthermore, even where the case is less serious or a party remains determined to avoid any public hint of less-than-perfect satisfaction with its elected representatives, much more could be done to keep legislators' attention focused on their parties' programs (rather than on the wishes of their more affluent campaign contributors) by simple, daily, organized party lobbying on behalf of those programs. And when some of a party's program *is* made into policy, local and state parties should never hesitate to claim at least some of the credit. Letting the world know an appreciated tax reform was a Democratic or a Republican measure is as necessary for party building at the local level as it is at the national.

Finally, state and local parties must assume more of the responsibility for education and litigation. Their role is almost indispensable in the latter,

---

42. Kayden and Mahe, *The Party Goes On.*

given the legal requirement that all litigants in a case must have "standing," that is, must themselves be suffering the injuries of which they complain. But state and local parties must also take on the task of community education, beginning with their own activists, who need help understanding that their part in a democracy is far greater than merely helping one candidate defeat another or "keeping the two-party system alive." Only when those who are active have this larger vision of party will they be able to persuade others to join the battle to rescind party-crippling state laws. And only activists with this larger vision will have the will to undertake the immense task of transforming our present parties, those much despised electoral machines, into the agencies of quotidian citizenship that every genuinely democratic government must have.

CHAPTER TWELVE

Is the House of Representatives Unresponsive to Political Change?

THOMAS E. MANN

THE contemporary House of Representatives, in contrast to the Senate, appears remarkably insulated from changes in political sentiments among voters. House incumbents enjoy an extraordinary degree of success in running for reelection: 98 percent of House members seeking reelection in 1986 won, topping the previous record of 96.8 percent set in 1968.[1] Fewer representatives were defeated in the 1986 general election than senators, even though 393 representatives were on the ballot compared with only 28 senators. During the postwar years, an average of 91 percent of House incumbents have successfully sought reelection. Not since 1974 has the rate slipped below 90 percent. And one has to go back to 1948 to find an election in which more than 20 percent of House incumbents were defeated. The contrast with the Senate is stark: 75 percent on average were reelected between 1946 and 1986, and there were three elections during the last decade in which a third or more lost their reelection bids.

The other sign of insulation of the House is the unprecedented lock the Democrats have had on the majority. House Democrats are presently enjoying their thirty-third consecutive year as the majority party, which more than doubles the previous post–Civil War record. The Democrats have controlled all but two Congresses since 1930, relegating the House

1. Jacqueline Calmes, "House Incumbents Achieve Record Success Rate in 1986," *Congressional Quarterly Weekly Report*, vol. 44 (November 15, 1986), pp. 2891–92.

Republicans to seemingly permanent minority status. Again the Senate offers a significant contrast: the 1980 Republican upset brought the twenty-six-year Democratic control of the Senate to an end. Even though the Democrats regained control in a stunning victory in 1986, the fact that the Republicans held their majority for six years makes it unlikely that the Democrats will settle into another quarter-century run as the majority in that body.

These two indicators—the success of incumbents and the dominant position of the Democrats in the House—while related to one another in several important respects, raise somewhat different concerns about the responsiveness of the House to the electorate. Questions raised by the advantage of incumbency operate at the level of the individual representative's relationship to his or her district. Do safe incumbents become insensitive to the needs of their constituents? Do disgruntled voters lack any realistic opportunity to express their unhappiness with the incumbent at the polls? Questions raised by the absence of shifts in party control are more systemic in character. Are changes in partisan sentiments among voters unable to alter the balance of power in the House? Will Republican presidents inevitably be forced to lead a divided government? What are the structural consequences for the House of having permanent majority and minority parties?

In order to address these questions, one needs to examine more closely the nature and sources of the incumbency advantage in the House, as well as the factors that account for the Democrats' uninterrupted control of the House. As part of that exercise, I shall gauge the extent to which the redrawing of congressional district lines protects incumbents and harms Republicans, and ask whether changes in the redistricting process would yield measurable benefits for challengers and the Republican party.

Advantages of Incumbency

Incumbents have long fared well in House elections. The uneven distribution of partisan voters across congressional districts has produced many safe seats in which incumbents were effectively insulated from challenges by the opposition party and voter reactions to adverse national conditions. Nonetheless, for most of this century there were enough districts in the marginal or competitive range, with voters evenly divided between the two parties, that a substantial shift in public sentiment could unseat incumbents and significantly alter party strength in the House. For example, it was common during the first half of this century for a party to lose well over fifty seats in an election, largely at the expense of its incumbents.[2]

The volatility of seat swings diminished shortly after the Second World War—the seventy-five-seat pickup by the Democrats in 1948 was the last time a party gained as many as fifty seats in a single election. After the 1954 midterm election, the Democrats settled into their majority position, which after 1958 became unassailable. At about this time, the number of districts supporting a presidential candidate of one party and a House candidate of the other jumped sharply, subsequently reaching a point at which a third or more regularly produced split results.[3]

Another alteration in the structure of competition in House elections first appeared in the 1960s. Incumbent candidates began winning a larger share of the vote, leaving fewer of them in the marginal range and presumably less vulnerable to adverse national tides in subsequent elections. The increased value of incumbency appeared in a number of forms.[4] The average vote won by House incumbents grew from roughly 60 percent in the 1950s to 65 percent in the 1970s. The percentage of House incumbents reelected with at least 60 percent of the major-party vote jumped from 60 to 75 percent during the same period (reaching a record-setting 85 percent in 1986). Freshman representatives contesting their first election as incumbents noticeably improved their performance after the mid-1960s. Changes in both this "sophomore surge" and the complementary measure that records the drop in support when the incumbent retires ("retirement slump") confirmed that the value of incumbency increased by roughly 5 percentage points from the 1950s to the 1970s.

This growth in the advantage of incumbency was related entirely to the individual House member, independent of and in addition to whatever benefit accrued to the incumbent by virtue of his party's strength in the district. It was facilitated by a decline in partisanship among voters during this period: the proportion of voters who defected from their own party in House elections doubled, and incumbents won the overwhelming support of those who strayed.[5] They succeeded largely by utilizing the increased

2. Norman J. Ornstein and others, *Vital Statistics on Congress, 1984–1985 Edition* (Washington, D.C.: American Enterprise Institute for Public Policy Research, 1984), pp. 34–35.

3. Ibid., p. 56.

4. Gary C. Jacobson, *The Politics of Conressional Elections*, 2d ed. (Little, Brown, 1987), chap. 3.

5. Thomas E. Mann and Raymond E. Wolfinger, "Candidates and Parties in Congressional Elections," *American Political Science Review*, vol. 74 (September 1980), pp. 620–21.

resources at their disposal (staff, the franking privilege, travel funds, and House television and radio studios) to cultivate their districts. Incumbents were able to enhance their personal reputations by advertising widely their concerns, positions, and accomplishments and by providing nonpartisan service for the increasing number of constituents who had encounters with the federal government.[6]

These efforts did more than increase the attractiveness of incumbents to voters. They also contributed to an aura of invincibility that discouraged serious candidates from challenging them. In an era of candidate-centered elections, when voters make their decisions largely on the basis of the relative attractiveness of the contenders, the surest route to victory is running against a weak challenger. The vast majority of House contests fit this description: the election is effectively over before the formal campaign begins. Of course, weak challengers were not unknown in the earlier, more partisan period, particularly in districts that were clearly safe for one party. But now incumbents representing more evenly divided districts often succeed in scaring away the strongest potential challengers. And as changes in the nature of House elections have escalated campaign costs, incumbents are better positioned than challengers to raise the necessary funds. Relatively few nonincumbents, even the most experienced politicians, are able to acquire the substantial resources needed to run a competitive race.

The increased advantage of incumbency in House elections after the mid-1960s is clear; its consequences are less obvious. Wider margins of victory should mean fewer incumbent defeats and smaller swing ratios— the rate at which changes in the national vote in House elections are converted into seat changes. But, as Gary Jacobson has argued, these expectations have not been realized.[7] The percentage of incumbents defeated in the general (and primary) election has remained constant over the last three decades. Moreover, the swing ratio showed little sign of decline from 1952 to 1980: a 1 percent gain in a party's national vote for the House translated on average into a 2 percent gain in seats.[8]

6. See Morris P. Fiorina, *Congress: Keystone of the Washington Establishment* (Yale University Press, 1977), pp. 19–23; and Jacobson, *The Politics of Congressional Elections*, chap. 3.

7. Gary C. Jacobson, "The Marginals Never Vanished: Incumbency and Competition in Elections to the U.S. House of Representatives, 1952–82," *American Journal of Political Science*, vol. 31 (February 1987), pp. 126–41.

8. Ibid., p. 132. However, the swing ratios in 1982, 1984, and 1986 were significantly lower.

Table 12-1. *Incumbent Defeats in General Elections, by Margin of Victory in Previous Election*[a]

Vote margin in previous election (percent)	Percentage defeated		
	1950s	1960s	1970s
50.0–54.9	19.7	18.6	16.3
55.0–59.9	7.4	8.2	7.4
60.0–64.9	2.7	3.3	7.6
65.0–69.9	1.7	1.5	4.8
70.0 or more	0	0.1	1.3

Source: Gary C. Jacobson, "The Marginals Never Vanished: Incumbency and Competition in Elections to the U.S. House of Representatives, 1952–82," *American Journal of Political Science*, vol. 31 (February 1987), p. 130.

a. Includes only incumbents who faced major-party opponents in both the current and previous elections.

Why did wider margins of safety not produce fewer losses? The answer can be seen most clearly in table 12-1, which shows, for each of the last three decades, the percentage of defeated House incumbents according to the margins by which they won in the previous election. Jacobson summarizes: "An incumbent elected in the 1970s with between 60 and 65 percent of the vote was just as likely to lose in the next election as was an incumbent in the 1950s who had been elected with 55 to 60 percent of the vote; incumbents in the 1970s with previous margins in the 65–70 percent range were more vulnerable than those in the 1950s with margins in the 60–65 percent range."[9] The additional 5 percent margin of victory enjoyed by incumbents paid no dividends in the all-important won-lost column.

This is because House incumbents are now subject to wide changes in support from one election to the next. As elections have become less partisan and more candidate-centered, the national partisan vote swing has become a much poorer predictor of change within individual congressional districts.[10] The source of change is found increasingly in the local district—in the quality of the challenger, public perceptions of the incumbent, and the dynamics of the campaign. As long as incumbents keep their reputation among constituents intact and discourage the strongest potential opponent from running against them, they are safe. But if feelings toward them sour and effective opposition is mobilized, incumbents' level of support can be sharply reduced. Incumbency is a resource to be exploited more or less successfully, not an automatic advantage. Incumbents are increasingly responsible for their own electoral fate. Fewer automatic

9. Ibid., p. 130.

10. Thomas E. Mann, *Unsafe At Any Margin: Interpreting Congressional Elections* (Washington, D.C.: American Enterprise Institute for Public Policy Research, 1978), chap. 5.

party-line votes give incumbents opportunities to build their advantage, but they also mean well-financed and electable opponents can cut deeply into their margin. Consequently, incumbents feel under increased pressure to build and maintain political support in their districts and avoid mistakes that might galvanize the opposition.[11] The new players in modern House campaigns—political action committees, national party campaign committees, and polling and direct mail firms—have increased the uncertainty felt by incumbents.[12]

In sum, the nature of the incumbency advantage in House elections has changed since the mid-1960s, but its value in staving off defeat has not significantly increased. Modern publicity-conscious, service-oriented members have used their "million-dollar" offices to strengthen their position back home, but the combination of adverse national conditions and vigorous local challenges can still be fatal for 10 percent or more of a party's officeholders. The threat is sufficient to keep incumbents concerned about their political future and responsive to the voters who send them to Washington.

This argument may not convince those more impressed by the failure of the Republicans to pick up a sizable bloc of House seats in the 1984 presidential landslide and by the remarkable durability of House incumbents in 1986. A continuation of the 1984–86 pattern in the next two or three elections would remove some of the uncertainty felt by incumbents and raise important questions about the case that I have made. But my major point is likely to remain valid: the increases in the advantage of incumbency that are associated with the decline of partisanship and the explosion of official resources and opportunities for publicity and service have made members of the House neither electorally secure nor independent of their constituencies.

One-Party Control of the House

Responsiveness to constituency sentiment is not the only value sought through congressional elections, nor necessarily the most important. Elec-

11. Richard F. Fenno, Jr., *Home Style: House Members in Their Districts* (Little, Brown, 1978); Mann, *Unsafe At Any Margin,* chaps. 2, 4; and Jacobson, "The Marginals Never Vanished," p. 139.

12. This argument is developed in Jacobson, *The Politics of Congressional Elections,* chap. 4.

tions also provide opportunities for the public to send a national message and to empower the president and his party in Congress to make changes in policy direction responsive to new challenges. In the American constitutional scheme of "separated institutions sharing powers,"[13] political parties have long served as the primary vehicle for converting shifts in public sentiment into new power arrangements in Washington. The classic example is the realigning election, in which voter unrest produces a presidential landslide and a sizable turnover in Congress, followed by changes in governmental action that permanently alter the structure of popular support for the parties.[14]

The U.S. system has ways short of a political realignment for responding to public demands for a new direction in government. Under the right conditions, more transitory shifts in public opinion can produce outcomes in the presidential and congressional elections decisive enough to create a mandate for action. Many factors contribute to the strength of this mandate: the clarity of the national campaign, the role of the political parties, the amount of turnover in the Senate and House relative to expectations going into the election, and the resourcefulness of the president in selling his interpretation of the meaning of the election to other members of the Washington community.

Changes in the electoral system over the last several decades—the decline in the volatility of seat swings in Congress, the increase in split-ticket voting, and the localization of political forces in House elections—all tend to push the president and Congress in separate directions and dilute the impact in Washington of whatever national message the voters may have in mind. These changes are by no means fatal; several presidents, most recently Ronald Reagan, have had some notable successes in acting upon their interpretation of the election mandate. Moreover, members of Congress have demonstrated an ability to respond to public concerns broader than their constituencies' particularistic interests even when there are no massive swings in party strength. This is accomplished through the recruitment of new members in both parties, the search for issues to revitalize party images, and the responsiveness of incumbents to perceived national needs. It is important to remember that Congress con-

13. This famous phrase is Richard Neustadt's. See his *Presidential Power* (Wiley, 1960), p. 33.
14. John E. Chubb and Paul E. Peterson, "Realignment and Institutionalization," in John E. Chubb and Paul E. Peterson, eds., *The New Direction in American Politics* (Brookings, 1985), pp. 1–30.

tinues to be a primary source of policy innovation in the federal government.[15]

And yet how responsive can the system be if one of the parties is relegated to permanent minority status in the House? The problem is partly one of the inevitability of divided government under Republican presidents, with the attendant though not insurmountable difficulties of building majorities on Capitol Hill. It also entails structural maladies associated with long-term, one-party dominance that affect both Democrats and Republicans. Large, stable majorities tend to become divided and complacent; they take for granted the rewards of majority status and lose sight of the importance of the party's collective performance. Permanent minority parties, on the other hand, can easily become demoralized and irresponsible, neither offering policy alternatives for voter consumption nor playing a constructive role in the legislative process.[16]

Reasons for Democratic Supremacy

The first and most important source of Democratic strength in the House is the distribution of party loyalties among voters. Since 1950 the Democrats have enjoyed a consistent and substantial advantage in party identification.[17] And while party attachments weakened noticeably during the 1960s, the vast majority of votes cast for the House of Representatives were consistent with party identification. The Republicans substantially narrowed the Democratic lead in partisanship during the 1984 campaign, but by early 1987, in the wake of the 1986 elections and the Iran-Contra scandal, the Democrats had regained much of their advantage.[18]

As the majority party in the House, the Democrats have also benefited from the advantages of incumbency and, more generally, the long-term trend toward the insulation of House elections from national politics. A similar pattern is present in state and local governments, where Democrats, buffered against adverse national tides, continue to win a substantial majority of elective offices.[19] Victorious Republican presidential candi-

15. See Nelson W. Polsby, *Political Innovation in America* (Yale University Press, 1984); and John W. Kingdon, *Agendas, Alternatives, and Public Policies* (Little, Brown, 1984).

16. Thomas E. Mann, "Elections and Change in Congress," in Thomas E. Mann and Norman J. Ornstein, eds., *The New Congress* (Washington, D.C.: American Enterprise Institute for Public Policy Research, 1981), p. 36.

17. Thomas E. Cavanagh and James L. Sundquist, "The New Two-Party System," in Chubb and Peterson, eds., *The New Direction in American Politics*, p. 43.

18. *The New York Times*/CBS News Poll, April Survey, April 5–8, 1987.

19. Chubb and Peterson, "Realignment and Institutionalization," p. 18.

dates have been unable to transfer their support to House candidates; the discrepancy in the Republican share of the vote is striking. This may result entirely from voters making separate presidential and congressional decisions, or it may be due in part to sophisticated ticket-splitting (a rational preference for divided government based on a discomfort with the policies and goals of both parties) by some fraction of the electorate.[20] Whatever the particular mix of reasons, the Democrats have been in a position to gain.

Two key elections—1958 and 1974—are also an important part of the story of Democratic control. Both the Eisenhower recession of 1958 and the political and economic troubles of the Nixon-Ford administrations in 1974 led to impressive Democratic gains in the House from which the Republicans did not recover in subsequent elections. The only big Republican gains during the past three decades came in 1966 and 1980, but they were neutralized largely by the effects of Democratic victories in 1964 and 1982. Less favorable national political conditions for the Democrats in either 1958 or 1974 might well have put the Republican party in a position to win control of the house in 1980, as it did the Senate.

Republicans have also suffered from certain self-fulfilling tendencies characteristic of a long-term minority party. In order to win many more House seats, the Republicans need to recruit strong candidates, capable of raising large war chests, to challenge Democratic incumbents election after election. Yet it is extremely difficult (for both candidates and supporters) to sustain serious challenges in the wake of repeated defeats. The problem exists at both the district level and the national level. Why run when defeat is almost certain? And why run if winning means never being in the majority? Minority status discourages strong candidates, which in turn ensures continuing minority status. In recent years the national Republican party has tried to break this cycle by investing considerable resources in candidate recruitment and campaign assistance. Their efforts, however, have been constrained by the national political climate.

Gerrymandering

The final factor contributing to the Democratic majority in the House, and one identified by Republicans as the primary source of their continued minority status, is redistricting or, more specifically, partisan gerryman-

20. Morris P. Fiorina, "The Reagan Years: Turning to the Right or Groping for the Middle?" Occasional Paper No. 86-5 (Harvard University Center for American Political Studies, December 1986).

Table 12-2. *Popular Vote and House Seats Won, by Party, 1946–86*

Percent

Year	Democratic candidates		Republican candidates		Change from last election by party that gained[a]		Difference between Democratic percentage of seats and votes won
	Percentage of all votes	*Percentage of seats won*	*Percentage of all votes*	*Percentage of seats won*	*Major-party votes*	*Seats won*	
1946	44.3	43.3	53.5	56.7	6.4R	12.8R	−1.0
1948	51.6	60.6	45.4	39.4	7.9D	17.3D	9.0
1950	48.9	54.0	48.9	46.0	3.2R	6.6R	5.1
1952	49.2	49.1	49.3	50.9	0.1R	4.9R	−0.1
1954	52.1	53.3	47.0	46.7	2.6D	4.2D	1.2
1956	50.7	53.8	48.7	46.2	1.5R	0.5D	3.1
1958	55.5	64.9	43.6	35.1	5.0D	11.1D	9.4
1960	54.4	60.0	44.8	40.0	1.2R	4.9R	5.6
1962	52.1	59.4	47.1	40.6	2.3R	0.6R	7.3
1964	56.9	67.8	42.4	32.2	4.8D	8.4D	10.9
1966	50.5	57.0	48.0	43.0	6.0R	10.8R	6.5
1968	50.0	55.9	48.2	44.1	0.3R	1.1R	5.9
1970	53.0	58.6	44.5	41.4	3.4D	2.7D	5.6
1972	51.7	55.8	46.4	44.2	1.7R	2.8R	4.1
1974	57.1	66.9	40.5	33.1	5.8D	11.1D	9.8
1976	56.2	67.1	42.1	32.9	1.3R	0.2D	10.9
1978	53.4	63.7	44.7	36.3	2.8R	3.4R	10.3
1980	50.4	55.9	48.0	44.1	3.2R	7.8R	5.5
1982	55.6	61.8	42.9	38.2	5.2D	5.9D	6.2
1984	52.1	58.2	47.0	41.8	3.9R	3.6R	6.1
1986	54.5	59.3	44.6	40.7	2.4D	1.1D	4.8

Source: Norman J. Ornstein and others, *Vital Statistics in Congress, 1984–85 Edition* (Washington, D.C.: American Enterprise Institute for Public Policy Research, 1984), pp. 41-42. Figures for 1984 and 1986 computed by author from data supplied by *Congressional Quarterly*.

a. R = Republican party; D = Democratic party.

dering. The case that a Democratic bias in redistricting has cost the Republicans a large number of seats in the House (perhaps even enough to deny them the majority) rests upon three undisputed facts: (1) the Republican share of the national vote for the House has not produced a proportionate share of seats; (2) the Democrats have largely controlled the redistricting process by virtue of their dominant position in state legislatures and governorships; and (3) the population shifts during the 1960s and 1970s that led to the reapportionment of seats among states and the redrawing of district lines within states did not produce the expected Republican gains.

Table 12-2 presents the relationship of votes to seats in House elections between 1946 and 1986. Since 1958 the Republicans have failed to win more than 44 percent of the seats in the House even though their percentage of the vote has reached 48 percent on several occasions. The Democrats have enjoyed a consistent seat bonus (difference between the percentage of seats and votes won) during this period ranging from 4.1 to 10.9 percentage points. In the only two elections since 1930 won by the Republicans (1946 and 1952), a Republican seat bonus was present but at substantially lower levels (3.2 and 1.6 percentage points, respectively).

The vote totals reported in table 12-2 include almost all congressional districts, even those that were uncontested.[21] If one examines only districts in which the two parties both ran candidates, the Republican vote nationwide appears more competitive. For example, Republican candidates won a majority of the votes in the 367 contested House races in 1984, yet 50.3 percent of the major-party vote in these districts produced for the Republicans only 46 percent of the seats.[22]

There are two major problems with using the relationship between votes and seats to detect partisan bias in redistricting. The first is the lack of correspondence between population and votes, due to differences among districts in the number of eligible voters and in turnout rates. Districts with high concentrations of ethnic and racial minorities, which generally favor Democratic candidates, have the lowest ratio of voters to total population.[23] An inner-city Democrat who wins 75 percent of the

21. Several states (for example, Florida and Oklahoma in 1986) do not report vote totals for uncontested seats. In addition, most Louisiana House races, settled in the first round of their bipartisan primary, are not included in the vote totals. In 1986, there were fourteen of these missing districts.

22. Data provided by Rhodes Cook of *Congressional Quarterly.*

23. Daniel H. Lowenstein and Jonathan Steinberg, "The Quest for Legislative Districting in the Public Interest: Elusive or Illusory?" *UCLA Law Review,* vol. 33 (October 1985), p. 50.

vote with a turnout of 125,000 will have 75,000 fewer votes than a Republican winning by the same percentage in a suburban district with a turnout of 225,000. By the standards of a population-based (rather than voter-based) districting system, the additional 75,000 Republican votes should not earn the party any additional representation in the House. The data in table 12-3 demonstrate clearly that districts with low turnout are disproportionately represented by Democrats. These partisan disparities in turnout account for part of the difference between Democratic votes and Democratic seats. As Daniel Lowenstein and Jonathan Steinberg argue, the mean district vote percentage for each party (the sum of the percentage of the vote won by a party in each district divided by the total number of districts) is a more appropriate measure of a party's vote than the aggregate tally.[24] The 1984 mean district vote percentage won by Republicans in the 367 contested districts was 49.4 percent. By this standard, the Republican share of the seats in these districts seems more reasonable.

The second problem concerns the expectation that under a fair or unbiased system a party's national vote will earn a proportional share of seats in the House. A single-member, winner-take-all election system will produce proportional outcomes only under conditions of extreme residential segregation. If, on the other hand, a majority party's supporters are evenly distributed across districts, a bare majority of votes can win 100 percent of the seats. Numerous scholars have demonstrated that under a normal distribution of political strength, the relationship between votes and seats will look like an S-shaped curve.[25] This means that the majority party will win an increasingly disproportionate share of the seats as its vote moves above 50 percent. Bernard Grofman calculates that in an electoral system like that for the U.S. House of Representatives, a purely random drawing of district lines produces a relationship between votes and seats in which 45 percent of the vote wins 40 percent of the seats while 40 percent of the vote translates into only 31 percent of the seats.[26] Estimates based on random or blind districting are not far from the actual figures reported in table 12-2.

These expected departures from a proportional relationship between

24. Ibid., p. 51.
25. See, for example, Bruce E. Cain, *The Reapportionment Puzzle* (University of California Press, 1984), p. 75; and Bernard Grofman, "For Single-Member Districts Random Is Not Equal," in Bernard Grofman and others, eds., *Representation and Redistricting Issues* (Lexington, 1982), pp. 55–58.
26. Grofman, "For Single-Member Districts," pp. 56, 58.

Table 12-3. *Party of Winning Candidate and Voter Turnout in 1984 House Elections*

	Democratic winners		Republican winners	
Number of voters	*Number*	*Percent*	*Number*	*Percent*
Less than 125,000	25	10.3	2	1.1
125,000–150,000	28	11.6	2	1.1
150,000–175,000	37	15.3	14	8.0
175,000–200,000	52	21.5	39	22.2
200,000–225,000	51	21.1	70	39.8
225,000 or more	49	20.2	49	27.8

Source: Norman J. Ornstein, "Genesis of a Gerrymander," *Wall Street Journal*, May 7, 1985.

votes and seats do not dismiss gerrymandering as a factor in the Republicans' long-term minority status, but they do shift the burden of proof. The two additional pieces of evidence mentioned above—the partisan control of the redistricting process and the political significance of population shifts—are relevant but far from sufficient to make the case. Democrats have had a clear advantage in recent decades by virtue of their partisan strength in the states. The round of redistricting following the 1970 census found the Democrats in control of both houses of the legislature and the governorship in sixteen states; the Republicans controlled only six states.[27] And in spite of the efforts of the national Republican party to strengthen its position in the states, the Democrats retained a clear advantage a decade later, controlling seventeen states compared with six for the Republicans. In many states, including several that enjoyed the largest increase in the size of their delegation, the Democrats were in a position to impose their will. The well-publicized California redistricting plan crafted by the late Representative Philip Burton convinced many observers they were doing just that.

Population shifts among and within states appeared to favor the Republican party. What began after the 1970 census as clear but isolated gains for California and Florida became by 1980 a dramatic shift from Frost Belt to Sun Belt. Not a single state in the Northeast or Midwest gained a seat; none in the Southwest lost one. New York gave up five seats, the largest reapportionment loss in the century, while Florida gained four.[28] In 1984

27. Amihai Glazer, Bernard Grofman, and Marc Robbins, "Partisan and Incumbency Effects of 1970s Congressional Redistricting," *American Journal of Political Science* (forthcoming).

28. Alan Ehrenhalt, "Reapportionment and Redistricting," in Thomas E. Mann and Norman J. Ornstein, eds., *The American Elections of 1982* (Washington, D.C.: American Enterprise Institute for Public Policy Research, 1983), p. 45.

President Reagan ran 4.3 percentage points better in the states gaining seats in the 1980s than he did in the states losing seats.[29] Just as important were population shifts within states. "In every region of the country, people not only were leaving the inner cities, as they had been doing for a generation, but also were moving beyond the first ring of suburbs to newly built communities that stood on land used for farming a decade earlier."[30] The fastest growing areas within states demonstrated a strong tilt toward the GOP; the correlation between 1970s population growth and the 1980 Reagan percentage of the total vote in House districts averaged 0.64 in the twenty largest states.[31]

The circumstantial evidence was strong. Population gains in areas of Republican strength produced few, if any, Republican seats. Since Democrats had the upper hand in the districting process, partisan gerrymandering had to be the prime suspect. And to the extent that partisan plans were blocked by divided state governments, the Democrats, as the majority party in the House, also stood to gain from the resulting bipartisan gerrymanders.

However plausible this argument, rigorous analyses of the partisan and incumbency effects of redistricting have largely failed to support it. The methodological problems of measuring the effects of redistricting are daunting, but several scholars have developed sophisticated methods for dealing with them. Their considered judgment is that redistricting has had little effect on the partisan makeup of the House. In a major reassessment of the redistricting following the 1970 census, Amihai Glazer, Bernard Grofman, and Marc Robbins concluded that districting changes had minimal consequences for the parties and for incumbents, both nationally (in terms of net shift in seats) and in particular states.[32] Richard Born, after examining ninety-one districting plans developed between 1952 and 1982, argues that partisan control of redistricting has had only a very modest effect on seat outcomes, a relationship that became even more tenuous over the thirty-year period. He concludes that one-man, one-vote requirements have weakened the ability of parties to devise favorable plans and that, in any case, voters are less inclined to behave as expected.[33] Both sets

29. John T. Pothier, "A Republican Takeover in the House?" (Yale University, n.d.), p. 1.

30. Ehrenhalt, "Reapportionment and Redistricting," p. 45.

31. Pothier, "Republican Takeover," table 2.

32. Glazer, Grofman, and Robbins, "Partisan and Incumbency Effects."

33. Richard Born, "Partisan Intentions and Election Day Realities in the Congressional

of findings are consistent with the earlier work of John Ferejohn, who found that gerrymandering did not account for the increased incumbency advantage in the mid-1960s.[34]

I do not mean to suggest that politicians are fools for believing that redistricting matters. Given the opportunity, a majority party will seek to maximize the number of winnable seats by increasing the efficiency of its electoral strength (shifting excess partisan strength from some of its safe seats to marginal seats controlled by the opposition party) and by removing or inducing the removal of minority party incumbents. Bruce Cain has demonstrated that the 1981 remapping of California seats helped swing five seats to the Democrats through an artful combination of partisan reconstruction and incumbency removal.[35] Similar though less radical post-1980 redistricting plans were evident in New Jersey, Indiana, and Pennsylvania, the latter two favoring the Republicans.[36]

Nonetheless, many factors conspire to dilute the net effects of partisan and bipartisan gerrymandering. Gerrymandering in states under one-party control is constrained by population trends in adjoining districts; the geographical clustering of party supporters; the unwillingness of safe incumbents to give up excess supporters or to alter in any substantial way their existing boundaries; the political ambitions of state legislators; the protection of racial minorities by the courts; the difficulty of predicting votes in House elections from party registration figures; and the intervention of national political tides that, when combined with the advantages of incumbency, can subvert the partisan intentions of those drawing the lines. Moreover, most redistricting is done in states with divided control or under supervision by the courts, both factors that tend to favor the status quo.[37] Finally, population shifts from inner city to outer suburb and from Frost Belt to Sun Belt should be expected to produce significant partisan changes only if the partisanship of the individual movers changes. There is little evidence to suggest the latter has occurred in any substantial way, reinforcing the view that the Republicans are the minority party in the House because they are the minority party in the country.

Redistricting Process," *American Political Science Review*, vol. 79 (June 1985), pp. 305–19.

34. John Ferejohn, "On the Decline of Competition in Congressional Elections," *American Political Science Review*, vol. 71 (March 1977), pp. 166–76.

35. Cain, "Assessing the Partisan Effects of Redistricting," *American Political Science Review*, vol. 79 (June 1985), pp. 320–33.

36. Ehrenhalt, "Reapportionment and Redistricting," pp. 48–54.

37. Glazer, Grofman, and Robbins, "Partisan and Incumbency Effects," p. 19.

The Future

In view of the several factors that have contributed to the long-term Democratic control of the House, what are the prospects for a Republican majority during the next decade? Would these prospects improve if the rules of the game were changed?

A Recipe for Republicans

In spite of the Democratic dominance in the House over the past three decades, I believe it is a mistake to assume that present patterns will extend inexorably into the future. The simple fact is that the Republicans now need to pick up forty-one seats to take control of the House. Even by contemporary standards this is not an unreachable goal. The Democrats gained forty-three seats in the 1974 elections, while the Republicans won forty-six over two consecutive elections (1978 and 1980). One can imagine a number of scenarios that would put the Republicans in the majority sometime during the next decade. All involve different combinations of the following ingredients.

First, the Republicans need to strengthen their support among voters generally, by increasing the percentage who identify with them and by improving their party image. As pointed out earlier, the impressive Republican gains in this regard appear to have been halted and partially reversed by the series of difficulties encountered by the Reagan administration in late 1986 and early 1987, most notably the Iran-Contra scandal. The Republicans need to get back on track, especially with the youngest cohort, toward parity if not realignment.

Second, the Republicans must strive to reduce the insulation of House elections from national politics by sharpening and heightening partisan differences. A party's ability to heed this advice depends partly on the context: 1980 provided a more hospitable environment for a unified national Republican campaign than 1982 or 1986. Nonetheless, Republicans would increase their probability of success by working to make some House races more like Senate contests, that is, less personalized and more ideological and issue-oriented.

Third, a party can succeed in House elections only by fielding able and well-financed challengers. Candidate recruitment is very difficult when a party appears mired in the minority; the problems are also formidable when national conditions turn sour on that party's watch.[38] The Republicans need to find ways of countering these natural psychological tendencies, particularly when the political climate is working against them, and of riding even higher on the national tides that roll in their favor. Their organizational and financial advantages should be directed toward ensuring sustained, vigorous opposition in the one hundred or so Democratic seats judged potentially most vulnerable.

Fourth, the Republicans need to continue their inroads in the formally one-party Democratic South. While there is an obvious lag between Republican success at the presidential and congressional levels, the fact remains that over approximately the past quarter century the Republican share of the South's delegation in the House has grown from 6 percent to 37 percent.[39] While continued movement toward parity is by no means assured (the Republicans suffered setbacks in both 1982 and 1986), the growing Republican loyalty among white Southerners makes the region an attractive target for House Republican strategists. As part of that effort, the Republicans will try to persuade selected Southern Democratic members to follow the example of Phil Gramm and Andy Ireland by switching parties. This courtship is likely to enjoy massive success only if the Republicans come within striking distance of a majority.

Fifth, the Republicans must avoid a blatant displacement of their incumbents in the post-1990 round of redistricting. As I argued above, gerrymandering accounts for relatively little of the Republican shortfall in the House. Nonetheless, the Republicans can help protect themselves against marginal losses in the redistricting process by reducing the number of states in which the Democrats control both houses of the legislature and the governorship and by using the courts to dampen partisan gains.

Sixth, the Republicans probably must lose a presidential election in order to position themselves to take a majority of the House seats. It is virtually impossible for a party to strengthen its position in the House at the same time that it occupies the White House. If the initial election that wins the presidency for a party does not produce a House majority, the window is effectively closed for the duration of that administration. One of the regular patterns of American politics—the loss of House seats at mid-term by the president's party—ensures that. In this sense, House Republicans have been victims of their party's success in presidential elections.

38. Gary C. Jacobson and Samuel Kernell, *Strategy and Choice in Congressional Elections*, 2d ed. (Yale University Press, 1983), chap. 3.

39. Pothier, "Republican Takeover," table 3.

With these ingredients, it is not difficult to prepare a recipe for Republican success. The Democrats win a closely contested presidential election in 1988 but fail to increase their House majority by more than a handful of seats. Republicans are encouraged by the economic problems that dog the new administration and recruit a group of exceptionally able candidates for the 1990 congressional and state elections. The Republicans win twenty new seats in the House and hold the governorships in California, Texas, and Florida, the states likely to reap most of the 1990 reapportionment harvest. The Democratic president is renominated in 1992 after a bitter primary struggle, only to face a strong Republican candidate leading a unified party. A new round of stagflation raises the specter of economic collapse, and the Republican presidential candidate wins in a landslide. The strong Republican tide gives the party the lion's share of the redistricting gains, and Republicans take control of the House with a pickup of thirty-three seats.

I offer this scenario not as a likely occurrence, but as a plausible one. It suggests that a Republican majority is not beyond the realm of possibility, and that no upheaval in the structure of House elections is required to change party control. The odds are clearly against the Republicans in any given election, but some combination of changing voter loyalties, successful candidate recruitment, and fortuitous national conditions could reverse their fortunes.

Institutional Reforms

Those who believe that a responsive and responsible government requires at least an occasional change in party control of the House might gain some solace from this analysis. They might also reasonably entertain various institutional reforms designed to improve the odds for a Republican majority in the short run and foster increased national party competition in the longer term.

One set of reforms addresses the reapportionment process. Some have proposed reapportionment by a nonpartisan blue-ribbon commission, arguing that apolitical, blind redistricting would produce district boundaries that are politically fair, favoring neither one party over the other nor incumbents as a class.[40] The major problem with this proposal is that

40. See, for example, Common Cause, *Toward a System of "Fair and Effective Representation"* (Common Cause, 1977). These and other reform proposals are discussed in Cain, *The Reapportionment Puzzle.* I draw heavily on his work in the section that follows.

apolitical commissions, however pure the intentions of their members, inevitably produce plans with political consequences. The 1981 experience of Iowa, recounted by Alan Ehrenhalt, is the most recent in a long list of illustrations that politics cannot be taken out of the redistricting process.

> In a burst of "good government" altruism, Iowa's Republican legislature voted in 1980 to turn its redistricting over to a computer operated by the state's nonpartisan Legislative Service Bureau and programmed to ignore partisan concerns and the wishes of incumbents. The only relevant concerns were to be compactness, population equality, and respect for traditional community boundaries.
>
> The computer did what it was told. It also happened to draw a map placing two of the state's three Republican House members—Jim Leach and Tom Tauke—in the same district. That caused a highly partisan uproar among GOP officials, who saw no reason why Iowa's major party should suffer disproportionately in the interest of good government. . . . "It looks like a Democratic computer wrote it," complained an aide to GOP Governor Robert Ray.[41]

It is difficult to argue with Bruce Cain's conclusion that "since all reapportionment plans inevitably have an impact on the parties, there is no such thing as an apolitical plan; and if plans are inevitably political, it is better to confront the political fairness issue openly rather than shove it under the rug of ostensible neutrality."[42]

A proposal to use a bipartisan commission accepts the political character of redistricting but seeks to improve the process in two ways: by making it difficult for one party to ride roughshod over the other and by removing the responsibility for redistricting from the hands of those personally affected by it. This proposal is not without its own problems.[43] Commission members would have less investment than legislators in preserving the continuity of existing districts, a value compatible with the democratic process. A relatively small commission would be unable to represent demographically the many groups whose interests are affected by reapportionment. It would tend toward bipartisan settlements, meaning less competitive, more homogeneous districts. A bipartisan commission, by definition evenly balanced between the parties, would also give the

---

41. Ehrenhalt, "Reapportionment and Redistricting," p. 55.
42. Cain, *The Reapportionment Puzzle,* p. 183.
43. Ibid., chap. 10.

minority party the opportunity to extort election gains through the redistricting process.

Another approach to improving legislative reapportionment accepts the present system as compatible with the pluralist character of American democracy and looks to incremental changes in the process. These include increasing the amount and quality of information available to the public before the legislature votes on the plan; dividing the negotiations into two stages, the first on the broad outlines of the plan, the second on its details; and reducing the amount of time spent struggling over reapportionment by closing off all unnecessary routes of appeal.[44]

The final reform strategy, and the one most relevant in the present environment, is to have the courts impose standards of political fairness. On June 30, 1986, the Supreme Court decreed in *Davis* v. *Bandemer* that political gerrymandering is justiciable, moving the grounds for constitutional challenges to districting plans well beyond those of population inequality and racial dilution. The Court failed, however, to reach a majority view on precisely what constituted an unconstitutional gerrymander. Speaking for the plurality, Justice Byron R. White wrote that a statewide political gerrymander is unconstitutional if "the electoral system is arranged in a manner that will consistently degrade a voter's or a group of voters' influence on the political process as a whole."[45]

The original suit in *Bandemer* was brought by the Indiana Democratic party against the 1981 reapportionment of state legislative districts. A three-judge district panel, guided largely by the view of Justice Stevens in an earlier decision,[46] ruled that the plan unconstitutionally diluted the votes of Indiana Democrats. Not surprisingly, the national Republican party, hoping to establish a precedent for challenging Democratic congressional gerrymanders, rushed to the defense of the Indiana Democrats. The national Democrats, in turn, argued the case of the Republican defendants.

The Supreme Court reversed the district court decision, concluding that the plaintiff had failed to establish the threshold showing of discriminatory vote dilution. The Court ruled that it is not sufficient to show that an apportionment scheme makes winning elections more difficult for a partic-

---

44. Ibid., pp. 188–91.
45. *Davis* v. *Bandemer,* 106 S. Ct. 2797 at 2810 (1986).
46. *Karcher* v. *Daggett,* 103 S. Ct. 2653 (1983). This point is made by Bernard Grofman in his editor's introduction to "Political Gerrymandering: *Badham v. Eu,* Political Science Goes to Court," *PS,* vol. 18 (Summer 1985), pp. 542–43.

ular group or that it fails to provide proportional representation. The real question, Justice White wrote, is "whether a particular group has been unconstitutionally denied its chance to effectively influence the political process. . . . Such a finding of unconstitutionality must be supported by evidence of continued frustration of the will of a majority of the voters or effective denial to a minority of voters of a fair chance to influence the political process."[47]

However demanding the burden of proof required by the Court, the *Bandemer* decision invites a flood of political gerrymandering litigation. A California case—*Badham* v. *Eu*—will likely provide the Supreme Court with its next opportunity to refine its standards for assessing gerrymandering claims. In attempting to develop workable standards, the Court faces substantive problems of incredible complexity.[48] My own view is that the inevitable spate of post-1990 redistricting litigation will primarily benefit the legions of political scientists and lawyers who are called as expert witnesses. If, as argued above, the net national effects of redistricting are minimal, partisan gerrymandering litigation is not likely to produce major gains for the Republicans. Nonetheless, as a party in search of forty-one additional House seats, the Republicans are well advised to pursue their new legal options, if only to protect themselves against California-style incumbent removal schemes.

Two other sets of reforms might increase the frequency of majority party change in the House. One seeks to increase the number of competitive House seats by altering the manner in which campaigns are financed. Partial public financing with high or no expenditure limits would lead to more sustained opposition in a number of House districts that are now effectively uncontested. Free television time and mass mailings for major-party candidates would produce similar results. Increased competition would partially close the separation that now exists between presidential and congressional elections, thereby making the latter more sensitive to national political tides. The obstacles to reform of this character are formidable: incumbents are reluctant to help their next opponents; Democrats have little incentive to endanger their majority status; and Republicans realize that if they can capture the majority under the present campaign

47. This excerpt is taken from Elder Witt, "Court Settles Voting Issues, Other Major Controversies," *Congressional Quarterly Weekly Report*, vol. 44 (July 5, 1986), p. 1524.

48. These problems are discussed fully by Lowenstein and Steinberg, Grofman, Cain, Richard G. Niemi, Martin Shapiro, and Sanford Levinson in a symposium on "Gerrymandering and the Courts," *UCLA Law Review*, vol. 33 (October 1985).

finance system, they will derive a long-term advantage from it (see chapter 7).

A final perspective on reform is offered by James L. Sundquist, who argues that the only effective way of forestalling divided government is through major constitutional surgery. Sundquist outlines two reforms—a presidential-congressional team ticket and bonus seats in Congress—that would very likely produce his desired result of unified government. But, as Sundquist notes, they would be certain to draw the strong opposition of congressional incumbents and the public.[49]

Those who believe the American political system works best when both elements of responsiveness are present—members of Congress to their constituents and the president and Congress to changing public sentiments about the direction of government—will be wise to place primary emphasis on encouraging positive developments already permitted by the current rules of the game.

49. James L. Sundquist, *Constitutional Reform and Effective Government* (Brookings, 1986), chap. 4.

Conference Participants

with their affiliations at the time of the conference

David D. Arnold *Ford Foundation*
Walter Dean Burnham *Massachusetts Institute of Technology*
Thomas E. Cavanagh *National Research Council*
James W. Ceaser *University of Virginia*
John E. Chubb *Brookings Institution*
Timothy Conlan *George Mason University*
Douglas Dillon *Honorary Trustee, Brookings Institution*
Shepard L. Forman *Ford Foundation*
Curtis B. Gans *Committee for the Study of the American Electorate*
Robert Goldberg *USI, Incorporated*
James L. Guth *Furman University*
Stephen Hess *Brookings Institution*
Albert R. Hunt *Wall Street Journal*
Robert A. Katzmann *Federal Judicial Center*
Samuel H. Kernell *Brookings Institution*
Everett Carll Ladd *University of Connecticut and Roper Center for Public Opinion Research*
Kay Lawson *San Francisco State University*
Bruce K. MacLaury *Brookings Institution*
Michael J. Malbin *University of Maryland*
Thomas E. Mann *American Political Science Association*
Milton D. Morris *Joint Center for Political Studies*

Alice O'Connor *Ford Foundation*

Paul E. Peterson *Brookings Institution*

A. James Reichley *Brookings Institution*

Stuart Rothenberg *Institute for Government and Politics*

Larry Sabato *University of Virginia*

Peter N. Skerry *Harvard University*

Larry H. Slesinger *John and Mary Markle Foundation*

Hedrick L. Smith *New York Times*

Steven S. Smith *Brookings Institution*

Gilbert Y. Steiner *Brookings Institution*

Donald E. Stokes *Princeton University*

James L. Sundquist *Brookings Institution*

Edwin W. Warner *Voice of America*

R. Kent Weaver *Brookings Institution*

Eddie N. Williams *Joint Center for Political Studies*

Index

285